ADVANCE PRAISE

for

The Joys and Disappointments of a German Governess in Imperial Brazil

"This insider's view of the final days of slavery in nineteenth-century Brazil captures her employers' lives and that of their enslaved servants. Expertly edited by Linda Lewin, her letters are a rich primary source for all historians of slavery and the family. Appropriate period photographs accompany the text."

—Mary C. Karasch, author of *Before Brasília*

"The German governess Ina von Binzer's letters provide unparalleled insights into the texture of Brazilian life in the early 1880s, from the condition and lives of slaves to the intimate family and material lives of their owners who employed her. Lewin's contextualization of these precious primary sources is consummate, moving from archival confirmation of specific details to concise summations of the general context that these missives illuminate."

—Peter M. Beattie, author of *The Tribute of Blood*

"This book is a fascinating window into nineteenth-century Brazilian daily life. The reader will enjoy the German governess's depictions of family relations in this first English translation and will appreciate her take on a society defined by enslavement in all its aspects. Linda Lewin's introduction weaves both realms, illuminating the inner works of the last slave society in the Americas."

—Maria-Aparecida Lopes, author of *Rio de Janeiro in the Global Meat Market, c. 1850 to c. 1930*

"This book wonderfully compliments a textbook account of nineteenth-century Brazil. *The Joys and Disappointments of a German Governess in Imperial Brazil* touches on many of the most notable events and paradoxes of the period, including the rise of coffee, waning slavery (that was not, however, weakening quickly enough in the regions where von Binzer visited), monarchical rule, and the start of a new wave of European immigration."

—Ian Read, author of *The Hierarchies of Slavery in Santos, Brazil, 1822–1888*

"Drawing on the personal letters of Ina von Binzer, Linda Lewin provides today's scholars with a lens to understand how wealthy families rooted in Brazilian coffee production struggled with the onset of abolition. Lewin's book integrates powerful photographs, including rare views of slaves, with von Binzer's letters that, together with Lewin's succinct, accessible introduction and explicating footnotes, will stimulate and complicate historical debates about slavery in Brazil."

—Theresa Alfaro-Velcamp, author of *So Far from Allah, So Close to Mexico*

"One cannot finish reading *The Joys and Disappointments of a German Governess* in Imperial Brazil without gaining insight into the economy, society, and beauty \that was Brazil in the 1880s, as well as developing some admiration for this intrepid governess, despite her flaws and prejudices. The translation flows nicely, and Linda Lewin's excellent introduction sets the stage."

—Francie R. Chassen-López, author of *From Liberal to Revolutionary Oaxaca*

The Joys and Disappointments of a German Governess in Imperial Brazil

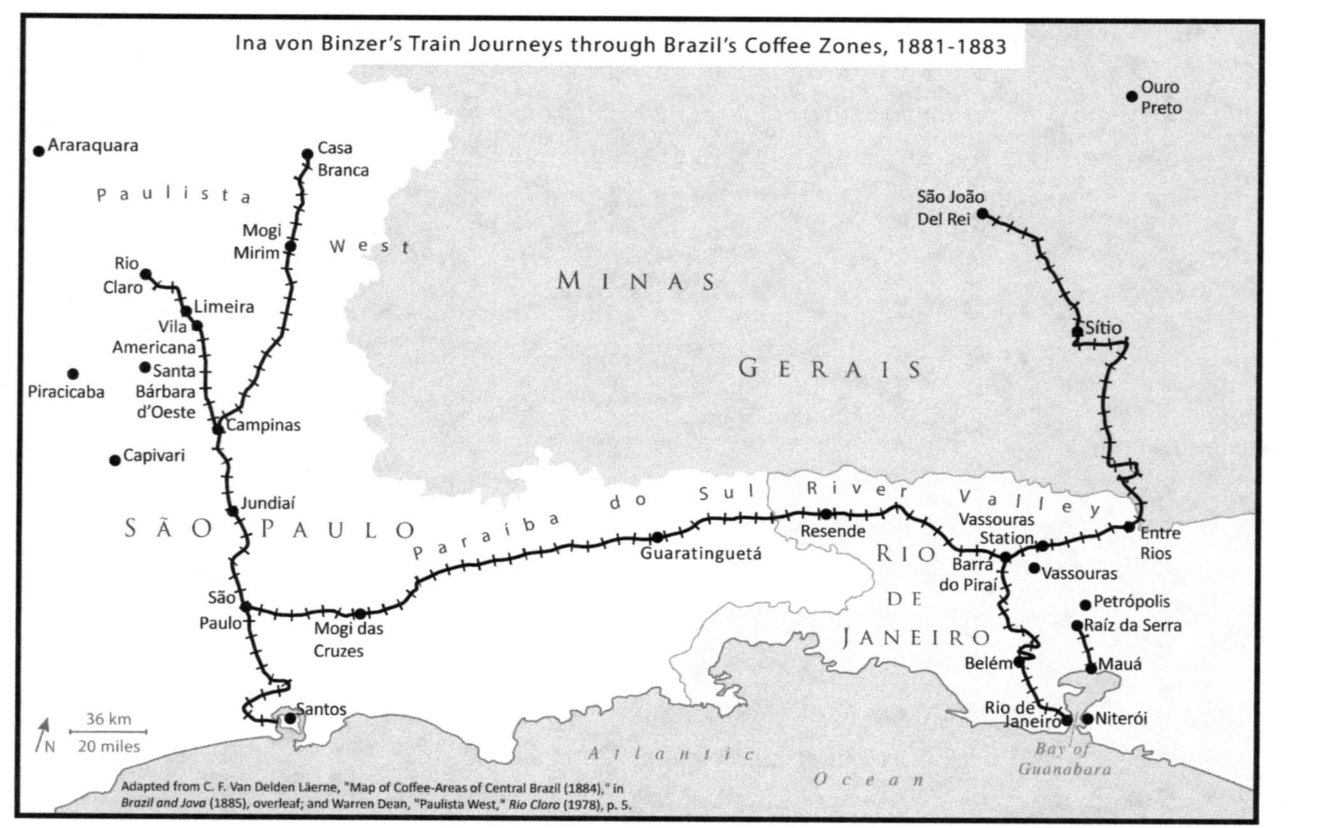
Ina von Binzer's Train Journeys through Brazil's Coffee Zones, 1881-1883
Araraquara
Paulista West
Casa Branca
Mogi Mirim
Rio Claro
Limeira
Vila Americana
Santa Bárbara d'Oeste
Piracicaba
Campinas
Capivari
Jundiaí
SÃO PAULO
São Paulo
Mogi das Cruzes
Santos
MINAS GERAIS
São João Del Rei
Sítio
Ouro Preto
Paraíba do Sul River Valley
Guaratinguetá
Resende
RIO DE JANEIRO
Vassouras Station
Barra do Piraí
Vassouras
Entre Rios
Petrópolis
Raíz da Serra
Mauá
Belém
Rio de Janeiro
Niterói
Bay of Guanabara
Atlantic Ocean
36 km
20 miles
N
Adapted from C. F. Van Delden Läerne, "Map of Coffee-Areas of Central Brazil (1884)," in *Brazil and Java* (1885), overleaf; and Warren Dean, "Paulista West," *Rio Claro* (1978), p. 5.

The Joys and Disappointments of a German Governess in Imperial Brazil

INA VON BINZER

Edited with an Introduction by Linda Lewin

Translated by Gabriel Trop

University of Notre Dame Press
Notre Dame, Indiana

University of Notre Dame Press
Notre Dame, Indiana 46556
undpress.nd.edu

Published in the United States of America

Originally published in German as *Leid und Freud einer Erzieherin in Brasilien* by Ina von Binzer (Ulla von Eck) in 1887; Richard Eckstein Nachfolger; Leipzig: Hammer & Runge, Berlin.

Library of Congress Control Number: 2021948783

ISBN: 978-0-268-20177-7 (Hardback)
ISBN: 978-0-268-20176-0 (WebPDF)
ISBN: 978-0-268-20179-1 (Epub)

In Memory of

Mariza Corrêa, 1945–2016,

and

Fernando Gasparian, 1930–2006

Contents

Illustrations

Abbreviations

ADP	Acervo Danda Prado, São Paulo
GFC/GOCPDI	Gilberto Ferrez Collection of Nineteenth-Century Photographs of Brazil, Getty Open Content Program Digital Images, the Getty Research Institute, Los Angeles
MIS/BN	Antigo Rio Collection, Museu de Imagem e Som, Biblioteca Nacional, Rio de Janeiro

Figures

Acknowledgments

This project could not have been launched without the initial encouragement of Mariza Corrêa. Although her search for a copy of the original edition of Ina von Binzer's *Leid und Freud* in Paulo Duarte's personal library proved in vain, Mariza's enthusiasm for the popularity of the German governess's little book of letters convinced me of the value they would hold in an English translation. Once the original edition could not be located in Brazilian libraries, Dr. Peter R. Frank, Curator of Germanic Collections for Stanford University Libraries, kindly assisted me in locating von Binzer's original text at the Staatsbibliotheck in Berlin. The photocopy of the 1887 edition that it generously supplied was the one on which Gabriel Trop based this English translation. Meanwhile, Fernando Gasparian, principal proprietor and director of Editora Paz e Terra, also had enthusiastically encouraged me to publish an English translation of Ina's letters, even sending me written authorization for the translation into English of his Brazilian Portuguese edition—should I not be able to locate the original edition. Gasparian's encouragement and infectious enthusiasm proved vital for my pursuit of this project. He recounted several sites in his native city of São Paulo that Ina's letters still called to mind, especially a homeopathic pharmacy once called "At the Golden Deer" (Botica Ao Veado D' Ouro), located on the Rua São Bento. After well over a century, this establishment, which had expanded into a half dozen locations, continued to embody the legacy of Ina's friend and benefactor, German vice-consul Gustav Schaumann, who had opened the pharmacy in 1858. I am very much indebted to Gabriel Trop for his tireless effort to render Ina von Binzer's letters into an authentic translation and for decoding some of her archaic literary references, which appear in footnotes. Otherwise, in authoring the one hundred forty, mostly expository, footnotes in this edition, I have drawn on many individuals and sources too numerous to mention. I would only offer my sincere appreciation for their collaboration or availability.

Once my research on Ina's biography was under way, I received valuable collaboration from a number of researchers whom I met online. Marly Ritzkat, author of a historical study based on Ina von Binzer's letters and a resident of Germany, generously offered to help. She ran down entries for Ina von Binzer in several parish registers recording baptisms, marriages, and deaths in that country, making phone calls and collecting copies of entries from archivists. Her collaboration clarified and corrected important parts of the factual record of Ina's personal life. Two more Brazilians further clarified Ina's biography, thanks to their genealogical websites and personal communications: Luiz Sérgio Heinzelmann, of São José dos Campos, Brazil, supplied information about Ina´s mysterious uncle, Christian Thomsen, especially regarding his marriage to a German immigrant, while Roberto Petroucic offered me a plethora of information about the final couple for whom Ina von Binzer worked in 1882: Bento Aguiar de Barros and Francisca Miquelina de Souza Barros. Margaret Anderson, my colleague in the History Department at the University of California, Berkeley, lent indispensable assistance by untying several knots in German history that Ina von Binzer's letters left convoluted. Robert Slenes helped me to decode *sos kiss*, while Luiz Bernardo Pericás offered special guidance on another conundrum I had to resolve. On an unforgettable afternoon, Ida Lewkowicz drove me through Higienópolis in order to tour Ina von Binzer's once illustrious neighborhood. We visited the Palacete Martinico Prado (opened in 1906), São Paulo's first office building, which still housed BOVESPA, Brazil's most quoted stock exchange, and we stopped off at Dona Veridiana's Chácara Vila Maria, constructed two years after Ina von Binzer departed for her rustic life in Santa Bárbara d'Oeste. Judith Hoffnagel, a real friend, accompanied me to Vassouras in 2018, where, together, we researched inheritance documents and parish registers that brought Ina's initial employers, the so-called Rameiros, into clear focus. The staff at the Vassouras IPHAN (Instituto de Patrimônio Histórico e Artístico Nacional) Office was simply wonderful in providing documents and valuable leads and in taking the time to explain anomalies and contradictions encountered in inheritance texts. Many thanks to Luciana Vale Pappacena and Isabel Rocha for making this visit so productive. Isabel, herself a published local historian of Vassouras, illuminated the identity of the elusive Dr. Lazzarini and pointed me toward additional printed sources. Judith also traveled with me to São João Del Rei, assisting with some photography and note-taking at the Museu

Ferroviária, while Douglas Libby recommended a superb *pensão* in Tiradentes for an unforgettable five-day visit.

As the introduction was nearing a final draft, a special session of LAHNOCA (Latin American Historians of Northern California) offered me important feedback and suggestions about revisions. I am grateful to a number of members, especially Myrna Santiago, Angus Wright, Maria-Aparecida Lopes, Heather Fowler-Salamini, and Ian Read, for their incisive comments. Mary Karasch, who generously vetted the introduction, together with Theresa Alfaro-Velcamp, offered me invaluable advice and suggestions regarding potential publishers for this book. Theresa led me straight to the University of Notre Dame Press. I am very grateful to Eli Bortz, editor in chief at the University of Notre Dame Press, who recognized the unique contribution that Ina von Binzer's letters represent and endorsed the inclusion of a generous number of historical photographs for this book. Eli enthusiastically guided publication through the initial stages and accommodated the delays I experienced in obtaining the photographs by offering lots of goodwill. I am also grateful to Peter Beattie and Glen Goodman, reviewers who served me well with the press and offered helpful suggestions on revisions. Zephyr Frank generously contributed the original map for this book.

Finally, the donors of the photographs featured in this book, which represent an important part of its documentation, deserve to be singled out for special appreciation. Danda Prado, whose paternal grandfather was Caio Graco da Silva Prado—at age ten, one of Ina von Binzer's seven charges during the five months in 1882 that she spent in the home of his parents, Martinico da Silva Prado and Albertina de Morais Pinto—deserves my deepest thanks. She allowed me to publish two photographs from her family collection that offer an intimate and unforgettable glimpse of what Ina von Binzer experienced in the household of Danda's great-grandparents. I am immensely grateful to the Getty, in Los Angeles, for its Open Content Program, which allowed me to reproduce digital images from the Gilberto Ferrez Collection of Nineteenth-Century Photographs of Brazil, recently made available online. The generosity of the Getty's Research Institute (GRI) has brought to English-speaking readers of this book a valuable selection of priceless photographs taken by imperial Brazil's premier photographer, Marc Ferrez. It was he who captured slavery's final shadow in the Paraíba do Sul River Valley contemporaneously with von Binzer's residence there. His rare photographic record preserves the faces and the details of the tasks associated with the last cohort of slaves to work the coffee plantations located in what colloquial speech readily acknowledged as Brazil's "River of Slavery." Rob McLaughlin offered crucial technical assistance with the photos and thereby moved things forward. I am also grateful to the Museu de Imagem e Som, Rio de Janeiro, for generous access to photographs in the public domain from its Antigo Rio Collection, housed at the Biblioteca Nacional. Finally, several Humanities Research Grants from the University of California, Berkeley, awarded over a long decade, financed the translation of Ina von Binzer's letters into English and promoted my research efforts in Brazil. It is my expectation that what has been for me a very fruitful collaboration will place in the hands of the readers of Ina von Binzer's extraordinary book a unique memoir of a time and a place that no longer exists, yet one that continues to resonate powerfully, thanks to contemporary issues that still engage our attention and continue to demand our efforts to resolve.

A Note Regarding Photographic Documentation

The first five photographs selected for this book arrived at the Getty Research Institute reflecting their nineteenth-century origin as images derived from a contractual obligation imposed on photographer Marc Ferrez. He was required to produce a series of photographs documenting the specific tasks that produced the sixty-pound sacks of coffee beans destined for Brazil's Atlantic entrepôts of Rio de Janeiro and Santos. No documentary notice, consequently, was taken of the human subjects who performed those tasks—not even their whereabouts in Brazil's Paraíba Valley was noted in the information that accompanied these photographs when they were placed on archival deposit at the close of the twentieth century. Nothing about those human subjects had been recorded in terms of archival notes that might have provided valuable information concerning who they really were, while only a single photographic title mentioned "slaves." That the photographic focus encompassed an enslaved work force would be registered only in the eyes of curious researchers. It would be left to historians to articulate who the human beings in these five photographs really were—or to wonder about the fate that brought them to a coffee plantation where they would be captured momentarily by a camera in a series of remarkably evocative photographs. The absence of any written notes describing the enslaved men, women, children, and infants preserved in these photographs deserves to be directly connected to a widespread cultural predisposition held by their contemporaries who were members of the free, property-owning classes during the 1880s. Namely, the silence over the identity of these human subjects amounted to a dismissal of their existence, even though the presence of a large enslaved workforce testified to the economic prosperity of the families who owned the plantations where the photographs were taken. Once abolition became a fact, successive generations of planter descendants would decline to speak of "slaves," of "slavery," or—more abstractly—of the "servile status" that formerly had proved inseparable from their families' economic well-being. While slavery had been in sway, the human beings shown in these photographs would frequently be spoken of as "captives," a choice of words that softened the outrageous nature of their forced servitude—the latter being rendered merely as "captivity." Alternatively, these same human beings might be spoken of as *negros* or listed in plantation records as *pretos*—terms ambiguously connoting blackness, but a blackness that concealed a terrible individual identity as chattel worthy of an assigned monetary value. These euphemisms of colloquial speech relieved their users of what "slave" or "slavery" would more truthfully bring them to recognize: their personal identity as the owners of human beings.

On a more fundamental level, these five photographs omitted any reference at all to their human subjects for yet a different reason. Beyond quite matter-of-factly erasing the identity of those human beings, the encoded silence accompanying these photographs altogether blotted out the existence of slavery. By not taking any account of their human subjects, by leaving them untitled, unreferenced, and even undiscriminated from their physical surroundings, these graphic images have managed, albeit obliquely, to deny the existence of slavery for the past 140 years. As such, they belong to a much larger collection of photographic documentation dedicated to preserving intact a certain historical context for the 1880s—the world of coffee plantations whose influential owners defined Brazil's ruling local elites within the Paraíba Valley as well as a powerful political bloc of legislators in the national parliament drawn from the same plantations. That their wealth had depended on the ownership of slaves thus could be left moot, thanks to what these photographs lacked in terms of titles, captions, or discriminating notes. Not to speak of slavery was to deny its existence. Thus did tacit dismissal—and successive generations after abolition concurred in that silence by means of a willingness to forget that such an institution had ever existed—ensure that the collective memory of slavery would fade in the national consciousness. Hence these photographs testify to a process of erasure not only for an enormous group of enslaved people but also for the troubling presence of a particular institution, one that unmistakably characterized all of Brazilian society for more than 350 years.

In moving these five images from pristine archive to the pages of this book, I favored calling it like it really was—140 years ago. I have chosen to follow the radical abolitionists who challenged national legislators on their working vocabulary—censuring the latter's oratorical preferences for "captives" and "captivity"—by demanding instead that "slave" and "slavery" become part of the national discourse. I have adopted their choice of words in entitling these photographs and composing their captions as the means of reversing what I found to be the awful archival silence that accompanied these images. Thus these five photographs herein disdain both ellipses and euphemisms. They deliberately employ the raw vocabulary favored by radical abolitionists in the years immediately preceding 1888, deeming the human subjects shown in these photographs to be exactly what they forced Brazilian legislators to confront: slaves (*escravos*) imprisoned by the legal institution of slavery (*escravidão*). Even as Gilberto Ferrez himself had to acknowledge, perhaps in a single moment of carelessness—or was it a flash of truth telling?—when he penciled two words of terse recognition on the reverse side of a single photograph belonging to his grandfather's amazing collection, the subjects of these photographs could be categorized as *todos escravos*—every one of them a slave.

SOURCES: In composing titles for these five initial photographs, I have consulted duplicate images archived at the Instituto Moreira Salles, in Rio de Janeiro & São Paulo, in order to verify the locale of the Paraíba Valley, certain dates, and precise tasks (although sometimes those duplicates proved less than completely silent on the slave status of their human subjects). Captions draw directly on Stanley J. Stein's classic study, *Vassouras: A Brazilian Coffee County, 1850–1900* (1957), for descriptions of work routines. During the 1940s, he and Barbara Stein interviewed certain older residents of Vassouras who themselves were among the last survivors to have been enslaved on local coffee plantations during the 1880s.

A Note on the Monetary Unit of the Brazilian Empire

The monetary unit of the Brazilian Empire was the *mil-réis*, written as 1$000 and consisting of one thousand *réis.* A single *real* amounted to so little value that it conversationally implied merely a cent or two, explaining why people usually spoke in terms of mil-réis as a monetary minimum unit. Larger amounts, quoted in exports of coffee, for instance, were expressed in *contos* or *contos de réis*—that is, in units of one thousand mil-réis, written as 1:000$000. (Do not confuse the plural, *réis*, with Brazil's monetary unit today, the *real*, whose plural is *reais.*)

The value of the mil-réis fluctuated considerably over the nineteenth century, although for most of the early 1880s it was quite stable. In her letter of April 21, 1882, Ina von Binzer noted that the value of five hundred mil-réis was one thousand German marks and that one conto equaled two thousand German marks. Elsewhere, she noted that one mil-réis equaled two German marks, or exactly the same value. In United States dollars during 1882, one conto was the equivalent of approximately $440 (two thousand German marks).

What was not stable price-wise during the 1880s was the value of slaves. On the one hand, the instability was owing to their declining numbers and advancing average age. Until the middle of the decade, their prices were rising, simply due to scarcity and the profits derived from coffee cultivation. On the other hand, by 1885, as large numbers of owners began to believe that abolition would soon be a reality, the prices of slaves began to decline sharply. Doubt that the imperial government would compensate slave owners actually delayed abolition and sent slave prices plummeting by 1886–87, such that by May 13, 1888, many slave owners already were bankrupt.

Introduction

But people have told me that I will find life on the plantation extremely primitive, as it is equipped according to the old style of the countryside. I am halfway scared about this "style," but I am also halfway curious about the true Brazilian country life, about which the many hundreds of people who visit Brazil never get an idea. In this way, we governesses have an advantage over the merchants and other Europeans, as very few of them ever leave the coastal areas, and most of them go back to Europe after ten or twenty years without ever having known in the most paltry manner the countryside or the life of Brazilians. We, on the other hand, who live directly with families, have to participate in all of their vexations.

—Ina von Binzer, São Paulo, 1 July 1882

A UNIQUE BOOK BY A SINGULAR AUTHOR

Among the many books authored by foreigners residing in nineteenth-century Brazil, Ina von Binzer's contribution stands out as unique for being written in the untried and novel format of a series of letters. *The Joys and Disappointments of a German Governess in Imperial Brazil* consists of forty-one letters written by the pseudonymous "Ulla von Eck" to her best friend, "Gretel," more frequently addressed as "Grete," that von Binzer published under her own name, acknowledging that she, herself, was Ulla. Those letters bear out the author's assertion that governesses possessed a certain advantage over other Europeans in getting to know Brazil. Given that they lived "directly with families," the vantage point for their observations lay within the domestic households of Brazilians themselves, a sedentary space that governesses advantageously occupied over considerable time. However fixed within a residence, whether rural or urban, Ina von Binzer did not neglect the world outside the confines of the households that circumscribed her daily routines.[1] In contrast, the male authors who produced the vast majority of the travel literature on Brazil usually were men on the move whose focus on domestic life was, at best, only tangential. They kept their eyes keenly on the horizon and mainly surveyed the public space, authoritatively parsing constitutional issues, appraising architectural landmarks, or capturing awesome geographical features. Otherwise, they rendered their conversations with the great men of the day into comprehensible summaries aimed at a male readership in North America, England, or Continental Europe. Von Binzer's book, consequently, can be deemed singular in the rich travel literature on Brazil because she belonged to a handful of writers who recorded the rare gaze of a woman. Hers was one of only seven accounts published by women in the nineteenth century that focused on Brazil and Brazilians.[2]

For the first time, this translation brings to the attention of English-speaking readers Ina von Binzer's unique rendition of the twenty months that she spent in Brazil between 1881 and 1883, when she worked as a governess and teacher for three upper-class households. Moreover, the historical context for her commentary proved particularly timely, because it coincided with the final decade of the Brazilian Empire (1822–89), crucial years that witnessed the abolition of slavery in 1888 and the proclamation of a republic in 1889. Entitled *Leid und Freud einer Erzieherin in Brasilien* (Disappointment and joy: A governess in Brazil), von Binzer's book was published in a modest

1. Having in mind Flora Tristan (1830s Peru) and Maria Graham (1820s Brazil), Mary Louise Pratt viewed women travel writers as defining a pattern wherein they "sallied forth" from the private space of their residences in "circular expeditions" that took them into the public space and "then back to the familiar"—the enclosed space of the household. *Imperial Eyes: Travel Writing and Transculturation* (London: Routledge, 1992), 5–6. She also remarked that "one is hard pressed indeed to find even an interior description of a house in travel books authored by men" (158).

2. Three of the seven authors wrote in English: Maria Dundas Graham (Lady Callcott), Elizabeth Cabot Cary Agassiz (whose husband's name appeared as sole author on the title page), and May Frances. Two wrote in French: Marie van Langendonck and Adèle Toussaint-Samson (whose daughter translated her account into English for original publication in the United States). And two wrote in German: Therese, Princess of Bavaria, and Ina von Binzer (pseud. Ulla von Eck).

printing in 1887, following her return to Germany in 1884.[3] Presumed by some to be fictive, Ina's epistolary account of her experiences appears to have been based on an actual series of letters that she penned to a close friend living in Germany. Certainly, her letters convey an authenticity of historical detail and contain specific references to actual individuals, including a number identified by their real names.

Ina's book remained largely forgotten until the mid-1950s, when it was published by Paulo Duarte in a serialized Portuguese translation in *Anhembi*, the São Paulo–based cultural journal that he founded and edited. A paperback edition appeared in 1956. However, Ina's volume of letters became accessible to a large number of Brazilian readers only in 1980, when Fernando Gasparian produced a second paperback edition. Editora Paz e Terra, his publishing house, launched *Alegrias e tristezas* (Joys and disappointments [inverting the terms of the German title]) as popular reading for a new generation of college students enrolling in Brazil's rapidly expanding university system. Between 1980 and 2004, Paz e Terra kept *Alegrias e tristezas* continuously in print. The relaunching of Ina von Binzer eventually made her letters known to thousands of Brazilian readers.[4]

Who was Ina von Binzer? Ina Sofie Amalie von Binzer was born on December 3, 1855, in Brunstorff, a village in the Duchy of Saxe-Lauenburg, where her father was in charge of the Forestry Administration (Oberförsterei). Lauenburg, not far from Hamburg, was an old principality inscribed within the new German Confederation created at the Congress of Vienna (1815–16); however, until 1866, it remained under the direct rule of the Danish crown.

3. *Leid und Freud einer Erzieherin in Brasilien* (Berlin: Richard Eckstein Nachfolger; Leipzig: Hammer & Runge, 1887), 227 pages. In November 2019, this 1887 edition became available online as Project Gutenberg EBook No. 60701, downloaded free at gutenberg.org. Travel accounts published in English can be found at the end of Ina's letters in "Suggestions for Further Reading."

4. *Anhembi* 19, no. 55 (June–August 1955), through 21, no. 62 (January 1956). *Alegrias e tristezas de uma educadora alemã no Brasil*, trans. Alice Rossi and Luisita da Gama Cerqueira (São Paulo: Editora *Anhembi*, Ltda., 1956); *Os meus Romanos: Alegrias e tristezas de uma educadora alemã no Brasil* (São Paulo: Editora Paz e Terra, 1980). Bilingual editions later appeared: *Leid und Freud einer Erzieherin in Brasilien: Alegrias e tristezas de uma educadora alemã no Brasil—Deutsch-Portugiesisch*, ed. and trans. Ray-Güde Mertin, Coleção Lusofonia 2 (Frankfurt am Main: Teo Ferrer de Mesquita, 1994); *Os meus romanos: As alegrias e tristezas de uma educadora alemã no Brasil, edição bilingüe* (Rio de Janeiro: Editora Paz & Terra, 1994). In 2008, the bilingual edition from Teo Ferrer de Mesquita (1994) was reissued. In 2017 the Paz e Terra original edition was reissued with a new cover by the Grupo Editorial Record (Rio de Janeiro), which had purchased the former publishing house in 2011.

Von Binzer was the third of six children, following two older brothers—Ludwig and Friederich—and preceding her younger siblings, Elizabeth, Max, and Sophie. Her birthplace in Brunstorff remained her early childhood home only briefly, during the years when her father oversaw the grounds as the forester in charge of this nature preserve. For the first ten years of her life, Ina moved frequently, due to her father's repeated transfers. By 1866, she was no longer living under Danish rule, but in the Prussian province of Schleswig. Her upbringing in a succession of rural environments may well explain why she took so enthusiastically to outdoor life during her final period of Brazilian employment, with the "Sousas," whose farm in Santa Bárbara d'Oeste she came to know from frequent excursions on horseback. In several of her letters, von Binzer reminded Grete that she was the daughter of a forester. Indeed, the almost phantasmagorical description of a locally uncut tract of pristine woodland in Santa Bárbara, conveyed in Ina's letter of July 11, 1882, testified to her firsthand familiarity with forests and a remarkable grasp of botanical detail.

When she was eleven, Ina's family moved to Arnsberg, Westphalia, where she completed her elementary and secondary schooling. Around the time that she finished high school, her mother died. As the oldest daughter, Ina stepped in to take her place, caring for her three younger siblings and keeping house for her father and two older brothers. She spent as many as five years carrying out those responsibilities. Indeed, this prolonged domestic interim probably accounts for why Ina deceptively passed herself off to the readers of *Joys and Disappointments* as only twenty-two years old when she arrived in Brazil. In fact, she was twenty-five. Around age twenty-three, Ina began to prepare for a career as a teacher, so she moved to Bonn. There she attended a residential normal school for a year and was indoctrinated in the *Vierzig pädagogische Sendschreiben*, the pedagogical "Bible" first published by Karl Bormann in 1859. A later edition of this foundational text for teachers made its way into Ina's suitcase when she packed for her trip to Brazil. Her gradual disillusionment with Bormann—she soon perceived that his pedagogy was very narrowly attuned to a northern European cultural background—made its way into her letters to Gretel. During a pivotal moment of great personal insight, laced with her characteristic mix of frustration and humor, Ina recounted how she quickly jettisoned Bormann, finding his pedagogical advice proved useless for the task of teaching Brazilian charges. In Soest, after passing her final examinations in late 1880 or early 1881, Ina was certified to hold a diploma as a governess and another as a teacher. Shortly after passing her certification exams, she left for her grand adventure in Brazil.[5]

Why did Ina von Binzer select Brazil as her destination? At the time she sought employment, the market in Germany for governesses was becoming saturated, thanks to the fact that a large number of well-educated young women were adopting Ina's career path, one that offered independence, respectability, and a taste of adventure. A regular job market existed, with advertised openings, but oversupply appears to have flattened domestic wages, rendering positions abroad financially more remunerative.[6] On the other hand, several of Ina's letters provide clues suggesting a special advantage that she possessed for securing a position abroad. They contain elliptical references to her "very rich" uncle, a businessman who had "lived for a long time in Brazil." Ina did not name him, although when she was presented to Emperor Dom Pedro II, he directly inquired after her uncle, demonstrating that he knew him. His name can now be disclosed: Christian Thomsen. Born in 1820, in Bredeneeck, a village in the Duchy of Holstein then part of Denmark, Thomsen immigrated in 1843 to Brazil's southernmost province, Rio Grande do Sul. There he established a successful import-export business in the port city of Rio Grande do São Pedro, and in 1847 he married a German emigrant from Hamburg. However, by the mid-1850s, Thomsen had moved his family to New York City, where he opened an office on Wall Street.[7] In 1869, the emperor ennobled him as Baron Cristiano de Thomsen. Eventually, styled "Baron de Thomsen" in New York City's newspapers, Ina's uncle made the social columns whenever he dined at Delmonico's or crossed the Atlantic to visit his wife's family in Hamburg.

The Thomsens appear to have kept in touch with Ina von Binzer and her siblings during their visits to Hamburg. At his death in 1898, the baron left

5. Ray-Güde Mertin offered new details on von Binzer's residences and education in "Nicht gar so starr germanisch," the afterword (*Nachwort*) in the German bilingual edition of *Leid und Freud* (1994), 259–64.

6. Ibid. Mertin commented on the "surfeit of the governess class" by the early 1880s, drawing observations from Irene Hardach-Pinke, *Die Gouvernante: Geschichte eines Frauenberufs* (Frankfurt: Campus, 1993), n.p.

7. I am grateful to Luiz Sérgio Heinzelmann, of São José dos Campos, Brazil, for information about Christian Thomsen's marriage. Emails to the author, 27 and 31 October 2016; 1, 16, 28, 29, 30 November 2016; 2 December 2016. The *New York City Directory* recorded Thomsen's residence and business addresses over four decades.

bequests in his will for Ina and all of her brothers and sisters. Presumably, Thomsen, or possibly his son Hugo, had earlier helped his niece to obtain a position as a governess by drawing on his extensive business network of Brazilian planters. A German librarian in the 1950s further supplied the information that Thomsen had financially helped Ina to launch a writing career when she returned to Germany in 1884, reinforcing his role as her benefactor. On her return to Germany, she was determined to earn her living as a writer. She did just that, moving to Berlin in 1885 and supporting herself there for a decade by writing books and articles.[8] In 1895, von Binzer married Adolph Richard Antonio Bentivegni, a career judge and amateur anthropologist. Eventually, in 1908, the couple settled permanently in Halle an der Saale, which remained their home until Ina's death in 1929. Von Binzer continued to publish articles through 1916, when ill health curtailed her writing career.

INA VON BINZER MEETS BRAZIL: A SLAVE SOCIETY IN TRANSITION

When Ina arrived in Brazil, in May 1881, she found herself in Latin America's only monarchy, one that had been in place since the country's political separation from Portugal in 1822. In a revolutionary era, independence had come about largely in order to preserve the monarchy as the institutional foundation for slavery. First, the Haitian Revolution (1791–1804) and then the independence movements of Spanish American countries (1810–25) determined that slavery would be nearly abolished in Latin America. By 1881, Brazil was singular in upholding slavery in the New World, for even the Spanish government had adopted a law that would end slavery in its colony of Cuba within five years. Following Cuba's lead, on September 28, 1871, Brazil's Parliament enacted the Rio Branco Law, popularly known as "the Law of the Free Womb," a measure of "gradual abolition" implying emancipation on an individual basis. The law stipulated that henceforth any child born of a slave mother would be free. Children "liberated by the law of September 28" were legally defined as "apprentices" or "wards" (*ingênuos*) bound to serve their owners until age twenty-one, unless manumitted earlier, beginning at the age of eight. The law

8. Von Binzer wrote two novels: *Zigeuner der Grosstadt* [Gypsies of the metropolis], 1895, and *Annelieses Hausstandssorgen* [Anneliese's domestic worries], 1900. She also published a children's book: *Tante Cordulas Nichten* [Aunt Cordula's nieces], 1896.

established an imperial fund to accelerate the process of manumission, considering eligible not only the children of slave mothers born after September 28, 1871, but also several other privileged categories.

Von Binzer acknowledged in her initial letter from Brazil that she had been mistaken in assuming that the Rio Branco Law abolished slavery altogether, a circumstance that her arrival in Rio de Janeiro abruptly corrected. Otherwise, she initially misapprehended much of that law's impact, especially the low rate at which slave owners availed themselves of the imperial manumission fund to indemnify themselves for freeing their "apprentices," starting at age eight. Thus she did not quite understand the scene that she so touchingly described in her letter of August 14, 1881, the baptism of eight infants born to slave mothers owned by "Sr. Rameiro," her first employer. Contrary to her assumption, those babies were not yet emancipated from slavery, for baptism validated only their status as wards, foreseeing future liberation automatically at age twenty-one. Alternatively, as children, they might have been emancipated as early as age eight, by payment of their purchase price to their owner. Yet this was a highly unlikely event where Ina was living in 1881, for in the Paraíba do Sul River Valley coffee planters were especially reluctant to part with their *ingênuos*. Coffee production for export explained why counties there still contained some of the highest concentrations of slaves in Brazil. Even more striking, those same counties registered the lowest rates of manumission in the country. Thus between 1872 and 1884, in the county of Vassouras, von Binzer's initial location, only 645 slaves were manumitted (slaves of all ages, including *ingênuos*), although 5,182 *ingênuos* were registered there during the same twelve-year period. The number manumitted amounted to about 3.1 percent of the county's estimated enslaved population of 17,891 in 1884. The profits to be made from coffee exports accounted for why so few slaves were freed by their owners. The closure of the Atlantic slave trade in 1850 had placed a premium on the domestic supply of slaves that would be felt until 1888.[9]

9. Ricardo Salles, *E o Vale era o escravo: Vassouras, século XIX* (Rio de Janeiro: Editora Civilização Brasileira, 2008), tables 11 and 14 (pp. 250, 267). In 1850, slaves in the county of Vassouras numbered 19,210, or 67 percent of the population. In 1872, they numbered 20,160, but only 52 percent of the population. By 1884, their numbers still showed little decline: 17,891 (percentage for the county not available, but below 50 percent). Thanks to an internal trade supplying slaves from Brazil's Northeast, there was little decline in the slave population over thirty years, but between 1850 and 1872, the free population (white and nonwhite) grew by 96 percent. Ibid., table 12 (p. 159).

Von Binzer arrived in Brazil at a crucial political and economic juncture. By 1881, slavery had long demonstrated irreversible decline, raising the specter of an impending abolition that, while still elusive, began to be taken into direct account by more astute planters. In 1872, the country's first census recorded an enslaved population of 1.5 million, 15.2 percent of Brazil's total population of 9,930,000 individuals. The province of Rio de Janeiro possessed the highest number of slaves. Nationally, by 1882, slaves had declined in number to 1,272,355, thanks to the 1850 closure of the Atlantic slave trade, passage of the 1871 Rio Branco Law, and the growth of private manumission associations. Fundamentally, however, the natural aging of the enslaved population foretold the institution's final crisis. Unlike in the United States after the 1808 closing of its Atlantic trade, Brazil's slave population had never been sustained, much less increased, by natural reproduction. Instead, a continuous supply of slaves from Africa fueled demands for labor. On the eve of abolition, in May 1888, five hundred thousand enslaved individuals would still remain, despite the 223,419 individuals who had crossed over to freedom during the preceding year. Brazil's official statistics never counted the growing population of *ingênuos* (wards) as slaves. Yet seventeen years after passage of the Rio Branco Law, they deserved inclusion in the official count. By 1888, approximately five hundred thousand *ingênuos* were still waiting to turn twenty-one, while at least one-half that number were working as de facto slaves for having attained the age of eight. Hence, practically speaking, Brazil's enslaved population still numbered one million individuals.

VON BINZER ADAPTS: THREE PLANTER FAMILIES, DIVERSE LOCALES, AND DIVERGENT OUTLOOKS

Von Binzer first worked in the county of Vassouras, Province of Rio de Janeiro, for a family of coffee planters in the Paraíba do Sul River Valley whom she identified as the "Rameiros." She thereby found herself in the heart of Brazil's "old coffee zone," the very first place where coffee had been cultivated for export. Strategically accessible to the Port of Rio de Janeiro from the 1820s onward, Vassouras had benefited from that connection to the global market via the Atlantic for both coffee and slaves. Next, Ina found herself working for two more planter families in the adjacent province of São Paulo who differed both from the Rameiros and from each other. The second family who employed Ina, the "Costas," had invested in coffee only in the late 1870s, although by the time Ina arrived in their city household they owned a huge plantation lying in the "Paulista West" (Oeste Paulista). There, thanks to the expansion of the railroad, coffee had arrived only in the late 1860s. Due to the rising price of slaves after 1850, planters like the Costas and their neighbors began to experiment with immigrant labor from Europe—Germans and Swiss, and, finally, Italians. In March 1882, when von Binzer joined the Costa family in their residence in the provincial capital of São Paulo, she began a uniquely urban experience, one physically removing her from the family's rural source of wealth, which increasingly would rest on coffee exports. Only in passing did she refer to the Costas's rural plantation; their city household, however, was serviced by domestic slaves. Von Binzer's final employers, whom she styled the "Sousas," once again deposited her in the remote countryside, several hours by train to the west of the city of São Paulo, where they resided on a farm carved from a much larger and older sugar plantation that historically had belonged to the wealthy father of Sra. Sousa, better identified as "Dona Maria Luísa." Located in the rural county of Santa Bárbara d'Oeste, this property depended short-term on migrant labor from the region of the Brazilian Northeast, rather than on slaves. Sr. Sousa nonetheless leased a substantial coffee plantation, which Ina located in the adjacent county of Piracicaba; however, it actually lay even farther west, in Dos Córregos. This more distant property, which Sr. Sousa visited about every three weeks, depended almost exclusively on a labor force of African and Afro-Brazilian slaves.

Consequently, in one way or another, all three of Ina's employers economically relied on slave labor, where coffee mattered, but to varying degrees. Their individual situations offer a stark contrast not only in terms of how coffee planters depended on slavery a mere six years before that institution collapsed but also in how they themselves viewed the servile institution—and anticipated the consequences of an approaching abolition.

The social prominence of Ina's employers dictated her attempts to conceal the real identities of at least the male family heads who employed her—as well as the names of their rural properties, which customarily served as colloquial "calling cards" for disclosing family identity in society. Landowners' given names often ended up attached to the name of a ranch or a farm, flagging them as men of considerable property while hinting at their ownership of slaves. Although Ina sought to cloak her three Brazilian employers and their families in anonymity, appropriating pseudonyms as the conventional literary device for respecting their privacy, their identities as well as the real names of their properties can now be disclosed. All three families occupied positions at the social pinnacle of their respective provinces. Each illustrated a particular path for investment in coffee production that differed from the others in terms of both timing and region, given the possibilities for exporting coffee, which had multiplied over the span of the entire nineteenth century. Yet in every case a fundamental dependence on enslaved labor proved characteristic, dictated by the circumstance that export production of coffee in Brazil was based on large-scale plantations—not on small family farms as elsewhere in Latin America.

The first family that employed Ina von Binzer, identified as the "Rameiros," diverged rather considerably from the impression that she conveyed in her letters. "Dr. Rameiro," assumed to be a native-born Brazilian and described by Ina as formerly a widower whose first wife had been Italian, actually was himself an Italian immigrant who had lived in Brazil for more than thirty years. His real name was Antonio Carlos Lazzarini. Far from being the holder of an ersatz law degree, as Ina sarcastically suggested, Dr. Lazzarini was a physician and surgeon who possessed a medical degree from the University of Lucca. His wife, Dona Alfonsina, or "Mme. Rameiro," was actually Afonsina Cândida Teixeira Lazzarini, Brazilian-born and a widow when she had married Dr. Lazzarini in 1866. She and her first husband had left their native Minas Gerais in the 1850s and joined his widowed mother, who previously had purchased a property called "Fazenda da Cachoeira" from the future baron of Vassouras (Francisco José Teixeira Leite), the mother's first cousin. Although Ina never revealed the location or the real name of the property—Fazenda da Cachoeira—she left the most knowledgeable of her readers to surmise (correctly) that it lay somewhere in the vast Paraíba do Sul River Valley, in the very heart of Brazil's "old coffee zone."

Fazenda da Cachoeira, about 120 kilometers over the mountains and due west of Rio de Janeiro, could be found in the famous coffee county of Vassouras. This plantation, which Ina called "Fazenda São Francisco," stood as a microcosm of the world that coffee planters in the Paraíba do Sul River Valley still vehemently defended in 1881, a mere seven years prior to the total abolition of chattel slavery. A half century earlier, the rise of coffee in the Paraíba Valley had breathed new life into slavery as a rural investment that, by the 1830s, paid very high returns. A network of intraprovincial roads, starting around 1820, economically enabled mule trains to carry sixty-pound sacks of green coffee beans to the port of Rio de Janeiro for shipment to Europe and the United States. In 1865, the railroad arrived in Vassouras, connecting the county directly to that international port. Contemporary parlance had long recognized the Paraíba Valley as Brazil's "river of slavery," given that since the 1840s it contained the largest concentrations of slaves in the country. In

1872, the year of Brazil's first census, Rio de Janeiro, though territorially a small province, still contained the country's second-largest slave population: 263,000 individuals, amounting to 31 percent of that province's total population. São Paulo, smaller in size, remained less dependent on slavery as a province due to coffee's later rise. Another 126,000 slaves amounted to 17 percent of São Paulo's population.[10] By midcentury, however, the writing was on the wall: reliance on Africa to supply a captive labor force for Brazil's coffee plantations was irrevocably sundered, foretelling coffee's future crisis.

As the New World's oldest and largest slavocracy, Brazil had been forced by the British to abolish the transatlantic slave trade definitively in 1850. Faced with the inevitable decline of the slave population, planters reacted differently to the crisis, depending on where they lived and when they had begun to invest in coffee cultivation. Whether they would cling to slavery indefinitely or devise schemes to attract a substitute free labor force framed the principal contrast between, on the one hand, the mentalities of the planters long invested in the Paraíba River Valley and, on the other, those who more recently had staked out plantations on the new frontier of the "Paulista West." The contrasting mentalities of Ina's employers toward slavery's future role in coffee production accosted von Binzer once she stepped, unknowingly, into the controversial scenario of impending abolition. In reading Ina's views about slavery, one must take into account that she still remained largely ignorant of the historical forces shaping both nineteenth-century slavery and the personal attitudes held by her employers about slavery and abolition. And, as a European, Ina von Binzer also brought with her the cultural baggage of a belief in the racial superiority of white people, notwithstanding her personal view that slavery was wrong. She trusted many of the attitudes and beliefs that her employers communicated about the intellectual limitations of slaves or their opinions on the dire consequences of abolition.

Von Binzer's letters from the Paraíba Valley convey the difficulties of her heavy work load supervising seven charges, the loneliness of her isolated situation, and her sporadic efforts to understand the world of slavery, mediated

10. Clovis Moura, "População Escrava," in *Dicionário da escravidão negra no Brasil* (São Paulo: EDUSP, 2005), 319. Daniel Mariani et al., "Censo de 1872: O retrato do Brasil," *Nexojornal*, 27 June 2017, 35, Nexojornal.com.br. In 1872, 38 percent of Brazil's population of nearly ten million was classified as white, and another 38 percent as *pardo*, or brown, while 20 percent was classified as *preto*, or black. The remaining 4 percent classified as *caboclo* was either indigenous Native Americans or of mixed indigenous and African descent. Mariani, "Censo de 1872," 30, 32.

by conversations with Dr. Rameiro. His wife, Dona Alfonsina, really did have twelve children, just as Ina von Binzer noted, and the governess accurately named the seven to whom she gave lessons. However, the five oldest of the twelve offspring had been fathered by João Nepomuceno Teixeira, Dona Alfonsina's first husband, who died in 1862. They, together with their mother, owned Fazenda São Francisco jointly with "Dr. Rameiro," their stepfather. Von Binzer's letters pay attention to the three eldest of her charges, those she scornfully christened "the Vehmic court": Maria Gabriela, twenty-two; Olímpia, twenty-one; and Emília, nineteen. Two older brothers no longer lived at the plantation. Her remaining charges, all daughters under eleven years of age, accounted for five of the seven children whose father was Dr. Rameiro: Afonsina, ten; Leonila, eight; Maria da Glória, five; Julia, around three; and the breastfeeding infant who remained nameless. She did not mention two other children of Dr. Rameiro, presumably absent, his oldest daughter and his only son. All seven of Ina's charges occupied her attention from 7 a.m. until 7 p.m.[11]

Rameiro expressed a standard planter view, that Brazilian slavery possessed a benign character, for he projected an ideological defense, the "good master." He offered the well-articulated argument that Brazilian owners treated their slaves much better than those in the pre–Civil War United States. Thus Ina's letters supported the image of Rameiro as the "good master," reinforced by the compelling anecdote regarding several desperate slaves who arrived in the middle of the night in flight from a cruel neighbor. They had begged Rameiro to intercede on their behalf against their owner. Yet by 1881 most Brazilian slave owners understood that slavery was on its last legs. It behooved them to avoid whippings and other cruel means of disciplining slaves in order to prevent their human property from running away or committing suicide.

Rameiro, however, pushed beyond the "good master" role by insisting that many slaves did not want their freedom anyway. What he failed to mention to Ina was his own reaction, a little more than two years earlier, to the

11. Inheritance documents confirmed the names and ages of the three sisters of the "Vehmic court" as well as the age of their half-sister Afonsina, who was ten or eleven in 1881. Neither Maria da Glória, Julia, nor the unnamed infant appeared in their deceased mother's 1887 inheritance documents, confirming that the three youngest children were no longer living, perhaps having fallen victim to a periodic devastation of yellow fever. Dona Alfonsina's two other children by Dr. Lazzarini ("Dr. Rameiro")—Adela (Adèle), age twelve, and Antônio, age seven—are not mentioned by Ina, presumably because they were living with relatives elsewhere. *Inventário* (inventory) of Afonsina Candida Teixeira Lazzarini (2 March–15 May 1887), IPHAN [Instituto do Patrimônio Histórico e Artístico Nacional] Archives, Vassouras.

flight of a valuable slave that he claimed as his own. He had offered an impressive reward for the man's capture: five hundred mil-réis, about US$220, perhaps 20 percent of the man's total market value. The advertisement that Rameiro placed in Rio de Janeiro's leading daily newspaper captured his personal determination to recover that property and hinted that the man may have escaped before:

> Ran away in the month of April 1878, from Fazenda da Cachoeira . . . the slave Venâncio, brown-skinned, born in Minas Gerais, occupation carpenter, 40 years of age, tall height, thin, gaunt face, beard on his chin and a mustache, startled gaze, hurried gait, leaning to one side with his arms swinging and head held high. He likes very much to play the guitar and passes himself off as free and thereby disguises himself . . . can be found hired out in some job in the city of Rio de Janeiro. . . . Whoever catches him and takes him to the above *fazenda* or to his owner, Dr. Antonio Lazzarini . . . will receive a gratification of 500 mil-réis. (*Jornal do Comércio*, 11 January 1880)[12]

Where Ina was concerned, Rameiro engaged in an exercise of friendly indoctrination, leaving little doubt about his own vested interest in the servile institution. Her letter of October 5, 1881, reported that the German botanist who was Rameiro's houseguest summed up with subtle sarcasm his own view of Rameiro's self-serving attitude: "I am afraid, Doctor, that I came to a place where I only get to see the positive side of slavery."

The second family to employ Ina von Binzer was the Silva Prados, whom she presented as "the Costas." They were the only family whose true identity could not be concealed from readers in the 1950s, due to her revelation of the children's real names. The latter proved a dead giveaway for disclosing their parents' identity. Martinho da Silva Prado Júnior and Albertina Morais Pinto had eight children in 1882—eventually, they numbered twelve—and their father was widely known to have named six of the first eight after celebrated figures in the Roman Republic. That circumstance explained why Fernando Gasparian revised the title of Ina's book as *Os meus romanos* (My Romans). All were Ina's charges: Lavínia, twelve; Caio Graco, ten; Plínio, eight;

12. Advertisement cited in Luis Costa-Lima Neto, "O teatro das contradiçôes: O negro nas atividades musicais nos palcos da Corte Imperial durante o século XIX," *OPUS* [Goiânia, Goias, Brazil] 14, no. 2 (December 2008): 38.

Maria Evangelina, seven; Clélia, five; Cornélia, four; Julieta, three; and the unnamed baby, one-year-old Vercingetorix (baptized Martinho da Silva Prado Neto [grandson] to perpetuate his father's lineage).[13] "Sr. Costa," or Martinico Prado, as he was universally known in São Paulo, was the son of a man worth over six million contos when he died in 1891. Martinico's maternal grandfather, the baron of Iguape (Antonio da Silva Prado), who had died in 1875, was the richest man in Brazil among his earlier generation. The story went that he liked to light his cigars with bank notes of one hundred mil-réis. The family's fortune initially came from commerce, but banking and plantations (mostly sugar, then coffee) later multiplied the original investment, topped off with Iguape's financing of the railroads that connected the Paulista interior to the provincial capital and then to the Atlantic port of Santos during the late 1860s.

Like Dr. Lazzarini, Martinico da Silva Prado was a genuine *doutor*, for he held a degree from the São Paulo Law Faculty, despite Ina's downgrading him to merely *Senhor* (Mister). Backed by an enormous family fortune and a father who became his main business partner, Martinico pursued an entrepreneurial and political career as an ardent member of São Paulo's Republican Party, founded in 1873. In 1875, Martinico became one of the founders of *A Província de São Paulo*, the newspaper that today is known worldwide as the *Estadão* (*O Estado de São Paulo*), the Brazilian daily analogous to the *New York Times* or the *Washington Post*. In March 1882, when Ina von Binzer joined his household, Martinico had just been reelected a member of São Paulo's Provincial Assembly, a post he would hold from 1878 to 1889. Raised in a family celebrated for its eccentricity—his mother had shocked São Paulo society by "divorcing" his father when they failed to agree on a bridegroom for their only unmarried daughter—Martinico was a lifelong rebel against his family's basically Conservative Party politics.[14] Brazil's great novelist Machado de Assis would draw on the contrast between Martinico and his older brother,

13. Vercingetorix was the nickname of a Gallic chieftain defeated by Julius Caesar. After Ina left the Silva Prados' employ, in August 1882, four more Roman-named children were born: Cássio (1883), Corina (1885), Fábio (1887), and Cícero (1888). When von Binzer's book was serialized in *Anhembi*, the Silva Prados were immediately recognized. Besides Corina (age seventy-one), Fábio (age sixty-nine) and Cícero (age sixty-eight) were still alive in the mid-1950s.

14. The *divórcio of* Dona Veridiana da Silva Prado (Martinico's mother) amounted to a legal separation. Civil marriage did not exist, and canon law prohibited divorce. Street kids stoned her carriage due to her "scandalous" repudiation of her husband (also her father's half-brother).

Antonio da Silva Prado, the Conservative Party leader, in his famous novel *Esau and Jacob* (*Isaú e Jacó*, 1904).

Although Ina von Binzer never visited his rural world, Martinico da Silva Prado was a man with one foot in the countryside, where coffee beckoned with new economic opportunities in the late 1860s and early 1870s. Correctly, he foresaw how investing in coffee along the dynamically moving frontier called the "Paulista West"—a frontier opening up northwest of São Paulo's provincial capital in the 1860s—would depend on a dramatic expansion of a railroad network connecting that frontier to the Atlantic port of Santos. He, along with his father and brother Antonio, was a major investor in the railroad, the Companhia de Estradas de Ferro Paulista, Ltda., simply called *a Inglêsa* (the English) by everyone. He experimented with a European, mostly Italian, labor force as a replacement for a portion of the slaves who customarily cultivated and harvested coffee. A professed abolitionist in the abstract and, in practice, an advocate for immigrant labor in São Paulo's western coffee fields, Martinico was not really averse to owning slaves, a circumstance von Binzer herself abruptly discovered while living in his urban household. Revisionist historians have now documented his decidedly slow evolution, such that he qualified to be counted among those they have dubbed São Paulo's "abolitionists of the eleventh hour."

The final couple who employed Ina von Binzer was the "Sousas," who lived with their children on a property roughly twenty kilometers south of "The Station." The latter denoted the railroad station of Santa Bárbara d'Oeste in the county of the same name, located 138 kilometers due west of São Paulo's provincial capital. Ina's experience of rural living there differed markedly from what she had encountered in the coffee county of Vassouras. First, her new employers, whose real names were Bento Aguiar de Barros and Francisca Miquelina de Souza Barros, had a much smaller family, with only three daughters under Ina's care: Maricota (Maria Rosa), fourteen; Isabel (Maria Isabel), eleven; and Albertina, eight. A son, Luís, age twelve, but mentioned only in passing, was already studying in Germany.[15] Second, slaves were few in number at the fictitiously named "Fazenda São Sebastião," where sugar and cotton were grown, lumber was milled, and foodstuffs produced for the family table.

15. I am grateful to Roberto Petroucic, of Curitiba, Brazil, for confirming the names and supplying the birthdates for the five "Sousa" children. (Eugênia, the youngest, was born after von Binzer left Brazil.) He corrected the location of Fazenda Vila Bela (in Dois Córregos), dubbed "Fazenda São Luiz" by Ina, and supplied information about it. Emails to the author of 26 and 28 September 2017; 2, 6, 7, 10, 29, and 30 October 2017.

This farm was a parcel carved from Fazenda São Luiz, an enormous plantation largely dedicated to sugar for most of its nineteenth-century history. Third and most important, Ina was made to feel like part of the Sousa family, instead of being treated as a servant. Her employers were down-to-earth people, the only ones whose friendship made Ina feel like she belonged. Yet, once again, "Sr. Sousa" (Bento Aguiar de Barros) really was a genuine *doutor*, having graduated from the São Paulo Law Faculty in 1863. Just as Ina had dismissed "Sr. Costa's" law degree, so, too, she never raised the circumstance that her third employer actually was a genuine *doutor*, although she certainly knew better. Reducing him to a mere *senhor* figured in her strategy of concealing not only Bento's prestigious identity but also that of his even more highly ranked wife. Uncharacteristically, Ina even gave the latter a pseudonym: "Dona Maria Luísa." Her easygoing relationship with the mother of her charges may have been fostered by the latter's ability to speak German. Formally cousins, but actually more closely related, husband and wife probably had been acquainted since childhood.

At first glance, this family belonged to a rural middle class, for their standard of living appeared rather modest. Von Binzer even described Dona Maria Luísa undertaking a number of domestic tasks that normally household slaves or servants would have performed. (Ina may have been trying to disguise Dona Maria Luísa's identity by taking her down a peg or two.) However, any conclusion regarding their social status that rested on their unremarkable rural property would be simplistic, given the role played by bloodlines, or family pedigrees. Both Bento and Francisca belonged to first families of provincial São Paulo. Bento's father, "Captain Chico of Sorocaba" (Francisco Xavier de Barros), had been a hero of the failed 1842 Liberal Revolt. Two of Bento's father's brothers, as well as one of Bento's own brothers, had been ennobled by Emperor Dom Pedro II; his father's sister had been a marquise.[16] Nevertheless, Bento's wife, Francisca Miquelina de Souza Barros, outranked him in prestige. Born in Rio de Janeiro, where she spent her early childhood before her mother's death, Francisca grew up in her father's mansion in the city of São Paulo after he remarried. She and her eight full siblings, together with their ten younger half-siblings, were schooled by Ger-

16. Bento's mother, Rosa Cândida de Aguiar, was the sister of Rafael Tobias de Aguiar, a principal leader of the failed 1842 Liberal Revolt. The latter is better recalled as the husband of the marquise of Santos (Domitila de Castro), notorious paramour of Emperor D. Pedro I who was left behind on Pedro's return to Portugal in 1831. Noble titles in imperial Brazil were granted for only one lifetime.

man governesses, speaking only German and French at home. Francisca's paternal grandfather had been the wealthiest man in the province at the end of the colonial era. Her father, Comendador Luiz Antonio de Souza Barros, São Paulo's first mayor in 1835, came into a huge fortune in the early 1830s, after graduating from law school in Coimbra, Portugal. In 1882, he still resided in his mansion in São Paulo's capital, renowned as the owner of nine large plantations in five counties, containing 3,630 hectares of land, 588,000 coffee trees, and numerous slaves, in addition to lands planted in sugar cane.[17]

Given that the Aguiars, Barroses, and Souzas had intermarried over three generations, it is hard, if not impossible, to disentangle the intertwined lineages of Bento and Francisca—Ina's "Sousas"—and, therefore, to distinguish their rural assets. Patrimonial power imposed parentally arranged marriages, explaining why families of wealth usually depended on intergenerational cousin marriage, or closer (uncle/niece or aunt/nephew) unions. Landed assets and slaves could thereby be kept among a closed group of kin whose children were numerous. However, those marriages functioned to keep pedigrees exclusively of European descent. Elite families disdained what they referred to as "mixed marriages," unions that might introduce African ancestry into their bloodlines. In reality, the small plantation that von Binzer called "São Sebastião" did not belong to either of her married employers, despite Ina's belief that it had been inherited from Mr. Sousa's grandparents. Instead, the owner was none other than Dona Maria Louisa's father, Comendador Luiz Antonio de Souza Barros. He had drawn up a contract with Bento ("Sr. Sousa"), designating him only the administrator, a pattern he applied to a number of his sons-in-law and even to his own sons. The father of eighteen children, he relied on those administrative contracts rather than dowries to secure his children's financial futures. As for the coffee plantation that Ina called Fazenda São Luiz, Bento either leased it or simply worked it as administrator. Ina made clear the couple's lack of a town house in the provincial capital when she noted in her letter written en route to Santos that the Sousas stayed in the mansion owned by Dona Maria Luísa's parents.

17. Zelia Maria Cardoso de Mello, citing the 1887 estate inventory of Com. Luiz Antonio de Souza Barros, in *Metamorfoses da riqueza São Paulo, 1845–1895: Contribuição ao estudo de passagem da economia mercantilescravista à economia exportadora capitalista* (São Paulo: Ed. Hucitec/Prefeitura do Município de SP, 1985), 132–33. I converted the 1,500 *alqueires* of land on the basis of one São Paulo *alqueire* = 2.42 hectares. (Ordinarily, one hectare equals 2.47 acres.)

It comes as a shock, consequently, to conclude that the Sousas did not own any real estate. Dowries were passing out of use by the 1860s, and Bento's father-in-law kept tight, patriarchal control over his children. Rather than an ideological commitment to abolition, the fact that Bento and Francisca owned few, if any, slaves may have accounted for their adherence to abolition. Most, if not all, of the house slaves that Ina encountered at Fazenda São Sebastião would have belonged to Comendador Luiz Antonio de Souza Barros, as owner of the property. At the distant coffee plantation called Fazenda São Luis, managed by Sr. Sousa, the enslaved labor force would have belonged to his father-in-law as well. Hence Ina's conclusion that the Sousas opposed slavery deserves reinterpretation in the light of their landless status, meaning their minimal ownership of slaves, if any at all. Notwithstanding this lack of assets, the Sousas availed themselves of Comendador Luiz Antonio's substantial largesse to enhance an otherwise modest lifestyle and maintain their elite status.[18] Thus Ina von Binzer's six weeks of vacation in Santos took place courtesy of Souza Queiroz & Co.—the actual owners of the *chácara*, or beach cottage, where the Sousas stayed. That seaside recreational property amounted to an important perquisite of the family's elite status.

READING INA'S CHARACTER AGAINST HER POSITION IN A PATRIARCHAL SOCIETY

It is against this backdrop of upper-class families and privilege that Ina von Binzer deserves to be appraised. How did she come to terms with her position as a foreigner, a woman, and a well-educated individual who, as a governess, ranked merely as a privileged servant? First, she always managed to keep her sense of humor, relying on a self-deprecating response that defined the other side of what even she acknowledged was her snobbishness. Hence Ina found wry humor in reading newspaper advertisements for runaway slaves that appeared side-by-side with the columns that listed openings for governesses. Or, in Petrópolis, she apologized to Mrs. Goldschmidt for her

18. Com. Luiz Antonio de Souza Barros had parlayed his inherited wealth into a massive fortune by the 1860s, originally by exporting sugar and importing African slaves. He and his brothers and cousins founded Souza Queiroz & Co. in order to compete successfully with English and German exporters based in Santos. This firm became the exclusive middleman for exporting the sugar and coffee grown by branches of his Souza Barros extended family in São Paulo's interior.

uncontrollable outburst of laughter at the woman's downright impertinent question: "Do you not have a job?" And she again erupted into uncontrollable laughter at Mr. Goldschmidt's even ruder reception of her, sarcastically concluding about her uncle's reference: "There is nothing like good recommendations for your compatriots in foreign lands—no one could possibly ruin that!!" Second, Ina proved to be a "survivor" whose independence and resilience allowed her to choose the terms on which she would be employed. Fairly soon, she found the isolation of the coffee plantation in Vassouras increasingly difficult to support; her three oldest pupils proved to be bored with their studies and, in Ina's view, rather boring themselves. In fact, they all had reached a marriageable age without having any prospects, at least in Ina's eyes.[19] Ina's serious illness—in November 1881, she apparently contracted malaria—persuaded her to change course and look for new employment. After recuperating for a month in mountainous Petrópolis and then trying her hand at teaching in a French boarding school for girls in Rio de Janeiro, she placed economic survival first and then bravely rolled the dice to look for a new job. Avoiding self-pity, she took herself to São Paulo in order to take charge of eight of that city's most notoriously spoiled children.

Finally, once established in the city of São Paulo, Ina focused on the goal at hand: to make the challenging situation presented by the household of Martinico and Albertina da Silva Prado work for her. Right away, her own "German" upbringing brought her into conflict with the permissive practices of those wealthy Brazilian parents whose children were famously deemed "uncivilized" throughout the city by their parents' own social peers. Ina took advantage of the social life that her new environment presented, an attractive urban milieu offering important contact with fellow expatriates from German-speaking lands. She understood that she could not challenge directly the children's "wild" behavior, but she could adapt—and do so with stubborn fortitude—as when she faced two of her "bad boy" charges seated on their English velocipedes across the dinner table from her. With Bormann's strictures long thrown out the window, Ina relied on guile and positive persuasion to cajole the children into focusing on their lessons, while she herself relied on

19. Although Emília never married and Olímpia became a nun, as did their much younger half-sister, Leonila, Maria Gabriela married Theodoro Peckolt 2º, a son of Dr. Theodoro Peckolt, the German botanist whose visit to Fazenda São Francisco Ina registered in comic relief (letter of 5 October 1881). Her younger half-sister Afonsina married Theodoro's brother Gustavo Peckolt.

letters to Grete as an escape valve for her frustrations over a brood of children who, for the most part, lacked even commonly accepted good manners.

Despite her European and cultured identity, von Binzer confronted strong class and gender prejudice, for basically she was perceived as a salaried servant whose intellectual accomplishments proved insufficient for earning universal respect. On a fundamental level, her very personhood stood as a silent indictment of the educational inferiority of privileged Brazilian women, for whom, as yet, no public secondary school existed in Brazil.[20] As Ina's letters detail, girls were expected to learn French and/or German, to play a musical instrument, and to sing and dance; above all, they were expected to learn how to administer a large household with efficiency and authority. That skill set, however, could be mastered through home schooling, while their brothers were sent to Europe for a costly, comprehensive education or apprenticeships in business. Ina's sympathy with the abolitionist cause and, implicitly, the condition of slaves deserves to be read against her own social inferiority in a society that located even well-educated European women as servants only slightly higher than slaves on the ladder of status.

Von Binzer's innate spirit of independence proved her salvation, once she extricated herself from the gloomy environment at Fazenda São Francisco. In the city of São Paulo, Ina exploited her identity as a foreigner rewardingly in order to build a new social life. She made contact with a large and important circle of German expatriates living there, thanks to invitations from the well-established Schaumanns. This couple had put down roots as permanent immigrants and opened a trusted pharmacy, while Mr. Schaumann served for many years as German vice-consul in São Paulo. The pivotal role that Germans played in the coffee export sector explained their large numbers in São Paulo by the 1880s, the high-water mark of their immigration. In fact, after Africans and Portuguese, who amounted to 79 percent of all foreigners living in Brazil in 1872, the 10.5 percent who were Germans ranked as the most numerous of any European immigrant group even in the 1870s. Ina's social life blossomed in São Paulo, and it was at one of the Schaumanns' many social events that she met Mr. George Hall, the English manufacturer of agricultural machinery. He would "coincidentally," but quite regu-

20. The campaign in the 1880s to admit adolescent girls to the prestigious Colégio Dom Pedro II, Brazil's elite public secondary institution, failed after an initial, limited success. June E. Hahner, *Emancipating the Female Sex: The Struggle for Women's Rights in Brazil, 1850–1940* (Durham, NC: Duke University Press, 1990), 60–62, 56–57.

larly, cross paths with Ina at the Schaumanns' house as well as in the countryside of Santa Bárbara d'Oeste or, eventually, even on the train to Santos. Dalliance with an attractive, if slightly enigmatic, beau thus salved Ina's ego. As the up-and-down romance blossomed between her and George Hall, Ina found her footing as the Sousas' valued governess, the genuine affection of their children amounting to her special reward.

As Ina was the first to admit, in both her tastes and dislikes, she was highly opinionated. Quite often, she came across as very funny in making her many frank utterances. Her comments about the "better sort" of white Brazilians indict her as a snob, albeit a snob whom she recognized in herself. Freely condemning the couturier styles or the piano artistry of elite Brazilian women, as well as the inability of men of any rank to make lively table conversation, she nevertheless mellowed as time moved on. Her situation as a governess captured the ambiguity of evolving Brazilian social class structure, which still rested on patriarchal authority and chattel slavery. An emerging urban middle class clung to the former if not to the latter, even as São Paulo teetered on the brink of transformation as South America's new industrial metropolis. Ina fully grasped her position as a well-educated woman conventionally regarded by her employers as someone incapable of attaining the level of their heightened position. Yet she could seize the advantage offered by her German identity as a foreigner. For instance, at a time when most respectable and wealthy Brazilian ladies rarely ventured alone into the city streets to visit the shops—but obliged the shopkeepers to go to their homes with their wares—Ina went into the streets by herself and bravely put up with the offensive behavior from men, who sometimes taunted her with insults and sexual come-on's. In Santa Bárbara, her sense of adventure led her to make forays alone into the countryside, once she discovered how delightful it was to ride horseback.

And what of the intrepid Mr. George Hall? Did he and Ina really get married, as the conclusion of her letters suggests? Or was George Hall simply a literary invention devised to make her letters more engaging—as critic Antonio Callado disdainfully charged? For now, an ambiguous reply is all that must be given, because the answer is not easily discovered. Ina von Binzer finished her letters on January 9, 1883, but she was said to have returned to Germany only in 1884. So why did she remain in Brazil for more than a year following the end of her work as a governess? Remarkably, in the early 1950s, an octogenarian resident of São Paulo, probably a younger half-sister of Dona Maria Luísa, disclosed to the Brazilian translators of Ina's letters that she had actually met Ina von Binzer. With the hindsight of seventy years, the elderly informant recalled, yes, the German governess had indeed married the English factory owner, although it had not ended well. Hence Ina's delay in returning to Germany may have been due to a brief marriage that ended in dissolution.

INA'S VIEWS ON RACE, SLAVERY, AND ABOLITION

However perceptive, Ina's commentary is not always enlightened. Although she believed that slavery in Brazil was doomed, like many Brazilians, she did not know when it would come to an end. An abolitionist in the long run, she displayed confusion in anticipating how free labor would replace slave labor, once abolition became a fact. Her assumptions about the limited capabilities of blacks fueled her pessimism over abolition's consequences. Her doubt over whether ex-slaves could successfully cope with freedom echoed that of her Brazilian employers, but Ina's characteristic bluntness makes her doubts sound very stark to us today. Like almost everyone, von Binzer believed in a racial hierarchy that just assumed those on top would continue to be of European ancestry. She never came into much personal contact with Brazil's growing population of free color, which, by the 1880s, was emerging as the foundation of both a lower middle class with artisanal skills and a smaller, professional middle class. The latter boasted journalists, teachers, printers, doctors, lawyers, civil servants, and career military officers. Fundamentally, Ina's express pessimism over the effects of "abolition now" was shaped not only by her limited contact with the free population of color but also by the attitudes of her slave-owning employers. They viewed the end of slavery as holding dire future consequences tied to their impending loss of human property or what they believed was the slave's incapacity for responsible action. Abolition, consequently, was a topic they fine-tuned as a theoretical benefit in a far-off future that, whenever it did take place, would still have disastrous social consequences. Fundamentally, abolition was feared as the event that would bankrupt the class of slaveholders.

Ina's use of *Negro* deserves historical explanation, given its frequent appearance in this translation. Readers of her letters should not let the word stand as a strict synonym for the same word in contemporary English. The term has reappeared today in contemporary Brazilian speech as a result of the broad impact of the *Movimento Negro* (Black Power Movement) in post-1970 politics, where it is used as a positive identifier in the struggle for civil rights to connote an inclusive African descent. The nineteenth-century connotation of the Portuguese word *negro*, however, carried a different meaning. This English translation of *Leid und Freud* carefully preserves von Binzer's use of *Negro* in the original German, while translating her use of *schwarz* and *schwarze* as "black." Von Binzer appears to have adopted the Portuguese word *negro* into her German simply by hearing Brazilians use it colloquially in everyday speech. In the early 1880s, the meaning of *negro* for Brazilians did not pertain to color or ethnicity, but to civil (legal) status. *Negro* fused blackness to civil status in order to connote a servile identity. Hence, the word operated in everyday speech as a synonym for "slave" (*escravo*).

Consequently, readers need to be aware that Ina's use of *Negro* referred to slaves rather than to black people. For example, when she described the "ten to twelve Negresses [who] sit and sew" in the big house at Fazenda São Francisco, she was registering their identity as slaves. Or when Ina described the driver of the carriage that met her at the Vassouras train station as the "Negro coachman," she was identifying him as a slave. Even her offhand observation about "the Negroes of all varieties of color" who populated the streets of São Paulo implied an exaggerated generic identity for them as slaves. On the other hand, Ina may not have grasped the subtleties of elite speech that otherwise might have led her to a different choice of words. *Negro* was susceptible to a wide range of nuance, for it directly relied on a speaker's carefully calibrated tone, a linguistic subtlety that may have escaped her. *Escravo* (slave) was usually avoided in polite speech, at least until the mid-1880s when a political movement finally focused abstractly on the subject of abolition. Instead, Brazilians preferred a different term for "slave": *cativo*, or "captive." In parliamentary debates, the age-old terms of "captive" and "captivity" [cativeiro] operated as euphemisms amounting to a legal dodge that derived from sixteenth-century jurisprudential arguments. On the other hand, by the mid-1880s, militant abolitionism would transform the national political debate to refocus on *escravo* and *escravidão*. However, among the slaves themselves, "captive" (*cativo*) was preferred for self-identification, in emphatic confirmation of the offensive sound of *negro*. Once abolition became a fact, popular speech quickly discarded *negro* altogether, replacing it with *preto*, an alternate term for "black," one that exclusively implied color in order to avoid the stigma of an ancestry linked to slave status. To the extent that *negro* continued to be used following abolition, the term passed into exclusively derogatory speech, amounting to a racial slur, one that polite and public speech did not tolerate.

As in the United States, being an abolitionist did not mean believing in the equality of the races. Ina's ethnocentric limitations emerged in Vassouras, where she first encountered Afro-Brazilians as a member of an upper-class white household sharing a plantation with over 150 slaves. Her early letters suggest that she had no firsthand contact with black people prior to arriving in Brazil. Initially, she may have felt fear on encountering the slaves who worked the coffee fields at Fazenda São Francisco, for their patois would have been largely incomprehensible to her if, indeed, they did not speak in African languages. Although the house slaves spoke an intelligible Portuguese vernacular, Ina still appears to have found them slightly bizarre, a sign of what she took to be their foreignness. Her own identity as *the* foreigner, however, may have led her to exaggerate their differences. Fundamentally, the daily contours of the institution of chattel slavery began to strike von Binzer as unreal; they constantly challenged her common sense.

One anecdote proved telling of Ina's intellectual evolution over a few short months—when she laughed out loud at eight-year-old Leonila, because the child urged her governess not to be frightened by little Jacob, the slave child who startled Ina, suddenly appearing with his irrepressible grin. Ina's laughter was elicited by Leonila's impromptu counseling that fear was unnecessary, because Jacob had been given to her by her grandmother as a birthday present. Ina, however, interpreted her own outburst of laughter as mocking the very notion of slavery itself. The child's comment cut to the very core of slavery's essential meaning for whites in Brazil, as she explained to Grete: "There is, in general, something comical about the dignity that even the children here assume automatically through the existence of slavery." Ina captured the basic reality of slavery. It was an institution that offered every white person, even at the young age of eight, the opportunity to claim a "dignity" based on ownership of another human being, thereby proclaiming a birthright derived from superior color. Do we not still speak today of "white entitlement" as an attitude—if not a "birthright"—one affirmed vehemently by those who today resent the exercise of equal rights by the descendants of African slaves?

Initially, in several letters, Ina freely expressed her aesthetic condemnation of the slaves' physical features, employing what today strikes us as no less than a brutal disparagement of individual physiognomies. Her words stand as truly insulting formulations worthy of condemnation. Some of those disparaging remarks, it must be pointed out, were not unusual for Brazilians themselves to express. Indeed, Ina may even have picked them up from her employers and their children.[21] By disparaging a slave's physical features, the speaker reliably removed, or distanced, that slave from a humanity that both of them shared. Ina's utterances of frank revulsion amounted, of course, to a stock tool in the assertion of white supremacy. On the other hand, Ina's deplorable remarks may also may have operated unconsciously to distance herself from society's lowest rung and, in her own mind, to elevate her to a position closer to her employers. Was not her own position as a foreign governess fraught with random humiliations? Yet she did not lose sight of the humanity of the slaves whom she saw on a daily basis; slowly, her ugly remarks ceased. As early as her second month of residence in Brazil, during the celebration of the feast of St. John the Baptist (Eve of São João, June 23), she described the slaves' behavior and attitudes with a degree of empathy that testified to her considerable admiration for several of them. Otherwise, in a letter written from Fazenda São Francisco, on August 14, 1881, Ina reflected on the multiple contributions made by slaves—"Negroes play the lead role in this country." Contemptuously, she charged, "The Brazilian [implying native-born whites] does not work." Once settled in São Paulo, Ina ceased her derogatory remarks altogether. Concomitantly, she no longer appeared angry, a state of mind that earlier characterized much of her commentary. Moreover, her letters written from Santa Bárbara contained genuine expressions of *simpatia* (friendliness) for several individual slaves. Finally, in writing about the slave who was a leper, Ina seems to have examined her own conscience to find herself wanting. Her soul-searching led her to confess to a serious moral lapse. She may have been moved to reconsider a number of her previous judgments, including those disparaging remarks penned so soon after arrival in Brazil. Certainly, von Binzer "mellowed"; those ugly comments disappeared entirely from her letters. Simultaneously, she joined a household in Santa Bárbara that received her with kindness and respect.

True, Ina never abandoned her penchant for disparaging individuals—of any color—when their lack of education or common sense complicated her personal situations. Resorting to ridicule always brought instant relief.

21. In the early 1900s, Martinico da Silva Prado's older brother Antonio Prado was watching a São Paulo soccer team play a match in Paris, together with one of his female cousins, a daughter of Ana Blandina da Silva Prado. She asked Antonio, in reference to the star player, a mulatto, "Who is that monkey?" "That is no monkey," he replied, "that is your cousin"—pointing to Joaquim Prado (the son of Dr. Eleutério da Silva Prado, a brother of Antonio's father), also Antonio's cousin. Darrell E. Levy, *The Prados of São Paulo, Brazil* (Athens: University of Georgia Press, 1987), 121.

The lack of educational opportunity in Brazil nevertheless deeply offended her. Where slaves mattered as a prima facie group denied education as public policy, contrary to the Law of the Free Womb's prescription mandating primary schooling for the children it "freed," Ina did not spare her contempt for upper-class whites. Even the Sousas, who failed to grasp how society would benefit from schooling the ex-slaves, did not escape her censure.[22]

AN INSIDER'S VIEW OF A SLAVE SOCIETY IN DISSOLUTION

In strictly political terms, Ina's musings over abolition provide a prism for viewing Brazilian slavery during its final decade. Her vantage point of living "directly with families" proved most significant for recording observations about slavery from the inside out. Indeed, she has been recognized as the inside observer on Brazilian slavery par excellence, given the sedentary, domestic perches from which she jotted down anecdotes specific to slaves or their owners. Her letters offer a unique window into the contrast between coffee planters in the Paraíba Valley who held on to slavery as long as possible and those in the Paulista West who pragmatically sought to foster a transition to free labor by promoting European immigration or availing themselves of migrant labor from elsewhere in Brazil. In the end, neither group genuinely embraced abolition as the solution for removing the stain of slavery on the body politic, a conclusion Ina's letters hinted at more than once. When abolition finally arrived, as the "Golden Law" adopted on May 13, 1888, it capped the efforts of the slaves themselves, who had engineered a mass desertion of the coffee fields in the province of São Paulo. Yet neither slaves nor their owners were offered any compensation. No government agency along the lines of the Freedman's Bureau in the United States was established to ease the transition to freedom. Nor were the former slaves given plots of land, as some Brazilian abolitionists advocated. The establishment of a republic in 1889 favored the interests of São Paulo's coffee planters and promoted their policy of replacing

22. According to Brazil's 1872 Census, the number of slaves who were literate or who were enrolled in school was unknown. So an arbitrary 1 percent was assigned as their literacy rate. As for the free population (all colors), the adult literacy rate was 17.7 percent in 1872 and practically the same in 1890: 17.4 percent. Boys enrolled in school in 1872 made up 17 percent of the free population, and girls 11 percent. Mariani et al., "Censo de 1872," 38–39.

slave labor with immigrants from Europe, consigning those who had been freed from captivity largely to marginal roles in the coffee export economy of Brazil's booming Center-South.

Von Binzer's letters deserve appreciation as a unique repository of primary source material for social historians of Brazil. Their somewhat limited commentary on the organization of elite family households, upper-class child-rearing practices, and the social behavior of children is offset by a compensatory amount of ethnographic material evocative of the world outside the household. Her visit to the tiny, shack-like church on the outskirts of Americana, at the invitation of the Sousas' *Confederado* refugee neighbors, stands as unique, quite probably the oldest account of a gathering of Brazilian Baptists. Ina's rendering of the *sos kiss* given by the slaves on Dr. Rameiro's plantation to the bumbling German botanist also illustrates how her letters delve into ethnography—if not always quite correctly recounting his "confusion." Those observations validated a ritual of dominance central to preserving the hierarchy of master-slave relations. Ina's delineation of the contemporary linguistic divide at Fazenda São Francisco, between the Portuguese spoken by whites—*a língua dos brancos*—and what later she correctly termed the "Negro-Portuguese pidgin" of the blacks, which in Petrópolis she likened to low German, stands as a rare observation in the travel literature. Her multiple accounts of St. John's Eve offer first-person descriptions of what then was *the* most important holiday in Brazil, one eclipsing both Christmas and New Year's. All of these descriptions today stand as fragmentary field notes testifying to her special talents. However much Ina's gaze fixed on domestic life, she also turned it outward to explore the world beyond domestic confines, recording events, impressions, and individuals from a multiplicity of positions—on foot or on horseback, in trains or from horse-drawn public conveyances, and even from a wagon driven by a slave coachman, while she was balancing a watermelon.

On the other hand, von Binzer was not deeply interested in the slaves as individuals—however much she recorded their collective behavior at festivals, at baptisms, or on the city streets. Much as the families who employed her, she took their household slaves largely for granted. Hence, for the most part, as individuals they remained unseen, just as in Victorian England the servants downstairs remained invisible to their social betters upstairs. In strictly political terms, however, Ina's musings over abolition came to view slavery as a moribund institution. By late 1884, when slavery was first abolished at the provincial level, in the northern provinces of Ceará and Amazônas, Brazilians would cease to place their faith in the Law of the Free Womb and turn instead to the progressive goal of "abolition now." Von Binzer offered her readers a great deal more than merely a sharp contrast between coffee planters in the Paraíba Valley who clung to slavery as long as possible and those in the Paulista Oeste who sought to foster a pragmatic transition to European labor. Beyond the confirmation that neither group viewed abolition as an immediate positive gain, she captured her employers' private opinions regarding the servile institution precisely as it was about to collapse. Thus Dr. Rameiro had pessimistically intoned, "Unfortunately, in the meantime, for us, there *must* be slaves." And Martinico da Silva Prado Júnior, who, by 1887, styled himself an abolitionist, had erupted into fits of rage in 1882, on discovering that his slave Tibério had appealed to a district judge to set his purchase price, thereby sealing his emancipation. Finally, even the Sousas, who, according to Ina, "don't like the slave economy" and favored abolition in the abstract, kept "an eye open to the danger that might threaten the country," viewing that impending event as spelling "economic ruin" or "impoverishment" for their neighbors.

The vignettes Ina von Binzer has left us memorialize her curiosity and powers of observation, offering a unique glimpse of the final days of the New World's last slavocracy. Given the uniqueness of her contribution, Ina's epistolary account deserves to be treasured and probed by twenty-first century readers. Her letters cast a unique gaze at a society that quickly passed away, yet whose long shadow has far from disappeared even today.

Ina von Binzer's Letters

Fazenda de São Francisco

May 27, 1881

My Dear Grete!

Fazenda means plantation. I'm sorry that the word for plantation is not *hacienda*, since this is probably what you believed until now. Sorry also that I must therefore disappoint you already with the first word of my first letter. But you may all console yourselves together with me, for I, too, was disappointed by this. And yet, it was so cute when we still innocently confused Spanish and Portuguese. One illusion breaks down after another!

That this is called São Francisco is not remarkable at all; on the contrary, it would be peculiar if it had a different name. Twenty-one localities in Brazil are called São Francisco, and the number of plantations that this popular saint must take under his protective wings are legion.[1]

I will present you with a second disappointment in this letter: I cannot report a single attack by Indians or a struggle with a tiger over the course of my journey here from Rio de Janeiro. At the very least, you might have expected an encounter with a giant snake—and I accept completely how much my stature must be diminished vis-à-vis other tropical travelers in all your eyes, given that I arrived here without any serious accidents.

But that is how it was.

At the train station, Dr. Rameiro* himself picked me up in—just imagine, Grete—a very comfortable European carriage! Seldom has a carriage annoyed me as much as this one. If only one of its wheels had at least broken on the way, or if only the Negro coachman had attempted to drive us into some sort of pit, perhaps as revenge for some punishment that he incurred—after all he, at least, was a real slave! But shamefully I have to confess again that he looked out at us over his flat nose with good humor and probably he was not thinking of any pit. Well, let's hope that fate shows us some understanding . . .

1. The fictitiously named "Fazenda São Francisco" was actually Fazenda da Cachoeira, a plantation dating to before 1820. Located just south of the city of Vassouras, on Rodovia RJ-27 at km 43, as the now beautifully restored and renamed "Fazenda Cachoeira Grande," this former plantation is today a tourist site and hotel.

*The *ei* in Portuguese words is pronounced with emphasis on the *e*, as two separate sounds. Editor's note: In Portuguese, *ei* is a diphthong pronounced as a long *a*, as in *rate*. Ina's footnotes are identified in this text by asterisks.

and allows me to end up in at least a mildly dangerous situation . . . but in such a manner that I will still be able to report it to you after the fact.

So Dr. Rameiro picked me up. They call him "Doctor."[2] I am not sure why, and I doubt that he himself or those who address him in this way could offer satisfactory information about this, except for the notion that every better-situated Brazilian man brings a natural birthright to this title, and that it must therefore appear either immodest or idiotic if someone demanded from him that he had to earn this title through some highly superfluous university study.

He spoke Portuguese, I spoke French.

There are supposedly hardly any Brazilians who do not speak French, but there are also a number who have a very incomplete idea of the conditions in the country affiliated with the language and of the fact that it also contains a number of other places than Paris. In the mind of my Negress, "Paris" is identical with every and all areas outside Brazil, and because I see her unlimited respect for this remarkable object, "Paris," from which I, too, come, I was careful not to allow my eight-day-old Portuguese to discredit "Paris" and the virtues of its sons and daughters.

"My Negress"—that is until now the best thing about my letter, isn't it? It does sound like something! Her name is Olímpia, which makes the matter decidedly more stately, and at every opportunity she submissively says, "Sim, senhora [Yes, miss]," even when I scold her. In confidence, however, I want to tell you, dear Grete, that she is the most repulsive, most thick-lipped black creature that ever went by a grandiose name, and that *senhora* is something very ordinary here, like "My lady" in Berlin. Furthermore, the eternal "Sim, senhora," becomes rather dull, since she uses it everywhere and always, particularly when she does not understand my Portuguese, which occurs several times a day. But don't tell the others this, all right?

Dr. Rameiro still owns about two hundred male and female slaves. Obviously most of them work outside in the coffee plantation, but there is a fair number here in the house, some of whom also have tasks to carry out. In a large hall with a skylight, which actually resembles a long corridor, a Negro and a Negress each sit at a sewing machine and chitchat the whole day.

2. *Doutor* was the title awarded to graduates from Brazil's two law schools, located in Recife and São Paulo, or, alternatively, from the two medical schools in Salvador and Rio de Janeiro. "Dr. Rameiro" was really an Italian immigrant named Antonio Carlos Lazzarini. Ina's disparagement of his use of *doutor* was completely unjustified, for he was actually a physician and surgeon at the local hospital. However, she concealed elements of his true identity to make him anonymous.

Around them and on the ground, and in an adjacent room that again looks like a corridor, and which lies next to the kitchen, ten to twelve Negresses sit and sew. And each one has a bamboo basket in front of her with a small child in it. Of course, one of the children in this collection is always screaming. Since for these sewing tasks they only use Negresses with very small children who cannot be left alone, it is obvious that when some are sitting around, the bamboo baskets are not absent and that there is crying from at least one of them.

The kitchen personnel consists of three individuals. I have not been able to ascertain which one of them does the cooking. Sometimes the food tastes as if their views with respect to the necessary ingredients diverged in the most diametrically opposed ways so that finally they all use their own particular approaches. At other times, it seems as if all three have withdrawn from the task of cooking to get some peace.

At noontime, a small, twelve-year-old mulatto with an insolent expression and a seemingly indefatigable passion for dirty suits and somersaults—which is his preferred manner of locomotion—has to chase the flies from the table with a small piece of cloth (which, at least now, is brown-grey, and it might have been earlier too), all of which I find far more insufferable than the flies. In addition to this, he serves coffee. Although that refreshment is consumed at least four times a day, this task is not regarded as sufficient occupation for a whole day, and it is hard to imagine to what levels of virtuosity in somersaulting this small, yellow creature could still rise, if he used only half of his free time for the perfection of this skill.

"Free time!" Oh, dear Grete, at the mention of this word I could begin grieving. Do you remember how we agreed that it was indisputable that the Brazilians do nothing the whole day except for looking smart and smoking, that their ladies, wrapped in the most delicate garments, swing in hammocks, fanned by small, interesting, Negro boys clad in white and red?[3] How orange and banana trees had a peculiar tendency to grow toward the windows in our pictures, and how colorful parrots and the "sweet" little hummingbirds flew around one like the pigeons in Lilli's park? What an idyllic place! And of course, such idyllic people would not demand something so coarse as rough "labor" from their governess—ugh!—one would rest with the children in the shade of the orange trees, teach them how to speak the precious mother tongue

3. Brazilians had adopted the indigenous hammock centuries earlier, substituting it for a bed.

while playing, taming parrots, eating fruit, writing poems, and adorning oneself with flowers. . . .

Oh, Grete! I say nothing but "Oh!"

Of course, Dr. Rameiro smokes—in fact, I have never noticed him not smoking—but for the life of me I could not call him posh! Neither when he stands with legs spread apart in front of the house, nor when he climbs around in the coffee warehouse. Nor does he have the least resemblance to the handsome Brazilians on the blessed stage of the Frederick Wilhelm Operetta House when he lies in the hammock in the evenings, doing nothing. It is quite depressing!

Madame Rameiro also sometimes lies in the hammock (here hammocks are like pieces of furniture and are attached to two suitably situated bedroom doors with strong hooks), but she is a somewhat lively lady, and cannot stay in one place for very long.[4] When she regains her energy, for example, due to bad sewing by the bamboo-basket women, I can hear her from the room in which I give my lessons. (What do I not hear from there?) She scolds the Negresses using words that strangely enough have a noticeable similarity to the strong, local curses. But tomorrow I will look up the amicable meaning of *diabo* [devil] or *canalha* [riffraff] to justify the good woman in my own eyes, which the dictionary will accomplish wonderfully.

More about the oranges and bananas later. Now just a word about the parrots. Whatever you do, dear Grete, never let them enter your idyll again. But if you do, satisfy yourself with only one and let it be deaf-mute! In the room with the musical bamboo baskets there are six of them on the walls and on top of small, half-foot-wide tin stands that look like little consoles. At four in the morning, they begin vigorously demanding their coffee and do not stop until they have achieved their aim, at the earliest and in good circumstances, after one-and-a-half hours. And then they chat, yell, squeak, scream, and nag the whole day long with a persistence that would be merely shameful were it not for the eleven other birds, the sewing machines, and the bamboo baskets which suffice to literally drive me mad! They are now my worst enemies. In the first few days, I nurtured an uncertain hope that they would soon die, but the day before yesterday, when I remembered Molière's hundred-

4. Subsequently identified by von Binzer as "Dona Alfonsina," "Mme. Rameiro's" real name was Afonsina Cândida Teixeira Lazzarini. Prior to marrying Dr. Lazzarini, in 1866, she and her five older children had inherited one-half of the plantation from her first husband, who died in 1862.

year-old parrot, I began to look at them only too often just as Mr. Pickwick regarded the stubborn horse—that is, in my mind I ruminate over the possible consequences of killing all six of them. Of course, I also hear them from the classroom.

Indeed, one hears everything in this idyllic house. The doors and windows are always open, and no rug, no curtain, and no upholstered furniture absorbs any sound that can travel through the air. Oh, dear Grete, these rooms resembling riding halls, this glaring light, these woven basket couches, and these Viennese chairs—it is all so appallingly unromantic and so un-idyllic![5]

And as for the *dolce far niente* [sweet idleness]! Let me be silent. We were astoundingly "young" when we convinced ourselves that this would be my main occupation here! I do not want to break your compassionate heart with further information. I will tell you about it gradually.

For today, farewell. Tea is being served, because I hear the "one, two, three"—that is, the somersaults of the mulatto boy. He needs three from the dining room to here, and of course, I hear them. Yes, right now he is mumbling something at the door—"Chá, Senhora" [Tea, Miss]—in other words, until my next moment of free time. I hope you do not become too bored in the meantime.

Yours, Ulla

5. "Viennese chairs" refers to the famous "café" chairs designed by Michael Thonet in his Vienna workshop, which mass-produced bentwood designs sporting caned seats—today still called "Austrian" chairs by Brazilians—perfect furniture for a hot climate.

São Francisco

June 9, 1881

Dearest Grete!

Do you know what I discovered in the depths of my suitcase today? Our Bormann, that is, his *Forty Pedagogical Letters*.[6] They don't work, Grete, they don't work here! And I had depended on them so much! When fear overcame me en route about how I would deal with my Brazilian pupils, I always thought about the helpful little book in my travel gear and said to myself calmly: "This is how you'll do it!" And now . . . ! Oh, Grete, I think Bormann himself would not have known what to do here. One gets angry about so many things, which is hardly comprehensible, but it always happens and again and again!

There are twelve children in this blessed family, and I have seven of them under my pedagogical rod. It starts at seven in the morning. That's when the "old ones" arrive to take their hour of German. Dona Gabriela, Dona Olímpia, and Dona Emília are already nineteen, twenty-one, and twenty-two years old, respectively, which is very close to old-maid age for female Brazilians, and which horrified me with my twenty-two years. And then, imagine, constantly having to address your student as "Dona"! In the first mornings, they regularly arrived late, so that I saw myself forced to beseech them to arrive on time, since at that time I lived according to Bormann. As a result, they now sit solemnly and silently around the table with their pale yellow, emotionless Brazilian faces when I enter. The dull, indifferent "Bonjour, mademoiselle" shows no expression of feeling from them, no early-morning freshness, no passion for learning, no personal sympathy. Oh Grete, this trio is horrendously debilitating! Upon seeing them, I am always reminded of the Vehmic courts, whose judges were famous for their coldness and gravitas.[7] I am cowardly enough to wish, already, that I had not beseeched them to be punctual. We drag ourselves drudgingly through this German lesson, naturally always

6. Karl Bormann (1802–88), German pedagogue, was the author of *Vierzig pädagogische Sendschreiben* (Berlin: Wiegandt and Grieben, 1859), which went to two more editions in 1862 and 1867. This pedagogical "Bible" was the standard manual in Ina's normal school training.

7. The Vehmic courts were secret, inquisitorial tribunals that dispensed vigilante justice in medieval Westphalia.

by means of the French language, and the latter is still the best part of the whole thing, because as soon as they start speaking German, I don't understand a single syllable.

I always feel slightly redeemed, but also already half-dead, when the "little ones" arrive at eight o'clock. Although they are naughty, they are at least children, and only the eldest girl among them has already acquired something of the holy tribunal in her. Oh Grete, they are all so "provoking" [original in English]! They do everything that I say, learn everything that I assign them, and nevertheless they irritate me to no end!

I am certain that they mean no harm, and sometimes I also find the "little ones" downright cute.

Thus, last Sunday, I was sitting on the bench, in the heavenly garden under an imposing mango tree, dreaming—oh, Grete—about German oaks. When I looked up, a disgusting little black creature from the jungle suddenly startled me. Imagine it about twelve years old, more ape than human, grinning from one ear to the other, with unappetizing woolly hair, a forehead as broad as a finger, a horribly fat abdomen, and club-like black legs, which glowed purple because of all the dust. Imagine all this, only dressed with the shortest conceivable version of a shirt of undefined color, and you will understand that I was not exactly enthralled by this noble fellow human creature. On the contrary, I probably drew back in fear, since the little eight-year-old Leonila immediately emerged from behind a bush to tell me calmingly and protectively, "N'ayez pas peur, mademoiselle, c'est Jacob" [Don't be afraid, miss, it's Jacob]. And then, when my face presumably still did not express enough enthusiasm, despite having been honored with the acquaintance of the holy patriarch, she added, half-indignant, half-elucidating, "Il est à moi, grand'maman m'en a fait cadeau à mon jour de fête" [He's mine. Grandma gave him to me as a present for my birthday].[8] I am telling you, it was too funny. The little slave owner was so proud of her live "birthday present," and the disgusting little piece of property grinned with such satisfaction upon hearing this declaration of ownership—which it, however, probably guessed at more than it understood—that I had to laugh out loud. There is, in general, something comical about the dignity that even the children here assume automatically through the existence of slavery. On the other hand, it is also touching how attached they are to the good and loyal Negroes and Negresses. The little

8. It was not unusual in wealthy families for children to be given a slave child as a birthday present.

five-year-old Maria da Glória, for example, always saves something from her dessert for her former nursemaid, a pretty mulatta, or she asks for something to give to the nursemaid's younger nursing-sister. And Alfonsina, who is usually wrapped up in her own appearance, would give away her most colorful ribbon if she thought that the old Ana wanted it.

They all like to give and to fulfill one's every possible wish—and yet—and yet . . . !

Oh Grete, did you know that I actually consider Peter in a foreign land to be a quite clever person now?[9]

Yours,
Ulla

9. "Peter in der Fremde" is a poem by August G. Eberhard in which the main protagonist resolves to wander out in the world, finds himself unable to decide which direction to take at the first crossroads, and, consequently, returns to his hometown.

São Francisco

June 20, 1881

Gretel, I wish you could be present at a Brazilian lunch! You would not be invited "to lunch," though, not even to the famous German "spoonful of soup," but to a "glass of water." However, you may venture there with good cheer, as this *copo d'agua* [glass of water] includes quite an extensive meal and has, as an encore, an evening filled with music as well as a place to stay the night.

Yesterday, we were invited by our neighbors, who, by the way, live five miles away. Two carriages drawn by four mules conveyed us to them at a brisk trot.

We found that a larger circle of guests had already gathered in the *sala de visita* [drawing room or parlor], a gigantic hall with seven windows. However, you have to understand the word "circle" only as a figure of speech, as the society here presented itself such that to the right and to the left of the large cylindrical sofa, visible in the foggy distance to those entering the room, a row of chairs branched off at sharp right angles which kept the space in front of the sofa free, thereby creating the impression that one was taking part in a social game. The initiated knows, however, that he can find these right angles in any Brazilian home. The coffee table stands in the middle of the hall.

Then, after I had occupied the left wing of one of these rows of chairs and sat next to Dona Gabriela for a while, a barefooted Negro boy announced that "lunch is served," and the mistress of the house rose in a dignified manner with the invitation "Vamos jantar"—that is, "Let's dine."[10]

On both sides of the table, barefoot and not all too clean, mulatto boys stood armed with long bamboo poles, on the end of which one of them waved a small red flag and the other a few copies of the *Jornal do Comércio* cut into strips to keep off the flies and mosquitoes.[11] I already had a quarrel with such a flag from São Francisco, but in the face of these revolting, rustling paper shreds, whose insulting tastelessness to the eye and ear no one in the company but me seems to have noticed, and which the others probably

10. "Lunch" was Ina's German usage. The nineteenth-century midday meal, often eaten at 1 or 2 p.m., was deemed "dinner" (*jantar*) for being the heartiest of the day. "Tea" (*cha*) was served as a light supper in the early evening.

11. *Jornal do Comércio* was Rio de Janeiro's leading newspaper.

regarded as an especially ingenious and lovely invention, I swore off my anger against the small dirty rag back at the house.

After the soup had been consumed, everyone began to pass around the dish of which he was in charge. For here, bowls are not passed around; rather, everything is set on the table at the same time and then offered and served by the person who is sitting in front of a dish, even if he is a guest. Everyone thus puts his courses together ad libitum. So I, too, bravely began to proffer my bowl of black beans, the beloved *feijão* of the Brazilians that is never missing from any meal: "A senhora quer feijão?" [Do you want beans?] "Um poco de feijão, senhor doutor?" [A little of the beans, Sr. doctor?] Very smart. I am telling you I impressed myself playing a "Brazilian woman." In between, I, too, was offered food. "Wollen Sie ein wenig Reis?" [Would you like some rice?] the daughter of the house beamed with a German sentence in which she emphasized the latter syllable of "wollen," pronouncing the *g* in "wenig" like a *k* and all soft *s*'s as sharp ones. "Um pouco de vinho, mademoiselle?" [A little wine, mademoiselle?] asked the good father, who had never learned another language than the *língua dos brancos* [the whites' language], as Portuguese is called here in distinction from the primordial African languages imported by the Negro slaves. "Vous offrirai-je des pommes de terre?" [Could I offer you some potatoes?] said a young man who had just returned from "Paris" (naturally he was also a *doutor*), and thus I tried to make as homogeneous a meal as possible out of roast pig, beefsteak, black beans, chicken, rice, cabbage, polenta, and sweet potatoes. But you will receive a warm lunch among Brazilians only by expending great calculation and skill, because, each time when you have uttered your "s'il vous plaît," one of the arms of the serving Negresses (here there were four) catches your plate with lightning speed and takes off with it to the proprietor of the bowl in question in order to bring you the desired object. You can see that you will be able to eat all the more calmly and warmly the less complicated you make your choice, as every new "s'il vous plaît" would again send your plate on a sudden journey around the table.

This matter of dining is in and of itself terribly disquieting, but the rustling paper strips, the occasionally energetic snap of the small flag, the loud, gesture-rich conversation of the Brazilians, the stomping around of the Negresses—all this had a deafening impact on my German nerves, which the blinding brightness of the curtainless rooms had already begun to assault, so that I could only look with shame at the indifferent faces of the other ladies. Although they, too, hardly participated in the conversation, their nervous systems nevertheless seemed immune to this noise entirely.

I was hungry from the journey, but I could not eat under these circumstances. I am actually still hungry, as I last ate on the ship. My stomach is only gradually accustoming itself to the monotony of the food and to the lard with which all the meals are prepared here. What initially made the whole thing even more intolerable was the complete absence of potatoes or bread on the table with which one could soften the aggressive taste of the lard. In this country, bread is replaced by so-called *biscoitos*, a baked good made with the flour of the manioc root. It tastes very good when it has just come out of the oven, but after two hours, it leaves much to be desired because of its toughness. After two days, it could compete favorably with small stones. Our good potato grows in these blessed lands only in sweet species, the *batatas*, which weigh up to nine pounds and are either cooked alone or enjoyed with sugar as a dessert. During my first days here, I found the large, bluish things, whose color and taste reminded me of their frozen brothers in the Nordic winter, extremely repulsive. But now I find the compote quite tasty, to my embarrassment. I am also starting to become better with the black beans and *angu*, a saltless, cornmeal pudding. Already, I am getting more attracted to the corn and manioc flour which is brought to the table in bread baskets, and which the Brazilians stir into the thick sauce of the beans—and how long will it take until I develop a passion for the sun-dried mutton that we are often served for breakfast?

Do not have contempt for me, Grete; there is nothing else here! Because if you add to the delicacies above some rice cooked in water, which comes to the table red like a brick because of all the tomatoes used to make it, there you have the whole menu for the entire year.

Dessert here is a big story. The *doces* [conserves] and the reputation of the Brazilians for excelling in preparing as well as in devouring them was yesterday proven to me again in full measure. Both gentlemen and ladies gorged themselves on unbelievable quantities of fruit conserves, chocolate and egg comfits, and so on, along with large pieces of cheese.[12]

And I must confess—I did as well!

Of course, on the first day that my European palate had to endure the new delight, I rejected this pleasure with indignation, requesting some bread and butter with cheese instead. Immediately, some *biscoitos* in stage number two appeared and a Danish brand of canned butter so soft, yellow, and salty

12. A comfit was a piece of candy containing a nut or a piece of fruit.

that . . . let me hold my peace! Bravely, I decided in favor of the combination that is customary here, and I believe that I made the right decision.

Thus, I was able at least to conclude my meal in good Brazilian fashion yesterday. And since I could also name nearly all the dishes in Portuguese (a great skill, given that the same meals are served twice daily) and bandy about a few incorrect but all the more elevated phrases, my new acquaintances found me *muito simpática* [very congenial] and honored me with a request to play or sing something for them immediately after dinner.

I played a waltz by Chopin, which they liked very much, and I sang "Little Ana-Kathrin," which they could not understand at all. Now I never sing German songs for Brazilian ears, only Italian etudes that will make an impression on them.

Our Dona Olímpia followed me with a few French dances. She plays well enough, but chooses her dances tastelessly. And then, a very quiet, very strong, and very dark-eyed lady sat down in front of the instrument and began to perform the second act of *Il Trovatore.* I was told before that she plays "perfectly," so I listened very attentively. . . . Oh, Grete, am I so staunchly Germanic that, as hard as I try, I can't find these Latins interesting and intelligent! But that is how it was—nothing that came out of the swift, disciplined fingers, and the static wax-yellow face of the pianist, whose eyes appeared like spiritless blots of ink, spoke to me. But it was true nonetheless: She played *perfeitamente* [perfectly]! I was angry with myself that the performance could not inspire me, and I looked around the circle, afraid that others would notice. But all the faces were pale, yellow, and, due to the great respect for this "perfect performance," motionless. All except one.

A few days ago, a young Italian architect was on a visit here, a nephew of the doctor from the latter's first wife, who was Italian. This unfortunate man seemed affected in the same way as I by the music. I smiled involuntarily when I saw his face. Our common European roots had already led us to many similar judgments about the local conditions, and now he raised his eyes toward the ceiling with an infinitely comical expression.

In the meantime, the "Trovatore" had become ever more aggressive; the quiet, strong lady had been playing for half an hour—did she intend to play the whole act? I carefully inched toward the door, but I did not dare to escape the hall, although I felt, at the same time, that a further quarter hour under the influence of this perfect performance would completely overpower me. Just then, the young Italian pushed past me. He looked completely exhausted—"Je n'en peux plus" [I can't take anymore], he whispered to me; "j'ai déjà une indigestion de musique!" [I already have musical indigestion].

And this in a country that is only beginning to become civilized and that has only one conservatorium! Woe to future generations when the piano-plague grows here in proportion to the population!

But hold on—my light is saying farewell! Just as if it had only allowed me this dark, prophetic lamentation, it is now flickering away on its last wick—for lamps do not exist here!

So good night, my Grete, or if it sounds more interesting to you: *Boa noite* [Good night].

I remain steadfastly yours,
Ulla

São Francisco

July 11, 1881

My dear and only Grete!

The first letters from home arrived today! I could have embraced the dirty little Negro boy, after watching him longingly for so many, many days, in vain, when one, two, three letters for the *professora* [teacher] emerged from his bag. Dr. Rameiro has the mail delivered every day, which is very rare here in the country. Most of the landowners send someone to check the post only once a week. Good news from home, a joyful letter from my Grete—God, how a page with some writing on it can make one so happy! And how patient one becomes! I am telling you, Gretel, I sometimes think that I am Salas y Gómez.[13] You know how it disturbed me in the seminary when we did not see the mailman for two days—and now, after nearly one and a half months, the first letters! I am going to acquire so many virtues here that I won't have any use for them in Europe! But today I needed a small refresher, everything was so deadening, starting early in the morning, and I felt so overburdened! First, I had one of the hardest struggles with my *biscoitos*, which I received in stage no. 3. Then the Vehmic court was more perturbing than ever, and, finally, I am suffering from an awful case of neuralgia in my face, so that I can eat and speak only with great effort. It's one of the common ailments of Europeans here, and even of the natives. It is excruciating torture, especially when one has to teach at the same time. They claim that I caught it because I was outside after six o'clock at night, in the *sereno*, the dangerous evening dew. But, Grete dear, I would have suffocated if I had not gotten some air, and, besides, having been outside from morning until evening all day on the twenty-four-day journey on the ship. But here I teach from seven to ten, then I have a hot breakfast. Madame Rameiro always needlessly keeps us waiting until ten thirty so that I cannot go outside afterward, but am forced to go back to teaching immediately following the last bite. After that, it continues until one o'clock, when there is a half-hour lunch break. At one thirty, the piano lessons

13. Salas y Gómez was shipwrecked on a Chilean island, where he survived for many years. Then, just as he was discovered in 1818 by the crew of the *Rurik*, which included the poet Chamisso, he died. The island was given his name. Salas y Gómez became the tragic hero of a romantic poem by Adalberto von Chamisso (Louis Charles Adelaide, 1781–1839), published in 1829 and long admired in Prussia, Chamisso's adopted country.

begin; they last until five, at which time we eat dinner. Now, I ask you, when am I supposed to take a walk other than after six o'clock? Can you think of a different possible time during the day? Here, they seem to want to swallow their "education" like soup, and they never have a free afternoon or day, let alone a weeklong break, for the whole year. I am dreading the thought of this—and the whole time not a single German word! During the lessons and at the table, French, and with the blacks, Portuguese. Oh, Gretel, it is much harder than one imagines from far away. Think again whether you want me to look around for something for you here—or at least take your bed with you if you come. Frugality is certainly a good thing, but one must not overdo it. I want to describe my bed to you—cry a silent tear for me! Imagine a rough, wooden bench with armrests but without a back: that's my bed frame. On it lies a "mattress," which, I discovered, contains a wild, dried grass, and some leaves graciously mixed with sticks and branches which were added for unknown reasons. Somewhere near the headboard of this torture bench, covered with a linen sheet, lies a miniature pillow, that initially I thought the little Maria had lost from her dollhouse. But it really is supposed to be my pillow, and it is stuffed with a dry, yellow flower called *marcela*, which is similar to our immortelles.[14] The whole thing is crowned with an English woolen blanket as a cover. Who knows whether I will succeed in befriending even this aspect of Brazilian life? I hope so! In the meantime, I am striving for the tranquility needed to become personally acquainted with several sticks in my mattress, and then I am hoping to coax just a little warmth out of this ascetic's bed, because, although it is hot during the day, the nights are noticeably cold.

I am surprised that the cool nights do not damage the plants in our captivating garden. Madame is a great botanist and keeps the garden under her special direction. She takes care that every rare plant is cared for and also arranges for tropical plants from India and Japan to be brought here at great cost. She has turned this spot of earth into a true Eden, a magical country full of fairy-tale splendor.

The gate to the garden, overgrown with lush, graceful clematis, leads first to small groups of rare conifers and beautifully sculpted flower beds full of tall, exotic flowers glowing in marvelous colors. Amidst all this stands a colorful Chinese-style kiosk. I am telling you, Gretel, with the deep-blue sky and the tropical sun above it, with the charming little hummingbirds, which really

14. *Marcela* was the alternate name for *macela*—in this case, *masela-do-campo*, a plant of the thistle family (*Achryocline satureioides*) used for stuffing mattresses and pillows.

do look like gems fluttering in the sun, this place is so exquisitely tropical that it seems like a dream! Then, you enter a splendid, shaded, cool bamboo boulevard. To the left of it, a little further down, is a small lake, full of colorful ducks. The area to the right, slightly elevated and gradually sloping upward, is populated with fragrant orange trees which often bear flowers and fruit at the same time. There is a new surprise at every exit: oranges, palm trees, and bananas everywhere. Cinnamon and almond trees give forth their scents, and pomegranates glow out of the ornate foliage. Here a tea plant, and there a coffee tree; now a lost cotton shrub, and then an anise or nutmeg plant. Indeed, you can even find vanilla and patchouli here. I was completely intoxicated at first, Grete, and I drank, as it were, this magical, beautiful, and strange world with all my senses . . . but do you know what impression is the longest-lasting for me? The sense that all this is strange, indeed, absolutely foreign! I marvel at it, all this southern splendor, I admire it, it intoxicates me immediately with its seductive magic—but I do not understand it. I do not know these great plants, and they do not know me. There is something wondrous about one's fatherland and all the things that belong to it. Even the flowers and the trees. At home, we know exactly what to sing under our magnificent oak trees; which young soul does not know our rich German linden poetry? And, as soon as we learn how to speak, we already begin babbling our homely, Christmas tune, "O Tannenbaum, O Tannenbaum!" Though the grand mango tree in the middle of the garden is very beautiful, I was nevertheless surprised when I recently began to hum this pretty little song while I was sitting in its shadow:

> I once had a beautiful fatherland,
> The oak tree stood tall there,
> The violets nodded gently.
> It was a dream.
>
> And when I came to distant foreign lands,
> There was an enchanting girl,
> Blonde-haired.
> It was a dream.
>
> She kissed me in German and spoke in German.
> You will not believe how good it sounded,
> The words: I love you.
> It was a dream.

And do you remember how at home we could never quite understand when Dranmor sang, "I would give up all this splendor—for a single, snow-covered pine!"[15] And now . . . but I am blathering, therefore I will be silent. Here, one can't be sentimental.

Your most German Ulla

15. Dranmor was the pseudonym of Ferdinand von Schmid (1823–88), a Swiss poet who went to Brazil in 1843; after making a fortune there, he settled in Paris.

São Francisco

July [*sic*] 25, 1881

Dearest Grete!

So, now I have to picture you in Elgersburg when I think of you—you, fortunate one, who is still familiar with the word "vacation" and who can actually put it into practice in the charming Thuringian Nest! For your poor Ulla, these kinds of things are increasingly turning into abstract terms—what does freedom, rejuvenation, cooling off in the summer mean . . . that is, no! With respect to "cooling off," I will definitely win the contest. I hereby solemnly declare that my teeth have chattered quite often because of the cold these days, and that I am writing to you with frozen fingers. Furthermore, I have full rights to this claim because yesterday was the coldest day of the year here, St. John the Baptist Day.[16] I felt savagely cold then as well, to the great amusement of the family, which denies to the "cold German" the right to suffer due to such conditions. I was so cold that I blessed my fondness for my old winter coat that made me take it along when I was packing in Berlin. The Brazilians themselves, strangely enough, hardly feel the cold. This became especially noticeable to me yesterday evening during the name day of St. John, one of the favorite saints of this nation. Every year on this day, which happens also to be the name day of one of Dr. Rameiro's sons who lives in Europe (Paris, of course), the doctor organizes a sort of harvest celebration for the slaves. It is around this time that the coffee harvest ends.

I had always been interested in seeing the carts full of coffee berries from the plantation being driven into the magnificent coffee-processing facilities and machine workshops set up by the doctor.

Last Sunday, we rode through a coffee field that encompassed half a square mile. The trees, or rather, the shrubs, were the size of large hazelnut

16. The Day of St. John the Baptist (Dia de São João) was June 24, but the celebration reached its apogee on June 23, the Eve of St. John (Véspera de São João), a night of bonfires, fireworks, and fire balloons. This festival falls just after the winter equinox of June 22 in the Southern Hemisphere and coincides with the coffee and corn harvests, which explains why it was more popular than any other holiday.

Editor's note: Ina makes clear from the content of this letter that she wrote on the day after St. John's Day (June 24); therefore this letter's date must have been June 25, not July 25.

plants, and many stood there full of berries between their sharp, shiny leaves. The doctor said that the planting was around twenty-five years old and that such a stand of shrubs could produce berries for forty years.[17] After that, a new piece of land had to be developed. It is bizarre and liable to arouse one's envy that for us such an area would be a very nice field or a very respectable garden, whereas here, it plays no noteworthy role at all. This plantation is three square miles large, but the management of the farm is a bit strange. Most of the land, of course, always lies fallow. But when a piece of the land is to be used, they burn down everything that had been growing there. This sometimes also unsparingly attacks the most splendid remains of the virgin forest, whose ashen remains and foul stems then turn into superb fertilizer.[18] Nothing looks crazier than a cornfield, for example, growing happily amid partially—sometimes completely—charred tree trunks strewn about wildly. At home, we can hardly imagine such disorder, and, more importantly, such waste. Here, too, people are slowly moving away from this cannibalistic manner of clearing the land. It has by no means become as rare as the Brazilians like to claim, and it was practiced by everyone in the past. Imagine, Gretel, on the plantation of Madame Rameiro's brother, a Negro slave died in one of these fires because he did not leave the woods in time, as it had been set aflame from all four sides! That's a horrifying and allegedly not too rare occurrence.

As we were driving through the plantation, the Negroes were at work because the slaves' Sunday at this plantation falls on Wednesday. The law only requires one holiday a week for the slaves, but leaves it up to the owner to choose a day. Usually what then happens is that each owner picks a different day, so that the holiday on one plantation does not coincide with that on

17. Coffee trees producing berries for forty years, at least for export production, amounted to a gross exageration. Historian Stanley J. Stein, in his classic case study, pointed to a consensus among foreign observers that in the second half of the nineteenth century fifteen years was accepted as the productive limit for a coffee grove: "A coffee grove of ten to fifteen years is, as a rule, completely lost and its soil forever ruined." *Vassouras: A Brazilian Coffee County, 1850–1900* (Cambridge, MA: Harvard University Press, 1957), 220, citing Miguel Alamir Baglioni, *O Eresipho do Cafeeiro* (Campos, Brazil, 1878), 48.

18. The burning (*a broca*), a standard practice derived from indigenous techniques, is known as "slash-and-burn," or swidden, agriculture. Besides removing vegetation for a cleared field, it returned nutrients to the soil. Burning, as Ina implied, became a major cause of deforestation. Soil exhaustion, well advanced in the Paraíba Valley by the 1880s, probably explained most of the land that she unknowingly described as lying "fallow."

the neighboring estate. This prevents the blacks from interacting with one another.[19]

It looked truly picturesque how the black figures in the bright shirts, picking diligently, stood with their baskets between the darkly glimmering shrubs. The Negroes are very well treated on this plantation, and whoever picks more than the required quantity of baskets receives a bonus.

On the tree, the coffee berry almost looks like a large blackthorn [small plum]. Inside the red-blue, juicy shell there are two beans pressed together on their flat sides, just like two seeds.

When a full cart leaves the plantation, it is emptied into a water basin, where the loose shells around the berry have already fallen off. Then the whole thing flows into a deeper-lying basin through crude pipes designed to strip the exterior layers. The extracted coffee beans arrive for further processing there, where the thin skins, which we can sometimes see at home on inadequately processed beans, are peeled off. Next, the coffee is spread out over a large asphalt terrace for drying.[20] Finally, the beans are brought to long, hall-like rooms, where the Negresses sort them. Only then does the coffee end up in sacks, to be shipped off after a prescribed time in storage. Dr. Rameiro gave me a whole sack as a present—imagine, a whole sack of coffee that has been aging for three years and which is, therefore, according to him, just right. He wants to help me send it home through his partners in Rio. So make sure you accept my invitations for coffee, Gretel!

The harvest has now finished for the year, having been concluded with yesterday's celebration. Already on the day before, Dona Gabriela proudly told me that on São João's Day they always slaughter an ox and two pigs, and that all this would be devoured by the Negroes at a feast. Indeed, yesterday there was great animation the whole morning, and even the Vehmic court took a personal interest in the organization of the whole affair—the preparation of the *doces* (sweets), the serving of drinks, and so forth.

19. Reference to "interacting" among blacks implied whites' fear of slaves conspiring to plot rebellion, a fear very specific to the Paraíba Valley's coffee plantations. A serious conspiracy of three hundred slaves had occurred in the county in 1838. The leader, Manuel Congo, was hanged. Historian Robert Slenes has identified a slave conspiracy in the lower Paraíba River Valley during March 1881 that local authorities exposed.

20. The drying terraces or patios (*terreiros*) in the Paraíba Valley were usually made by applying a plaster of Portland cement, asphalt not yet having been introduced. Otherwise, the ground was floored with paving stones or square red bricks that were manufactured on the plantation. After drying, coffee beans were stored and shipped "green"—i.e., unroasted.

When it grew dark, the celebration began.

In the yard, enclosed on three sides by the building and on the fourth by palm trees, they arranged tables in the shape of horseshoes, festively covered with white table cloths. The Negroes are very proud of the fact that at least once a year they can eat on real linen cloth like the *senhores*. On the tables, there were huge, carved-up roasts, mountains of rice (naturally red, like bricks, because of the tomatoes), gigantic bowls with black beans and their ever-present companion, *angu*, the cornmeal pudding. But there was also sweet potato compote for dessert, fresh corn cooked in milk (*canjica*) accompanied with molasses; *goiabada*, a magnificent *doce* made from the *goiaba* [guava] fruit; and even—wine—*à discrétion*![21]

How nicely the blacks dressed up! First hesitant and embarrassed, then with more confidence, and finally surging forward, pressing against one another, the older people and the adults arrived according to rank. The young people had to wait, since only a hundred people could sit at the same time. It was amusing to see how some of these good, simple people had "adorned" themselves. The men apparently satisfied their ambitions by wearing jackets, which they had either received as presents or bought from a traveling secondhand clothes vendor. One of them was even wearing an old tuxedo. Those, however, who could not manage to wear a jacket at least had a hat, preferably a top hat.

The women presented themselves a little more gracefully, having decided to use colors. Some of them wore all the colors of the rainbow with grand airs; wearing a red turban with a blue dress and a green belt does not disturb them at all.

The scene became especially pretty and peculiar after a large number of colorful little lamps were lit, enchantingly illuminating the area with their glimmer. The luminescent Southern Cross became visible in the cold-clear sky. We observed the whole thing from the windows of the house, and you can imagine how captivating the scene was, especially for us Europeans.

The blacks even had a dinner speech and a toast. As a joke, the little Leonila handed a page from the newspaper through the window to an old Negro, telling him: "Read, Porfirio!"

Porfirio, a splendid old Negro with gray, woolly hair, grasped the page, examined it with half-comical, half-melancholy pathos from all sides and

21. Again, Ina's ear for Portuguese proved unequal to the task, for she speaks of "*gunabada* [*goiabada*] and *gunaba* [*goiaba*] fruit," her mispronunciations herein corrected.

then began to speak: "My little *senhora* has ordered me to read, but Porfirio cannot read. But Porfirio can speak and he has something to say. I have to confess something to Senhor and Senhora—May they live very long." "Viva!" the Negroes yelled.

"I have to confess that I spoke ill of Senhor a year ago, because he did not give us a harvest festival. I said, 'Why has Senhor counted the sacks, but forgotten about us poor Negroes?' And I was filled with wrath inside. But this year, Senhor has remembered us and Senhora too—Viva, Senhor!"

"Viva!"

"Viva, Senhora."

"Viva!"

"And we want to thank them for this. And we want to thank them for something else. Namely this. Formerly, how much did we poor blacks have to torture ourselves with cleaning the coffee, how hard did we have to beat the bean of the castor-oil plant to extract a little bit of heating oil? But now our Senhor has brought in machines from foreign countries, which they call England and Germany, and now we have it much better. We want to express our gratitude for this: Viva, Senhor!"[22]

"Viva!"

"Viva, Senhora!"

"Viva!"

Thus it continued with the vivas for a little while, until the adults made room for the adolescents and children, and they, in turn, began their beloved dances in the open space in front of the house.

They assembled themselves in a circle, and then the ear-splitting music began. Two drums made from barrels, played by two Negroes beating them monotonously, and a tin rattle performed the accompaniment as unharmoniously as possible. To this, they sang a monotonous melody consisting of two strophes, which the singer repeated without getting tired—I was able to count it sixty-four times. They danced to the sound of these "harmonies," and in such a manner that only one person at a time performed the dance in the middle of the circle, designating the next person to relieve him.[23] I have to

22. "Dr. Rameiro," actually Dr. Lazzarini, was a heavy investor in modern agricultural machinery who looked to it as a solution for a dwindling slave workforce.

23. She is describing a variation on the *coco*, a dance in the round identifiable from its repetitious two verses and the drumming—the quintessential dance of nineteenth-century slaves who brought it, together with the drumming, from Central-Southern Africa.

confess, to the disgrace of the female participants, that they lagged far behind the men in grace and rhythm. Especially our small, insufferable somersault-*muleque* [*moleque*], Tonino [Toninho], was brilliant in his skillful, snake-like movements.

Those who were not dancing occupied themselves with the fireworks, for that is the real celebration that St. John seems to have claimed for himself on his name day in Brazil. There were two fires similar to our Easter bonfires in front of the house, and they lit up the scene, flickering and shining marvelously. Dancing Negro boys threw flares and rockets in the air, and, under the cold-clear, sparkling starry sky of the coldest day of the year, all this appeared exquisitely picturesque and poetic on the wide, open lawn.

A small scene during the course of this evening will remain especially unforgettable to me. I wish I could have captured it with brush and paint in order to reveal its charm to you. Stirred by the ongoing noise of the drums and tin rattles, a graceful mulatta with her face turned toward the stars, her eyes closed, and her right arm stretched out, walked barefoot over the embers of the fire, while colorful flares went off and descended again from the dark night. She was walking with such self-assurance that we thought we were watching a somnambulist. I could hardly believe my eyes and looked at her with bated breath and a silent sort of horror. Alone, smiling calmly, she put on her shoes again afterward. On St. John's Day the fire does not hurt you, the Negroes say.

Gretel, I now become very jealous when I even think of a fire. With what great respect will I greet the first coal heater! Dona Gabriela, who is still the friendliest member of the Vehmic court, recently offered to heat my room using big tubs full of hot water. But that would surely only raise the already unhealthy humidity of the room and help very little. If someone had told me that I would experience the greatest cold of my life in Brazil . . . ! My neuralgia still will not disappear, and I have been suffering from toothaches for weeks as a result.

Yours,
Ulla

São Francisco

August 14, 1881

Dearest Grete!

The Negroes play the lead role in this country, and I think they are basically more the masters than the slaves of the Brazilians. Every task is performed by blacks, all the riches brought forth by their hands; the Brazilian does not work. And being poor, he would rather go around sponging off affluent relatives or friends than lift his hands honestly. Even all the domestic chores are done by Negroes. Here the black coachman drives you, there the Negress waits on you, there the black cook stands beside the stove, here the slave suckles the white child. I would merely like to know what these people intend to do when the slaves are finally emancipated! In Europe, we had no clear concept of the law regarding emancipation and believed, in fact, that the law had abolished slavery outright. But that is not so. It prescribed only that from the day of its proclamation forward—that is, from September 28, 1871, onward, no further person will be born a slave in Brazil.[24]

Whoever was then [before September 28, 1871] alive and a slave must remain so until he dies, or until redemption [by a fund], or until manumission [by the owner]. But now, whoever was born [into slavery]—these insignificant black "chattel" have no worth for the masters. They are merely people who consume resources. Therefore they reap no benefits from the legislation; they are not even taught this or that skill as they were previously, and "one really has nothing to show for it." On the other hand, as "free" people they are for their part treated with somewhat greater respect by the Brazilian than those born slaves.

Thus, this afternoon, eight such insignificant, free citizens of the world were ceremoniously baptized here![25]

24. The reference is to Brazil's Rio Branco Law, colloquially known as the "Law of the Free Womb" (inspired by Cuba's Moret Law [1870]), which meant no more slaves would be born in Brazil. As of September 28, 1871, all children born of a slave mother would be free-born. The law also established a national emancipation fund for the partial "redemption" of those still in slavery—those who had accumulated, or in the future would accumulate, most of their purchase price and would be redeemed by owners legally obliged to free them.

25. Ina's reference to "citizens" implies the Law of the Free Womb, which required baptismal registers to serve as a civil registry for recording the names of those infants born of a slave mother, who were thereby "freed by the Law of September 28, 1871." The vast majority of those "freed" children, however, remained de facto slaves until reaching age twenty-one because at age eight their owners chose not to free them.

At breakfast, I had already noticed a wonderful little old man who seldom spoke. Whatever he did say, it was spoken in a language completely mysterious to me, one to which Dr. Rameiro responded in his fluent Italian. But what stood out for me was an enormous red handkerchief to which he seemed greatly devoted, and also the fact that he consumed—I could have nearly written "devoured"—innumerable bananas. How astonished was I when later he turned out to be an itinerant Catholic priest—something I never would have guessed, the less so as he traveled in ordinary civilian clothes. He was born an Italian, but he had already been to every part of the world, and he had already invented the universal language, which he now speaks, before anyone in Europe ever thought of such a thing.[26]

About twelve o'clock in the great *sala de costura*—or, more commonly speaking, the sewing room—an imposing, buffet-like cabinet was opened. I was always curious about the contents of this cabinet. Lo and behold, there appeared the Mother of God together with the Christ child, ribbons, a crown, necklaces, bracelets, and earrings. The Negro Felício, whom I otherwise was used to seeing only at the sewing machine as the house tailor, officiated as altar boy. He functioned as an aide to the priest, who was dressed in full regalia. The whole thing was strange for my Evangelical [Lutheran] soul, Gretel!

Then, one after another, the Negresses showed up with their young offspring, all very nice-looking, some even outfitted with white embroidered costumes and colorful ribbons. The women were preparing to become the *madrinhas* (and indeed, as one might discern from the goodness of the Vehmic court, I should probably not call them this!), which means the godmothers of these small black Christian children.

Incidentally, I was amazed at the barely dark, indeed nearly white, skin of most of these children. "They become black," a man told me with a smile intending to scorn the Negro on the one hand, my ignorance on the other. "Only the inside of their palms and the soles of their feet remain white. They say that when Ham migrated to Africa he touched the water of the Jordan with his feet and palms at the Lord's command, which then receded before him. From that touch, those parts remain white for him and his descendants, even with the sunburn of Africa."

The ceremony began. I was a mute witness as these eight flat-nosed, woolly, dreadful little things received the names César, Felício, Messias(!),

26. This is apparently an early reference to Esperanto, for its founder, L. L. Zemenhof, did not publish a text of the language until 1887. The Italian priest must have been an early follower of Zemenhof.

Elias, Angélica, Maria Salomé, Marcela, and Ruth. And why shouldn't they, too, get the most beautiful names? And yet these baptismal names, which the old Portuguese-, Italian-, Latin-, gibberish-talking little priest granted to them according to the requests and choices of their masters, are the only ones with which they must make do for the rest of their lives. For, even if most of these mothers are married, they have no family names. Hence the freed slaves, since they lack family names, simply take that of their previous master after their manumission—how nice for him, isn't it!![27]

But as now I have come to the subject of the Negroes, I have to tell you another story that happened here the other day.

One evening last week, it was so completely "cool and refreshing" that a cup of tea made it quite cozy inside.[28] Suddenly, in front of the house, I heard a timid clapping sound that set all of our dogs in motion and caused all of us to prick up our ears. Here, clapping replaces the house bell, and whenever someone wishes to enter or has entered a house, he must make himself noticeable outside or in the corridor in this way—if he doesn't want to be taken for a thief. Everyone was naturally curious about who could be coming so late, and Tonino was sent out to have a look. He went somewhat anxiously, but then somersaulted merrily back to the threshold.

"There are two uncles outside, master," he reported. The old blacks are called *tio*, uncle, and *tia*, aunt, by the young, even when they don't know each other at all. I find something touching in the expression of this feeling of affinity among these pariahs, don't you?

Two slaves? It was hardly to be expected that a neighbor sent a message this late, but what could they want otherwise! Dr. Rameiro went out and came back after a while, his usually so jovial face completely clouded over!

"Well then?" we all exclaimed.

"Two unfortunate blacks," he said, "who are begging me for the sake of Jesus to buy them."

"Where do they come from?"

"From Dr. Albu's plantation."

"Oh, the poor things! That one is known for tormenting his Negroes," Madame said. "My husband has only to threaten to sell a rebellious black to Dr. Albu, and he immediately turns obedient."

27. Former slaves did not necessarily take the surnames of their former owners. In fact, last names were not so common among the free poor, including those who were white.

28. She is quoting from a folksong called "Santa Lucia: Kühl und labend."

"What will you do, Papa?" Dona Olímpia asked.

"What can I do, my child?" the old master said excitedly. "He won't have any interest in selling them, and, in any event, he will propose that I pay an exorbitant price. Besides, he will be my irreconcilable enemy if I get involved against him, and you know well that he is responsible for that terrible forest fire last year that no one could account for."

"So the poor wretches have to return?" I asked.

"I cannot keep them in the house. They are property, and if I kept them even one night under my roof, I would appear to be concealing runaway Negroes. One ought not to expose oneself to that, particularly when one has to keep blacks oneself. These demonstrations of confidence are, of course, in themselves quite nice and flattering, but how dreadfully awkward! This is not the first time I've been through this."

"So then there really are actual plantations where those awful conditions from *Uncle Tom's Cabin* are still to be found?" I inquired.

"It's probably nowhere so terrible around here, and probably hardly ever was. The Brazilian is better natured than the North American, and the black race in general occupies a different position here with us. You see, as soon as the Negro is free, he is treated here with equal rights: we have colored teachers, artists, doctors, representatives, even ministers, and the princess also gives orders for colored folk to dance for her.[29] The contempt on the one hand, the corresponding bitterness on the other—it isn't so great here as it is with our northern brethren. Certainly there are some brutal creatures among us as well who do, in fact, mistreat the poor blacks, of which you have just had proof."

"What will now become of these two poor devils?" I asked.

"If anything, they will receive a hearty beating this evening, but only in order that they be kept more strictly; such pranks are quite foolish. Then I will see whether I can either redeem them myself or recommend them to an abolitionist society."

29. Dr. Rameiro was reciting a common defense of slavery, as an institution upheld by humane, even enlightened, coffee planters who pointed a condemning finger at their counterparts in the land of *Uncle Tom's Cabin*. He refers to Princess Isabel, heir to the throne, who, at a court ball, had recently danced with the French-trained structural engineer and abolitionist André Pinto Rebouças (1838–98), a talented freeborn man of color. More to the point, Isabel commissioned talented free men of color for important tasks undertaken on behalf of the government, the most notable being Rebouças and his brother, French-trained engineers who were in charge of modernizing all of Brazil's Atlantic port facilities.

"But if their master doesn't want to sell them?" I interjected.

"He must, as soon as he is offered an acceptable price."[30]

"Why didn't they think to contact such a society themselves?"

"That's too difficult for them, since its members would be very unwise to let themselves be seen on plantations, and since the blacks cannot write. They simply have no means of communication. But also, most of them are only after good treatment. Freedom is more of a secondary concern; they have no ideals."

"I have thought as much myself," I said, "after the little I've been able to observe, for otherwise even those who are treated well would be forever full of resentment and discontent."

"Yes, and you will never, I dare say, find that. On this plantation you will not come across any rebellious slaves. I am strict about their humane treatment and good accommodation. I have some Negroes, women especially, who could have bought their freedom a long time ago."

"Really! How do they earn the money?"

"Whoever asks for it receives a small piece of land to cultivate, and then people here in the main house like to buy good vegetables from them. They can also raise chickens and sell the eggs when I send them to the post office, among other things.[31] They are paid to work on Sundays and also are paid for work in excess of the lawful number of hours, and the house Negroes and Negresses frequently obtain monetary gifts, particularly the latter if they were ever wet nurses for the children. For example, our broad-grinning Ana there is quite a prosperous rich aunt, but she stays because she has it good here and she loves the children. Freedom, that noble possession, she does not understand."

I was pleased with this explanation as one is always pleased with statements that confirm one's own thoughts and conclusions. Thus could I visualize the matter: I could imagine that barbarism and beastly cruelty vis-à-vis the slaves often lead to very sorrowful incidents. But then again, to expect the enlightened views of profoundly civilized men among a race that has been enslaved through generations, to presume our concepts of freedom among

30. The 1871 Law of the Free Womb required slave owners to emancipate a slave when he or she, often with the assistance of a manumission society, offered to pay the fair market price. It designated imperial judges as final arbiters of a slave's price.

31. On large coffee plantations where soil erosion had occurred, such as in the Paraíba River Valley, planters were usually more inclined to grant slaves plots for growing their foodstuffs, often on marginal land. Of course, this "privilege" also benefited owners of slaves.

mankind, of honor among womankind—that, I well realize, would constitute a mere vain, poetic illusion.

But I see that I am expecting you to put up with a formal disquisition on national finance under the cover of a simple letter—well, you can take your revenge by allowing it to be printed, can't you? Or you can read it in your reading circle; shared pain is half the pain.

Now I will go to sleep while contemplating which direction the neuralgia will have pulled my face in the morning. My mirror and I are no longer surprised!

Good night—but by you it is now no longer night, so good morning!

Your Ulla

São Francisco

September 1, 1881

Dearest Grete,

Yesterday we came back from an "expedition into the interior"—that is, from a journey to the province of Minas Gerais. We went there for the inauguration of a railroad. When I recall, Grete, how we always pronounced this name in geography class, especially the *gerais*! And we didn't even know what we were saying, when in fact it is so easy: *gerais* is the plural of *geral*, "general," and Minas Gerais means nothing other than general mining-land or mine-rich land.[32]

For Southern Brazil, this province corresponds approximately to what an arrogant Westerner from our country refers to when he speaks of "Farther Pomerania" or "East Prussia": a rather primitive territory, one that harbors more good humor than civilization, and one that is just as reviled as it is unknown. Minas nevertheless has an advantage over these German provinces: an abundance of precious metals, especially of gold. The capital city of the province carries two names: Ouro Preto, which means black (dark) gold, and Vila Rica, which means rich city, named after the treasures of its mountains and rivers.

It was extremely interesting for me to travel through these areas, areas that are so very different from those that one sees in the province of Rio. All around, you can see the sides of the mountains jagged and lacerated as if made by countless mole tunnels. Through the binoculars we even recognized black and white men who were busy seeking the precious metal. Along the river, which cuts through broad and grassy valleys, we saw bent figures patiently washing the gold out of the sand day and night. Some become rich,

32. As the "General Mines," Minas Gerais entered Brazilian history in the 1690s, when gold was discovered there. In the early 1700s, diamonds were discovered. The cycle of gold mining defined the first fifty years of the eighteenth century and generated Brazil's first "urban revolution," causing thousands of slaves from the Atlantic coast to migrate to this interior province, in addition to gold-greedy Portuguese immigrants. In 1881, Minas Gerais was Brazil's most populous province, but Ina's visit to São João Del Rei took her to an old colonial mining town in full decline rather than to a dynamic urban center. The diocese of São João Del Rei was the birthplace of Dona Alfonsina, her first husband, and their three oldest daughters (Ina's "Vehmic court"). So the trip was to have been a family reunion of sorts.

others submit themselves to torture for their daily bread. It all depends on whether or not they are lucky. Afterward I bought a half thimble full of gold for twenty-two marks from a poor black beggar in São João—this was the fruit of eight work days, according to what he told me!

Earlier, the yield was supposedly more consistent and, above all, more considerable.[33] Precisely this richness in gold probably provided the first impulse for the Portuguese conquerors to construct larger settlements in this inhospitable area, an area far less hospitable at that time than it is now. Every transport, whether it carried men, food, or anything else, took place on the backs of donkeys. This manner of transportation still happens today for the most part, in a place where twenty years ago bread was practically unknown. Indeed, the town still lacks a hotel.

All the guests that the town of São João d'El Rei had invited for the inauguration of its railroad were therefore lodged in private houses. It seems to me uncommonly characteristic for Brazil, where disparity constitutes the main order of things, that a town of about seven hundred inhabitants had invited about eight hundred guests, including Emperor Dom Pedro II, who kindly granted an appearance.

They were expecting six people from Dr. Rameiro's family. Since, however, the lady of the house (or Dona Alfonsina, as she is called according to the customs of the country) came down with a hefty cold and therefore did not wish to travel, she asked me to take her place—and, as you know, wherever there is anything to see, I'm on my way! We all left in good cheer, the doctor, the Vehmic court, little Julia, and my own humble self.

First we traveled on the large railway "Dom Pedro Segundo," which was already in operation. This is the railroad that the new line connects within the province of Minas. With characteristic Brazilian generosity, the railway conveyed its guests free of charge not only in its own region—it had also made arrangements with the large railway so that we traveled over one hundred miles without paying one penny.

The new railway's domain began four hours before our destination. As soon as the train stopped, someone shouted, "Transfer as quickly as possible!" The speed must have meant something, because otherwise in Brazil people are always saying, "Paciência," and no one rushes. Everyone was then rushing to the other platform with unusual haste—the reason will become

33. By the 1750s, the exports of gold began to decline rapidly. However, by the 1850s, introduction of English technology revived Minas's gold mining industry.

clear! There you would have seen the smallest train that you have ever seen, Grete: wagons and locomotives, everything *en miniature*. As fast as lightning we were seated, only to wait patiently—or impatiently—three-quarters of an hour until the little train started moving. To pass the time, among other things, we measured the wagon: it was 1 meter x 65 centimeters.[34]

Finally, it started moving, at first slowly, then faster and faster, going boldly through mountains and over bridges. It was as if the little train were afraid of nothing. Moreover, it seemed to be able to do more than its clumsy brother. With amazement and admiration we saw our little train wind itself around the cone of the mountain deftly like a snake, gradually, but safely, climbing upward, appearing three times on the same side. When we reached our destination—that is, the town of São João d'El Rei—it was 11:30 a.m. instead of the expected arrival time of 7 a.m., but that didn't matter. On the contrary, when something happens on time in Brazil, it is quite unusual. So everyone was happy.

The train station was covered with flags and decorated with garlands. A band (mostly Germans in this country) was blowing merrily away, and a

34. The destination of São João Del Rei was accessible via the Dom Pedro II Railway (Estrada de Ferro Dom Pedro II/EFDPII), departing from the Vassouras Station for Entre Rios Station and then northward to the Sítio Station, where Dr. Rameiro's party changed trains. At Sítio, they boarded the more recently created West Minas Railway (Estrada de Ferro Oeste de Minas/EFOM), which used a much narrower-gauge track (2'6") than the Dom Pedro II Railway (5'3"). Hence, Ina's impression of a "little train" was due to the petite engine required by the narrower-gauge track. Her train was pulled by one of two imported wood-burning Baldwin locomotives manufactured in Philadelphia in 1880 that operated between the newly constructed stations of Sítio, Barroso, São José Del Rei (today, Tiradentes), and São João Del Rei, a distance of ninety-nine kilometers.

Today, the West Minas Railway (EFOM) is the oldest line (est. 1878) operating in Brazil, because locals and tourists still ride the train between São João Del Rei and Tiradentes, a thirty-five-minute trip of thirteen kilometers. Furthermore, Maria Fumaça (Smoky Maria) designates the two original Baldwin locomotives that pulled Emperor Dom Pedro II's coach from Sítio to inaugurate the São João Del Rei Station. Maria Fumaça also promotes the Railroad Museum (Museu Ferroviário) in São João Del Rei Station, opened in 1981 to commemorate the 1881 inauguration of that station, attended by Ina von Binzer. For a taste of Ina's ride from Sítio (today, Antonio Carlos Station) to São João on the narrow-gauge train, see Pedro Tacorakani, dir., *Tiradentes - Maria fumaça-saindo de Tiradentes para São João Del Rey-Minas Gerais*, video, 8:34, YouTube, 26 September 2014, https://www.youtube.com/watch?v=IYczRXE5WSI; *TV Estrada Real: Maria Fumaça (documentário)*, video, 6:58, YouTube, 26 August 2013, https://www.youtube.com/watch?v=NLwEdlqzd-0. For a historical narration in English, see David Corbitt, dir., *Ferrovia entre São João del-Rei e Antônio Carlos—1976 e 1979 (VFCO/SR-2)*, video, 14:14, YouTube, 5 January 2011, https://www.youtube.com/watch?v=V17RmQ6Y8iA.

chaotic crowd of people was crowding onto the platform in order either to welcome the guests, to receive them, or to stare at them. Some benevolent saint let us catch a wagon that carried us across the dangerous street pavement, which was a threat to both men and horses, before depositing us, to my surprise, safe and sound at the dwelling of our hosts. I was introduced to them and mustered my best Portuguese in order to excuse my uninvited appearance, yet their surprised faces and strong handshakes, as well as the usual two kisses of greeting, let me know that my appearance was considered perfectly natural, which was, of course, that much more desirable for me. There were even more guests there, and we tortured ourselves for a little while sitting on the right-angled rows of chairs and chatting. Then we went to bed.

There were six companions in the room, but only a single washstand, and I was freezing terribly in the more than primitive "bed," especially since the crevices and tears in the floor ensured that the cold air from an open hall beneath us could penetrate our room without any hindrance. I was not at all surprised to learn on the following morning that the small house of our hosts was lodging twenty-seven guests that night. In our country, people praise Brazilian hospitality, and they do so rightfully—it is just that one should by no means judge the matter according to European standards. The Brazilian guest needs no more than a mattress and a wool blanket. He cares not a whit about coziness (not to mention comfort), and the Brazilian host is released from his duties when he gives his guest these basic provisions and lets him partake of his coffee, his black beans, and his dried meat during mealtimes. I am convinced that the people mean well, but in our country, we would see a great inconsiderateness or a certain simple effrontery in these mass invitations and in the perfunctory manner of treating the guests. But, as I said before, their intentions are certainly good, and therefore they should not be met with ingratitude.

In the morning, a cheerful mood prevailed. All of the guests were on their feet to see the town, and everyone, even the poorest inhabitant, was proud and amicable because he considered himself to be a host.

Then we saw the churches. The small area had no less than three large churches, a fact that must have caused astonishment and approval among the Europeans, above all among the Protestants, especially considering the primitiveness of the other conditions. And these churches were not mere wooden chapels or houses of worship, but massive stone buildings made from Portuguese marble. Their style, neither decidedly Byzantine nor the least bit Gothic, was usually tasteless and gaudy, approaching for the most part the so-called Jesuit style.[35] On the inside of the churches, horrifying pictures of the Holy Trinity—life-size representations in colorful wooden figures—frightened me everywhere.[36] Also the paintings, especially in their use of perspective, were the most astonishing sight that I have ever seen.

And yet, I feel a greater admiration for these testaments to a people's piety than I ever felt for the looming towers of the charming cathedral at Ulm or the miraculous cathedral in Köln [Cologne, Germany].[37] Conjure up in your mind mighty stones, one foot thick and often longer than two feet, all

35. São João Del Rei had no fewer than a dozen principal churches, mostly constructed in the "Minas Baroque" style, what Ina correctly attributed to Jesuit influence. The three that she visited lay near her lodgings and counted among the most renowned: St. Francis of Assisi and probably both Our Lady of Pilar (the parish seat) and Our Lady of the Rosary. Ina's comments focus on the church of St. Francis, begun in 1774 and completed early in the nineteenth century. More than fifty-five meters long and fifteen wide, the church possesses two towers rising to thirty meters. Capt. Richard Francis Burton, British consul for Santos-São Paulo (1867–71), commented on its architecture: "It has been said that the architect of the São Francisco [church] used no rule but a compass; there is not a straight line save the vertical; the chosen form is the oval." *Highlands of Brazil* [. . .] (London: Tinsley Brothers, 1869), 1:122. The architect was Francisco de Lima Cerqueira, although the original plan (subsequently discarded) for the church is attributed to Aleijadinho (Antonio Francisco Lisboa), colonial Brazil's most acclaimed artist. He definitely sculpted the ornamental façade of the St. Francis Church, where he carved the date (1774) over the doors. Magnificent, life-size wooden statues adorning the six side altars are also attributed to him. For videos about the "City of the Bells," see *Sinos da Igreja de São Francisco de Assis - São João Del Rei - 09/03/1991*, 4:53, YouTube, https://www.youtube.com/watch?v=fYFqx-u4ojw, where teenage bell-ringers do their work. Interior and exterior views of the Saint Francis of Assis Church can be seen in *Igreja de São Francisco de Assis (São João del-Rei MG*, 4:53, YouTube, 28 November 2015, https://www.youtube.com/watch?v=3hG5jDbhyiE. For views of São João's historic churches from a drone, see *Sao Joao del Rei em 4 k, filmado com drone (parte 1)*, 4:51, YouTube, 24 April 2017, https://www.youtube.com/watch?v=FQSTAix7ogY.

36. Aleijadinho (the Little Cripple) carved the life-size wooden sculptures of the Holy Trinity which compose the retable for the high altar of the Church of St. Francis of Assisi that so "horrified" Ina. Acknowledging that "the Brazilians have to a considerable extent inherited the art of wooden statuary, in which Ebro-land [Portugal] has excelled the world," Capt. Burton left a description of the Holy Trinity statues twelve years before Ina's visit: "The Creator is distinguished from the Preserver by a red cloak and a gold triangle for a crown, a Dove in red and white hovering between them." He referred to Aleijadinho, who sculpted these "very laborious alt[ar]-reliefs," as "a handless man" whose affliction of leprosy caused him to chisel soapstone and wood with tools his assistant strapped to "the stumps which represented arms." *Highlands of Brazil*, 1:123–24. Recent research now questions whether leprosy was the disease that afflicted this accomplished sculptor.

37. Cologne Cathedral, begun in 1448, had been completed only in 1880, shortly before Ina's departure from Germany, prompting her to recall its "miraculous edifice," as the world's tallest building.

around massive columns, stairs and ramparts, and then ask yourself how they got here! Then tell yourself that each of these stones made its way on the back of a mule from the coast into the interior of the country, a journey that would have taken sixteen to eighteen hours with a train, but for which the animals probably needed four to five months.[38] Ask yourself then, apart from the astonishing amount of labor, how much such a project would have cost, and then you would certainly be surprised along with me. You would admire the spirit of their piety, these people who gave priority to building altars for God and appropriately housing his saints.

The following day, the twenty-ninth of August, was the actual day of the inauguration, scheduled to coincide with the arrival of the emperor. Early in the morning, the Brazilian beauties had already clothed themselves in finery, and, indeed, some of them appeared in the most elegant Parisian society clothes. Whoever had some money and connections really did procure gorgeous clothing from Paris, or, at the very least, from Rio, and they put them on display. You could see ladies who had otherwise worn nothing but a calico dress for the entire year now wearing bright red or deep blue, or even yellow and green, silk clothes.[39] I will never forget the niece of our hosts who was wearing a chamois-colored gown that was practically competing with the color of her own skin. It was draped with red velvet and had a quadrangular cut. The train of her dress, whose white tip was half torn away, whirled in the dust. Her brown hands, adorned with rings, were holding one of the most colorful fans, and, instead of a hat, she had a wild new hairdo, one that she had doubtless arranged especially for this event. The day before, she appeared to me as a completely good-natured creature in spite of her blemished face and the braids hanging down in a mess. And no one had said to her foreign visitor, "How are you, are you doing well?" in such a sincere fashion as she. But in this

38. Ina saw white marble imported from Portugal used in the balustrades of the uncompleted atrium for the Church of St. Francis of Assisi or its interior decorative elements. However, she was mistaken about the origin of the ordinary stone masonry used there and in the town's other churches (rather than the customary bricks). It was locally quarried granite and limestone. More famous was the decorative stone of Minas that Burton identified geologically as "steatite, bluish, and at times of an apple green, which, when the usual bits of octohedral iron are rare, takes a high polish." *Highlands of Brazil*, 1:122. This steatite is more commonly known as soapstone (*pedra-sabão*). When polished, it can resemble certain types of marble, although Ina apparently was unaware of this feature, nor had she learned that Minas Gerais was famous for its huge deposits of soapstone.

39. Green and yellow were Brazil's national colors, a detail Ina may not have learned until she arrived in São João Del Rei.

costume, she looked terrible! Did she sense this instinctively? At any rate, at a certain point she brushed suddenly, and yet very respectfully, against my velvet dress, whose warmth I am able to bear quite well, and she said from the heart: "A Senhora está muito civilisada!" (You are so sophisticated!)

On this day, the gates of honor, which had been lying around in the streets half-finished since the day of our arrival, were finally put up. They consisted of rounded arches made out of bamboo reeds, constructed in the most simple of ways with a larger reed in the middle and two smaller ones on the sides. Lying on the street, they were wrapped in colorful gauze, and in the spaces in between they were bound with a quantity of bright ribbons. Here and there, people set up little lamps. The avenue of the triumphal arches that led to the emperor's lodging could have appeared quite graceful if it had been fittingly decorated. But with its formal decorations and poor lighting, this avenue made a thoroughly pitiful impression. Finally, on the third day, it emerged from the dust of the street. Where the arches were driven into the ground, the pavement was torn up and the stones lay wildly around. In front of the house which was meant for the emperor, a gate closed off this archway made out of wood and paper, crude and compact in design, nevertheless creating quite a sturdy impression. In another street, a gate was erected that was almost two feet wide and made from dark blue, brightly colored paper that had been pulled over wood. This gate achieved the highest degree of tastelessness that is humanly possible. An entire street had deigned to "decorate" itself patriotically, with barrels painted yellow and green placed in front of the doors. Here a little torn flag was waving, and there a little greenery from palm trees was peeking through. Only the street from the train station to the city, encircled by light columns bearing slender verdure and delicate flags, made a pleasant impression.

I was completely taken aback by so much tastelessness and awkwardness! What we could do in Germany just with this treasure trove of natural adornment that Brazil has ready at hand! Give us nothing more than these bending palm branches, these stately banana leaves, these bright oranges in their dark verdure, give us the delightfully slender pine trees of Brazil, these vines often larger than ten to twenty meters, these large, glowing, richly colored flowers, the silk-cotton *paina* [kapok] tree, whose white flakes you can blow like snow—give us all these things in such abundance as here, and the smallest German city would, without these impoverished tarlatan rags, without help from wood and paper, wrap itself in a fairy-tale garment. Do you not think so, Gretel? But now you would probably like to hear about the emperor. So:

At seven o'clock in the evening, everyone, both local and foreign, surged to the train station where Dom Pedro was supposed to arrive. Since the train was late by about four hours and no guard or any other peace officer was hindering the good citizens from their patriotic "thronging," the crowd had the time and the liberty to shape itself into a rather decent wall.

Finally the train arrived. The locomotive had broken down en route, and they had to fetch another one. This meant that the emperor had to wait two hours at the Entre Rios Station, where people were busy painting and decorating.[40] All this did not, so it seemed, ruin his good mood: "Did anyone make arrangements for a concert or a ball?" we heard him asking.

He continually greeted everyone with his hat and his hand, the empress nodded right and left, and then the little company gradually made its way with patience and good words among the emperor's beloved, multicolored subjects. They were finally received officially by the train directors in the "waiting room." (I offended a Brazilian when I asked him if this room was the main thoroughfare.) Our party used this delay to hurry back to the emperor's lodging in the city as quickly as possible, where we, for our part, were allowed to "greet" the regal pair.

In the meantime, the main square was illuminated. Some transparent lights—and *entre nous*, rather dreadful ones—were doing most of the illumination work. Many houses were content to attach sorts of wagon lanterns on both sides of their windows. One street had put up a rope on one side and hung little lamps on it; the other side was dark. The gate in front of the *logis imperial* was lighted by a row of small lamps, which almost looked nice, but the little lamps were not all lit, and the interruption in the row of lights was basically just distracting. Sometimes it really seems like the Brazilian would not be happy—given all of his inclination to put things on "display"—if he actually did something that looked right. It is as if it would contradict his essence to do this, for it is often not that difficult to do something thoroughly and effectively. Or do they not see such things?

We arrived, we waved our hats and scarves, and we took off our right glove, for Brazilian etiquette does not allow one to touch royalty wearing gloves.

40. Emperor D. Pedro II's inauguration of the West Minas Railway's extension to the São João Del Rei Station officially took place on August 28, 1881. However, Ina presumably dated it accurately, as August 29. Inauguration of the station was a major event, marking the railroad's expansion as interprovincial infrastructure that would soon tie together the provinces of Rio, Minas, and São Paulo into an integrated national rail grid, promoting both the export of coffee and the growth of an internal market for foodstuffs.

Then we waited in the corridor—only twelve people! The crowd seemed already to have cooled off or to have satisfied its curiosity.

We—twelve people (just think about it, your Ulla was among the twelve!)—"played the host." The house was private property and only "loaned" for the sake of the imperial guest; it belonged to a widowed baroness who lived in Rio.[41] The house's contents were not much better than wicker furniture by European standards and belonged partly to this lady and partly to other patriots. Whoever had anything nice brought it by. First we went quickly through all the rooms. Nowhere did it seem appealing to me except in the dining room, where a small table had been covered and prepared by a French cook.

When we went down again, a corporal was screaming out commands that were incomprehensible to me to a company of soldiers. They had completed an "about-face" that put me in the best of moods. Gretel, our most-recruited recruits do it better! The corporal pulled a man forward by his button and used his saber to push another man back. Then he left it to their discretion whether or not they wanted to remain like that.

Then a wagon came rattling over the pavement. . . . "O Imperador [The emperor]!" a voice thundered, and "Viva," screamed the crowd outside, although it was not a very big crowd. I stuck my head outside in curiosity. A tall, stately man with a white beard was cordially shaking the hand of Dr. Rameiro, who was standing in the door. Then the stately man stepped into the hallway, shook the hands of the ladies, who bowed discretely, and then shook the hands of the men. I had positioned myself—probably wisely—as the last person in the row so that I could imitate everything that the Brazilian women did. A very small, somewhat crooked lady came behind the emperor, wearing the most simple black clothes, and she let her hand be kissed by everyone in turn with a benevolent smile. That was the emperor and the empress of Brazil![42] You cannot believe, Grete, how I felt at that moment. It was so terribly simple. And I had imagined a reception for the emperor by the pomp-loving Brazilians to be completely different—there was nothing at all that made an impression!

41. The owner was the baroness of São João Del Rei (Guilhermina Cândida de Carvalho), whose husband, the baron of São João Del Rei (Dr. Eduardo Ernesto Pereira da Silva), had died two months earlier. The beautiful, two-story house, known as a *solar*, still stands today (having once housed the Superintendency of Schools), recalling in local memory the building that von Binzer had informally called the *logis imperial*. (The word *logis* is used in both French and German to mean "dwelling" or "lodging.")

42. Emperor D. Pedro II, often referred to as the "bourgeois emperor," was known for his simple taste and down-to-earth manner—for being a monarch who normally dismissed pomp and circumstance.

Dom Pedro gave his arm to his wife, and the simple pair slowly climbed the stairs. We followed them. Once we were up above, the empress sat down on the sofa in the *sala de visita* [parlor]. The women then lined themselves up following the example of the only lady of the court, right and left in a rectangular row of chairs, and the poor, tired princess tortured herself just to say a friendly word to everyone. Meanwhile, the emperor was standing amid the men like a boy without the slightest trace of fatigue. And, imagine, Grete, he spoke with me as well! At first, I was afraid when he spoke to me. He asked about my uncle in New York, who had lived for a long time in Brazil and was spoken of with great fondness by Dom Pedro.[43] The emperor supposedly speaks German very well, but he spoke French to me. After a short stay for the sake of decorum, the "guests" left the house. The noble guests were not in the mood for a formal dinner, and then everything became silent and dark in the house of the widowed baroness.

But the noble guests were not permitted to rest for a long time. The emperor's agricultural minister, Buarque de Macedo, suddenly fell sick with a grave illness. And at midnight the emperor was informed, and the news was announced that the man was probably nearing his end. The emperor went to the place where the sick man was being held. Dr. Rameiro's brother, a doctor who was staying at our house, was called. Too late! There was nothing to be done. For some time, the sick man wavered between life and death, and then he finally sighed: "My poor family!" The emperor barely had time to comfort him with a hasty word guaranteeing him their well-being. At dawn, Dom Pedro went back to his *logis* across from the decorated streets; the following day at dawn, his wagon led him to the train station. All further festivities had been canceled.

I do not believe, however, that we lost anything because of the premature departure, for the performance of the *Bell of Corneville* that we saw during his stay was horrible. At this musical matinée, the orchestra was playing with a metronome. And, when this didn't help, they played according to the energetic beat of the conductor's foot—and we laughed so uncontrollably that we attracted the most intense malevolence of the devout "natives."

By the way, if I let this letter get any longer, I am afraid of the one that I will receive from you. So for today, that's the end!

Your loyal Ulla

43. Ina's uncle was Baron Cristiano de Thomsen (Christian Thomsen), ennobled by Emperor Dom Pedro II in 1869, but permanently residing in New York City.

São Francisco

September 17, 1881

Oh, dear Grete, if you only knew how angry I get here sometimes on days such as these! How the hours crawl by, how everything appears so heavy! The children are naughty, the Vehmic court is lazy, the entire house is loud, and I feel so alone, so indescribably alone! Furthermore, the entire matter is beginning to take a physical toll on me. The neuralgic pains are constant, even if, thank God, they are less intense than before. I have migraines quite often, which I attribute particularly to the noise and the total discomfort of the domestic facilities. The nerves of these people must be like ropes—unfortunately! Otherwise they would know how to be considerate with others!

Imagine the following scene and then ask yourself if your own nerves would be able to bear it.

I gave the little Leonila a piano lesson in the so-called office of Dona Alfonsina, as the children do not have their lessons on the grand piano in the *sala de visita*, but rather, on an honorable upright.[44] The "office" that I just referred to is situated in the middle of the house, and all rooms lead to it, including a food storage room, the bathroom, the bedroom of the children, the room belonging to the Vehmic court, a closet, and the sewing room. You can imagine a little bit how much noise can be heard in this pleasant room even under normal circumstances. Today, however, it seemed like "Old Nick" was playing his game![45] Someone discovered mice in the food storage room, and, without hesitation, Dona Alfonsina commanded two black women and a black man to empty the entire room to find the mouse holes. I counted out my "un, deux, trois" with resignation on the badly tuned upright, Leonila continuing to make the same mistakes; and a corral of boxes, barrels, sacks, and so on was being built around us under the loud commands of Dona Alfonsina. The noise that was caused by this procedure—the loud orders and the occasional exclamations of discontent by the mistress of the house—was, in and of itself, deafening. In addition to that, the door to the sewing room was open next to the piano, and two machines were in that room clattering away. In the neighboring room, there were screams coming from a bamboo basket, and,

44. A better translation for *oficina* ["office"] would be "workroom."

45. The reference in German is to "the old gentleman," presumably to the Devil ("Old Nick").

all the while, parrots and other birds were screeching. Finally, the ever-growing pile of boxes forced a little mulatto girl, whom Dona Gabriela was teaching to read, from the corner where she was "studying." She then stood behind my chair, monotonously murmuring her "b—a ba, b—e be, b—i, bi." That was the last straw! Enraged, I sprang up, snatched the music, called Leonila to follow me into the hall, and declared the lesson to be over. The people here took that very poorly, and they consider me to be the inconsiderate one in the whole matter!

Yes, I know, if people have sensitive nerves, it is probably bad, but if they have none at all, it is even worse for others. And this is how the Brazilians seem to me to operate. I doubt that I will last all that long here with my health! Be sure to write often to me, I feel very lonely and isolated. If only I could somehow get to see anything or anyone German!

Your poor Ulla

By the way, I have changed rooms; in the previous sunless room, the dampness made it unbearable. Furthermore, I saw a snake right in front of my window one afternoon—shoo, you disgusting animal! We often see such beasts.

São Francisco

October 5, 1881

My dear Grete!

It is as if divine providence had received the final sigh in my last letter to you, face-to-face! The "German person" is here! And moreover, he is the most whimsical person that you could possibly imagine—the joy of the entire house, I must confess. Mine too. He is a scientist, an older man. At the recommendation of an Italian colleague, Dr. Rameiro has placed the house at his "service" during the length of his stay in this part of Brazil.

Our good countryman, whose French is terrible, and who struggles rather in vain to adapt his German-accented Latin to Portuguese, would have been completely lost without me as his translator. He is a "learned man," the sort that you find in books, and with his pedantry and his whimsical clothing he would even be strange for us Germans. But here, I can see that the Vehmic court, despite their immobile faces, enjoys being able to make fun of something German. Furthermore, I am sure that they are convinced that all Germans are like this professor. He is not at all suited to what one could call chatting, but he is nevertheless a fellow countryman, and once again I hear German words! What a source of bliss, Grete! I could just kiss the mean little pedant simply because he is German!

But I would like to tell you a story that happened to him yesterday. I laughed like I have never before laughed in my life.

Yesterday was Sunday, and, as I was sitting on the porch in the afternoon, enjoying my leisure, suddenly standing before me was the most strangely dressed creature. Big, blue glasses on his nose, a white straw hat on his head, a mighty botanist's box at his side, a green butterfly net on his shoulder, in the right jacket pocket a "handbook of botany," in the left a voluminous work about entomology—who could possibly be dressed in this type of array other than a German scholar! Our good professor invited me to be the companion of his first expedition on the plantation, but the matter had little interest for me, and the sun was too oppressive. I asked him to excuse me this time. The children came and played by the door, and Dona Gabriela and the doctor sat down next to me on the bench. We had been sitting there for barely forty-five minutes when something startled us all of a sudden.[46]

46. In all probability and unbeknownst to Ina, the visitor was Dr. Theodoro Peckolt, a renowned botanist who had immigrated to Brazil in 1847. The author of *História das plantas*

It raced around the sharp corner that the path makes next to the house, breathless, sullied up to the neck, one boot covered with a layer of mud, the other one having been totally replaced by mud, no glasses, no hat, no botanist's box, the empty butterfly net like a flag in the hand—the remains of a German scholar that had set out to investigate nature! Wheezing, he sank down onto the bench; the doctor stared at him horrified and looked over at me pleading for help with translating—yet even before he asked, I had already cried out, "What happened?"

"What happened!? Alas! Oh! Somebody is chasing me! Somebody is trying to kill me! Murder! Uff! Oh, my beautiful plants—what an orchid! And these interesting chigger fleas, oh, I had such a glorious specimen under my magnifying glass. . . ."

"But who in the world is chasing you?"

"Who? The savages, the cannibals, the—Alas!"

"What savages?"

"There, there, just look how the chap is rushing toward us, even his master won't be able to tame him, let's save ourselves in the house!"

"But that's a Negro from the plantation!"

"Yes, yes, indeed, for all I care, but I'm telling you that he is a savage and that I just barely managed to escape from him," cried the poor little man, clearly in despair. And then, gathering together his last ounce of strength, he plunged into the house.

Smiling and shaking my head, I translated these hot-headed sayings for the doctor, who listened and shrugged his shoulders. The Negro then arrived, completely out of breath, holding in his left hand the handbook of botany and in his right hand the book about entomology. He gave one to me, the other to the doctor, wheezing out the words two times, "Sos kiss, sos kiss."[47]

---

alimentares e de gozo do Brasil (Rio de Janeiro, 1871), he was also personal pharmacist to Emperor Dom Pedro II. His visit to Fazenda São Francisco was on behalf of his son and namesake, Theodoro Peckolt 2°, who would later marry Dona Gabriela, one of Ina's "Vehmic" judges. It is possible that the botanist was pursued by wasps he had disturbed with his butterfly net. Even today their hives pose a problem for visitors to the plantation.

47. *Sos kiss* referred to the ritualistic exchange of blessings that was a form of greeting between slaves and white authority figures. The term is a transliteration of the vernacular contraction for [*Nosso Senhor*] *Jesus Cristo*, used by slaves, whose native tongue usually was one of a number of Bantu languages—the *kiss* or *kisto* derived from *Christo*. During the 1940s, Stanley J. Stein heard elderly Vassouras informants, former slaves, recall that when they saw the master appear on horseback in the fields, they stood erect, doffed their hats, touched their foreheads, and uttered, "Vas Christo" [Go with Christ], to which he responded,

"What's going on?" his master barked at him.

"Senhor, *sim*, senhor," the black man said, "the German man who is visiting senhor is crazy." The two of us could barely suppress our laughter.

"He says that you are savages. What did you do to him?"

"Nothing, master, nothing. We were working in the coffee grove and the German man came along. We ran up to him in order to offer him *sos kiss*. The gentleman did not see us and was coming quickly. Then we walked somewhat closer to him. He began to run, quickly, quickly, quickly. He threw down his case, his hat, his books, and kept running toward the mud, next to Saint Jerome's pond, *sim*, Senhor. We were shouting to him not to run into the mud, but the man kept rushing in that direction, *sim*, Senhor, and finally he ran through the mud."

This report was given with many pauses and was interrupted and stuttered out with countless—and often meaningless, as you see—*sim*, senhors. During this speech, an entire company of the slave's black comrades was gathering behind him. One held the hat, another his botanist's box, a third his crushed pair of glasses, a fourth the muddy shoe of the poor scholar. And each one was holding out these various objects to us with a concerned expression and their habitual *sos kiss*.

The scene, which had already been half explained, was so unbelievably funny that I broke out into hysterical laughter, and when Dr. Rameiro finally began to laugh with me, this threw our poor honest black man into confusion. "Just put those things over there," the doctor said at last. The good men took their leave, pondering the events and leaving behind the nature excursion's sad remains in a row on the bench. "What is it that could have frightened your compatriot in such a manner from the very beginning?" said the doctor, wiping off tears of laughter.

"I can think of some reason," I said, repressing my own gaiety. "Could it have been the stretched-out hands and the *sos kiss*, which seemed so mysterious to me as well, when I first came here?" The doctor began to laugh again.

"By Our Dear Lady—that must be it! Ha-ha-ha! It was precisely their politeness—their greeting! I agree that it is difficult to recognize a gracious gesture of greeting in their stiff, flat, stretched-out hands and in the 'mysteri-

---

removing his hat, "Seja sempre louvado" [May He always be praised]. *Vassouras*, 164 (also citing Louis Couty, *L'Esclavage au Brésil* [Paris, 1881], 47).

ous *sos kiss'*—you are right, who would recognize a polite greeting in these gestures: *Louvado seja Nosso Senhor Jesus Christu* [Praised be Our Lord Jesus Christ]!"

I went up to the professor full of good cheer, but I bore the most empathetic facial expression possible. The man was gasping and calming himself in his rocking chair. The doctor followed me.

"What frightened you so much?" I asked clearly.

"Frightened, frightened! Oh, that is absolutely outrageous! Is that hospitality? The black beggars! The entire community wanted to beg from me! I can't believe this is tolerated! You should have seen the number of the hands that they were stretching out! But who takes money from a botanist? I pretended not to see the cannibals, but then they began to run after me and chased me, screaming, right up to the house. You should have heard their voices!"

I began laughing again. The doctor stood by, embarrassed. The professor shot enraged and disdainful looks at me.

"Forgive me," I finally managed to say, "but it is too funny. . . . "

"Funny!!"

"Just listen"—and I told him what the Negro had told us and the meaning of the whole incident. The professor's face began to take on different expressions, moving from distrustful rage to surprise, embarrassment, relief, good-hearted humor, then culminating in honest self-irony and cheerfulness. And finally, all three of us began to laugh.

"So, now your compatriot should take a look at our Negroes up close so that he can rid himself of these cannibal ideas," said the doctor in the afternoon. And we all went out to teach the professor not to be afraid.

Everywhere near the huts of the Negroes, little black half-monkeys came up to us, muttering their "sos kiss," and now our brave professor answered "Para semper." We looked into the huts.

There was a most crude sort of bed area made out of boards, as well as a mat made out of corn husks and a red wool blanket, a small lead coffer, and an indescribably primitive table. These objects, except for some pots, bowls, and small gadgets, made up the entire interior of the windowless room. A woman was cooking a meal over a fire in the corner.

"How terrible this fire must be in this hut," I said. "Do you not allow them to light the fire in front of the house, especially when it is so hot?"

"Allow it? I have tried to implement this a hundred times, but the black man is unhappy—no, sick—when you take his fire away from him. He needs it in the winter as well as in the summer and never sleeps without glowing coals in the hut."[48]

"How awful," groaned the professor, "and no windows, in addition!"

"At first, huts were probably made like that in order to prevent attempts to escape, since you cannot lock windows like you can doors. But then the Negroes got so used to it that, even when they are free, they don't put any windows in their huts."

"What are all these women cooking?" I said. "The slaves are all fed on the plantation, right?"

"The married ones only get fed at noon. The women generally cook dinner, as they are apportioned rations."

In front of one of the last houses, a pair of extremely old, fragile Negroes got up: "Sos kiss," they stuttered as we approached. "What do you still use them for?" the professor asked, horrified.

"For nothing," smiled the doctor, "but I can't let them die. They turned gray in my service, now they receive charity. I would also set them free, but I didn't have the heart to send old, used-up Negroes, free and yet incapable of work, into misery or destitution—let them die here."

"Do many plantation owners think like this?" I asked.

"Thank God, yes, and it is right that way. To say to old people like that: 'You are free. I don't have to take care of you anymore, go on your way'—this would be barbarism. One of our sayings goes, 'Whoever eats the meat gets the bones afterward.'"

"I am afraid, Doctor," said the professor tactfully, "that I came to a plantation where I only get to see the positive sides to slavery!"

"That wouldn't be so bad!" said the doctor amicably. "So much has been written about the other side of the story, and so much has been exaggerated that it would be good to emphasize the better aspects. By the way, you are wrong if you think that I am alone in the way I behave. Many plantation owners here in Brazil keep their slaves as well as I do, some even because of self-interest! The drawbacks to slavery are primarily the lack of freedom, the ethical corruption of many slaves, and the ignorance of all of them—all of this will remain as long as there are slaves. Unfortunately, in the meantime, for us there must be slaves."

48. The obvious practical explanation was that a lack of windows and the presence of a fire discouraged mosquitoes and other night insects from entering the slaves' shacks after sunset.

"It is odd how the dark sides to slavery obtrude upon me far less here than in Europe and perhaps than in every other place," I said, contemplating the matter.

"Maybe you saw only the dark side," the *senhor de escravos* [slave master] said, laughing.

You know, Grete, I forgave him a long time ago that he doesn't look posh and that he doesn't dress colorfully like the small glove maker's Brazilian in the operetta.[49] He is really a good person, and as far as he and his wife are concerned, I am being well taken care of here—but the Vehmic court, the Vehmic court!

Your Ulla

The professor is leaving tomorrow.

49. This is a reference to Jacques Offenbach's operetta, *La vie parisienne* (1866). However, sadly, slave quarters normally lacked windows, unless fitted with bars to deter escapes.

São Francisco

October 22, 1881

My dear Grete!

You asked in your last letter if I had a friend nearby with whom I could talk. My dear woman, there is nothing at all "nearby"; the next plantations are four to six miles away, and there is no city that can be reached from here without traveling very far. Moreover, as my bad luck would have it, all of the plantations that are at all close by only have grown-up children or the owners are so simple that they wouldn't take on a *professora* [teacher]. So I am quite alone here at work, a lonely and sensitive soul. Sometimes I cry terribly, but you can't tell that to my mother!

I would love to get out of here, at least to go to Rio so that I could experience the city that I saw so hastily when I arrived and that appeared so beautiful to me. I still have a letter of recommendation for a German family living there, as well as one from a friend of my uncle from New York, who is very rich. It would be such a solace to me just to have any foothold at all in this foreign country . . .

But forgive me, Gretel, if I end my letter right here—I am deathly tired and lethargic, and I just wanted to send you a greeting.

Your Ulla

S. F., December 3, 1881 [postcard]

That was a long break, wasn't it, my dear Grete? But you will forgive me when you hear that I was sick. A terrible bout of malaria grabbed hold of me, and along with the overexertion that this position (especially because of the music) demands of me, I was incapable of serving in any pedagogical capacity for four weeks.

Finally, I was able to get up today—on my birthday (oh Grete, nobody knows about this, I received no happy birthday greeting, no flower, no letter, nothing!)—and in the following days I will go to Rio to consult a doctor. The most sincere greetings from—

Your Ulla

Give this card to your little brother for his collection.

Rio de Janeiro

December 24, 1881, Evening

Christmas Eve and 25 degrees Celsius in the shade! How strange, how far from home, and, oh Grete, how sad! Nobody in this colorful, noisy city seems to think about Christmas. Public life is not even touched by it, and nothing reminds me of the holy time that is so familiar at home. Maybe some German families, even in the tropical city, will decorate an exotic little Christmas tree. (There is nothing resembling our pine trees over here—nothing of that sort for me to see here!) The Kleins received me in such an unfriendly manner that I will not go there again. I was even more surprised at this since Mrs. Klein had once been a governess and knows how such lonely creatures feel. I haven't been able to meet my uncle's friend thus far. So imagine your Ulla in a lonely hotel room on Christmas Eve, thinking about you in my homeland and longing indescribably for you and our beautiful, dear Germany!

Outside, the city is noisy with its evening traffic. Through the open windows, the strange, warm, damp tropical air comes inside, and I see the stars in the twilight evening sky; in the frame of the side windows, the palms of the Corcovado can be seen, that airy cliff behind the Botafogo Bay whose famous springs furnish Rio with delicious drinking water.[50] The inhabitants of Rio are also very proud of this splendid gift of nature, and they have a saying: "Quem bebeu a água de Carioca—Nunca toma outra água na boca." Whoever has once drunk the waters of the Carioca spring will never lift any other water to his mouth.

So many impressions could be so poetic here if one were able to enjoy them calmly, but I have never visited another city as noisy as Rio de Janeiro. In comparison with Rio, staying in Berlin is like pure summer freshness and relaxation for one's nerves. Not even in London did it seem to me so noisy. So many horses travel the roads, and there are omnibuses and frequent warning whistles causing such a loud clatter. Little one-person coaches, called "tilburies"

50. An aqueduct was built in the mid-eighteenth century to carry spring water from the mountain of Corcovado (today the site of the iconic Christ the Redeemer statue synonymous with Rio de Janeiro) to the city center. Slave laundresses went to the public fountain at the Largo da Carioca, where the aqueduct terminated, in order to wash clothes. At the end of the nineteenth century, the Roman arches of the deactivated aqueduct were used to support the tracks for a trolley line between downtown and adjacent Santa Teresa. It continued in operation throughout most of the twentieth century.

by the English, rumble over the terrible pavement, something that you can probably imagine. If somebody is riding, they do so mercilessly and at a gallop. Already a couple of times, just recently, I almost jumped out of the window because I thought a horse was coming through the walls. People selling water, newspaper vendors (these are for the most part just as bad as the parrots on the plantations), candy, cigarette and sorbet vendors, Italian fishmongers, and also hurdy-gurdies, along with other instruments, notwithstanding the sound of countless pianos coming through open windows—all of this noise clamors punctiliously in the narrow streets, where every sound is twice as loud. In addition to this, the people here, especially the adult Negroes, have completely inhuman voices, so that one almost collapses when one happens to be in their immediate vicinity. You can get a sense of the treat to your ears by imagining the din of fireworks going off day and night. And then, of course, you take for granted the monotonous, hard-voiced Negro conversations in front of your window and the inept guitar playing not that far away, and—envy me if you can! But here again, the nerves of the locals surprise me. In spite of this deafening noise, people live on the street, or practically on the street. If one were to follow the principle of that famous old Berlin professor backwards and forwards—"The educated person belongs in a room!"—then it is certain that one could bargain for educated men here just as Abraham did so for good men in Sodom. The idle black man can always be found in front of his house door, smoking and spitting; the children roll around from morning to night in the alleyways. The small grocer, the vendor, yes, even the more well-off merchant, stand in front of their doors in the more elegant streets when there are no customers present and chat with the passersby—and as long as the sun permits it. Every balcony and every window is occupied by idle people gaping at the scene in front of them.

The house seems to hold absolutely no attraction, nor does it require anyone's attention, or else it would not be so amusing for these people to go off into the tumult of the streets. The street has the effect of forcing its way in a terribly plebian manner into the space of the household. In a good Brazilian room, people sit around as if they sat before a stage. All windows are open, since Brazilians believe that open windows always make a house cool—and all the doors as well. I do admit that the opening of the doors is necessary in order to let in a draft to make up for the foolishness of the open windows—but why don't people create a more thorough and more pleasant coolness by keeping the windows covered against the sunlight of the daylight hours?! I have come to a better understanding of why the Brazilians do not yet have anything to show in the way of scientific achievements. Their way of life does not permit any sort of organized thought. In order for proper thoughts, you need a properly enclosed space, one in which a thousand outside things do not pull you away from the issue with which you are attempting to grapple. This is the meaning of that Berlin professor's original dictum.

Of course, Rio is not the place for me at this time. The doctor was not satisfied with the condition of my nerves, tortured as I was by work, noise, and neuralgic pains. He advised me urgently not to return to my work in São Francisco, but rather to say farewell to the Vehmic court, the parrots, and the five hours of piano lessons per day. He urged me to go to Petrópolis (the famous spa and sanitarium beyond the bay) for four weeks in order to recover from my fever. Petrópolis is also the summer residence of the emperor, and all of the politicians flee there during these months in order to avoid the heat and yellow fever.

Then Mrs. Carson, the wife of the innkeeper, asked me to eat dinner with her in her private room. The Carsons are English and they are nice people. Their children are being raised in England, and even if they are not really celebrating "Christmas" because of this, at least they seem to understand how difficult this day must be for a lonely German soul over here. And our own compatriots—!

Write to me extensively how everything is with you at home, describe everything to me, everything that we did as children, every gift that you received—every word will be a piece of Germany for me! Send your letters here to the Hôtel Carson, Rua Catete, and may there be many of them!

Your Ulla

Fig. 1. Slaves harvesting coffee on a steep hillside, Paraíba Valley, ca. 1882. *Photographer*: Marc Ferrez. Digital Image Courtesy of the Getty's Open Content Program. Planting coffee on steep hillsides provided drainage for tropical rains, but it made harvesting more arduous. By the 1880s, the sharp decline in the enslaved population meant that more women filled the ranks of field hands, where, formerly, men had predominated.

Fig. 2. Slaves departing for the coffee harvest, Paraíba Valley, ca. 1885. *Photographer*: Marc Ferrez. Digital Image Courtesy of the Getty's Open Content Program. Slaves were awakened before dawn by an iron bell or the blast of a cow horn and lined up for the morning prayer and then roll call, prior to departing for the coffee groves under the supervision of an overseer. Mothers took their babies and young children with them. On average, Stanley Stein reported, each slave was expected to pick from five to seven *alqueires* of coffee berries per day, between seventy-two and one hundred quarts.

Fig. 3. Early morning lineup for the coffee harvest, Paraíba Valley, ca. 1885. *Photographer*: Marc Ferrez. Digital Image Courtesy of the Getty's Open Content Program. Slaves generally spent all day in the coffee groves, breaking around 10 a.m. for a midday meal and again at 1 p.m. for coffee and leftovers. They ate supper in the groves around 4 p.m. and went back to work until sundown, around 6 p.m. Returning home, they lined up for the day's final roll call.

Fig. 4. Younger slaves working the coffee harvest, Paraíba Valley, ca. 1882. *Photographer*: Marc Ferrez. Digital Image Courtesy of the Getty's Open Content Program. Posed by the photographer during a meal break, these mostly teenagers convey in their expressions an immense sadness. Expected to do a day's work from the age of eight, this group was born before passage of the 1871 Law of the Free Womb and was therefore destined to a lifetime of servitude.

Fig. 5. The drying terrace (*terreiro*) of a coffee plantation, Paraíba Valley, ca. 1882. *Photographer*: Marc Ferrez. Digital Image Courtesy of the Getty's Open Content Program. Once picked, the green coffee berries were deposited onto a large drying terrace. They were then raked and turned over to dry in the sun for several days. Either they were immediately bagged for rail transport to the ports of Rio de Janeiro and Santos or, if equipment and labor were available, the berries were dehusked and sorted for quality as beans, before being bagged and sent to an Atlantic port.

Fig. 6. European immigrants harvesting coffee, São Paulo, 1890s. *Photographer*: Marc Ferrez. Digital Image Courtesy of the Getty's Open Content Program. Contracted for sharecropping exclusively as family groups, European immigrants rapidly replaced former slaves, once abolition was a fact. Their most common destination was the coffee frontier known as Paulista West, where entrepreneurs like the Silva Prados had already invested in both large-scale plantations and the railroad linking the province's interior to the Port of Santos.

1
Memorial
Manuel
Congo
Manuel Congo
A LUTA PELA LIBERDADE
ETERNIZA O HOMEM

MEMORIAL
MANUEL CONGO
GOVERNO-RENATO A. IBRAHIM
VASSOURAS, 06 DE SETEMBRO DE 1996.

Fig. 7. (*Top-left*) Vassouras museum devoted to Manuel Congo's 1838 slave revolt. (*Bottom-left*) Commemorative plaque at the museum, marking where Manuel Congo was hanged. *Photographer*: the author, 2018. This modest museum was erected by the Municipal Government of Vassouras in 2016, in commemoration of Manuel Congo, an African slave convicted of leading a revolt in the parish of Paty do Alfares in 1838. The revolt was the largest ever to occur in the Paraíba Valley, at a time when 75 percent of the slave population came from Africa. The sign outside the museum reads: "In tribute to the memory of Manuel Congo, 178 years after his death—a figure of great importance in Vassouras memory. The struggle on behalf of liberty renders man immortal." The bronze plaque, erected on September 6, 1996, by the Government of the State of Rio de Janeiro, is positioned on the site where Manuel Congo was hanged in 1838. The Brazilian Empire reserved the death penalty for those who led insurrections, including slave revolts.

Fig. 8. (*Below*) The *logis imperial*, home of the Baroness of São João Del Rei, São João Del Rei, Minas Gerais. *Photographer*: the author, 2018. Ina von Binzer was presented to Emperor D. Pedro II and Empress Teresa Cristina inside the mansion she christened the *logis imperial* when she visited São João Del Rei for the inauguration of the city's railroad station in August 1881. Imperial fêtes celebrating the expansion of Brazil's railroad networks underscored the national importance of infrastructure projects principally dedicated to exporting commodities—above all, to sending coffee to Atlantic ports.

Fig. 9. Inauguration of the Mantiqueira Tunnel, 25 June 1882. *Photographer*: Marc Ferrez. Digital Image Courtesy of the Getty's Open Content Program. Attended by Emperor Dom Pedro II, Empress Tereza Cristina, Princess Isabel, and her husband, the Conde d'Eu, the inauguration of the Mantiqueira Tunnel (a kilometer in length), connecting the provinces of Rio de Janeiro and São Paulo, offers a suggestion of the similar celebration anticipated by Ina von Binzer in São João Del Rei a year earlier. Above the royal party, flanked by cabinet ministers and important businessmen on the ground level, can be seen the ubiquitous decorative palm fronds that so captured Ina von Binzer's attention in São João Del Rei. The upper level of this photo features a privileged cohort of railroad workers invited to the party as a socially discrete contingent.

Fig. 10. Maria Fumaça (Smoky Maria), the 1880 Baldwin locomotive on the West Minas Railroad. (*Below*): Factory medallion mounted on the locomotive's side. *Photographer*: the author, 2018. This locomotive was one of two brand-new locomotives carrying the royal party and guests to the inauguration of the São João Del Rei Railroad Station in August 1881. This steam engine still operates today, transporting local commuters between that city and Tiradentes, a distance of twelve kilometers, and the station doubles as a railroad museum. Used on the final stretch of track from Sítio (today, Antonio Carlos) to São João Del Rei, this locomotive on the West Minas Line (E.F.O.M.) pulled the "miniature" carriages that Ina von Binzer so carefully measured for her notes. The medallion mounted on the side of the locomotive indicates its place and date of manufacture.

Fig. 11. Marc Ferrez (*upper row, far left*) and crew on the Rio-Minas Railroad, ca. 1880. *Photographer*: Marc Ferrez. Digital Image Courtesy of the Getty's Open Content Program. Marc Ferrez (1843–1923), born in Brazil of French parents and educated in France, returned to his native country in his early twenties. In 1865, he opened his own photographic studio in downtown Rio de Janeiro, after briefly apprenticing with Swiss lithographer and photographer George Leuzinger. Beginning in the 1870s, Ferrez traveled the country for over thirty years, carrying out contracts with the imperial government to photograph infrastructure projects (especially railroad and dam construction), natural landscapes (prompting him to invent his own wide-angle lenses), urban building projects, ports, and ships. Today, his photographs, preserved by his grandson, are the largest repository of Brazil's nineteenth-century visual documentation.

Petrópolis

January 15, 1882

My dearest Grete!

Be happy with me, for I have found again the humor that I had lost—or rather should I say the mischievous, pessimistic humor that I grabbed by the collar in bad situations?

I am writing in an environment that would be a pretty good candidate for a rummage den. My clothes and my jackets are hanging on the wall in picturesque disorder; there are bows on the bed, hats and fabrics spread out; on all of the chairs, laundry is sunning itself. Five pairs of boots and shoes are looking out wistfully from the windowsill onto a bunch of bananas, and all my gloves, hanging on a clothes line, are fluttering in the zephyr of the afternoon.

My wardrobe and I find ourselves in this condition once every three days. This procedure became necessary after I discovered that in this fecund land, boots and clothes become covered with the most plentiful vegetation.[51] The fortuitous overgrowth of vegetation is quite nice in many respects, only it doesn't agree with my wardrobe. Fate has particularly harried my boots, gloves, and silk garments; all of the beautiful, refined leather gloves that I bought in Antwerp are splotched!

At any rate, I want to tell you my adventure from the beginning:

When I went back to São Francisco on the second day of Christmas and declared that I could no longer stay, the people there were unpleasantly surprised. But my four-week-long sickness and my miserable appearance softened their hearts so that they did not prevent my departure. We said "Adieu" to one another, and I was gone. Grete, I have never said such a farewell in all my life! I was not sorry at all to leave. On the contrary, I felt that none of them would be hard to miss, and I was also aware that in the hearts of the children, there was no real attachment to me. Really, the only thing that bothered them was that they had to look for a new governess. It's not exactly all warmth and good feelings over here!

I came here on New Year's Eve, and there were three different legs to the journey. First, by steamer over the bay, then by train until the mountain

51. Ina is referring to the mildew and mold that grow very quickly in humid, enclosed spaces.

where Petrópolis lies, and then in a group carriage, although on quite well-traveled roads. I managed to get quite a good place in one of the five wagons and was also comforted by the fact that my suitcase seemed to have just as much luck.[52]

Around the halfway point, we took a break. Everyone went to a shack where we could find coffee, baked goods, and fruit. I was hungry and drank my cup of coffee greedily. And I was just as eager to bite into a biscuit that I had snatched up. It tasted somewhat bizarre, and as I looked more closely at the second bite, I noticed that it was swarming with ants, of which I had almost certainly just swallowed a considerable amount. Blech! Right? Yes, you know, I was already so integrated into the Brazilian way of life that I indifferently brushed aside the rest of the little guests from my biscuit and then consumed it comfortably along with a second cup of coffee. This will probably provoke your disgust just as much as it provoked the astonishment and admiration of a young Frenchman. He directed some sort of ridiculous phrase to me, and I idiotically chose to answer with good cheer. For since that moment, this gallant "arch-enemy" (who was luckily sitting in another car) began to pester me. And if I had eaten and drunk everything that he wanted me to eat, delicacies that he had offered to me one after the other, I probably would have barely made it alive to Petrópolis.

When I arrived, I went to the German Hotel and then started on my way to the house of Mr. Goldschmidt, my uncle's business friend. He had a house here—more like a castle—with a spectacular park. He lived here during the hot season with his family. Since I had met the family when I was staying in Rio, this visit was not my first.

I was led into the hall and asked to wait for a moment.

"Do you not have a job?" somebody screamed suddenly behind me, and Mrs. Goldschmidt, an extremely lively Brazilian woman who spoke German quickly and incorrectly, stood before me with a half-laughing (she always laughs), half-skittish countenance.

Grete, the fear of this twentyfold millionaire—I wouldn't mind having a fraction of what she has—was so indescribably funny that my humor came back to me in a magical stroke, and I laughed out loud. Dona Albertina looked at me rigidly.

52. In 1883, the year following Ina's visit, the stretch of railroad track connecting Raíz da Serra, at the base of the Serra do Petrópolis, to the summit (where the city is located) was completed—eliminating the group carriage.

"Forgive me," I said now also somewhat curtly, "but it is too funny that that was your first question! No, I don't have a job, but I will find one when it becomes necessary."

Then her husband arrived.

"You see, my lady," he pontificated, "I was always a rich man because I only used half of what I earned. I came to Rio with fifty marks, and today I own many millions. All of this from this method! But what I wanted to say: Go now to Miss Dahlmann, as we do not have our governess in our house with us. It is uncomfortable for me to have foreign people in my house. She is a German-English woman and lives with a simple German family in the village. Perhaps she can advise you where you can find cheaper accommodations. You would spend too much money in a hotel. That is wrong—always act according to my principle, my young lady, always according to my principle!"

The small man amused me immensely with his "mezza voce" flood of words and with his thumbs constantly snapping the lining of his vest. I nevertheless decided to follow his advice—which I had not asked for—regarding possible accommodations. I intended to seek out this Miss Dahlmann, in whom, at the very least, I would find a colleague.

Dona Albertina asked me to take part in the breakfast that was being served. "You see, my young lady," began the husband again (he seemed to love this way of beginning a speech), "I only invite people to breakfast, never to lunch. We eat at six; afterwards the evening mail comes, which I have to take care of in peace, and it disturbs me when there is someone there. Do you understand? But anyone can come to breakfast who wants to, it disturbs me less." Swoop! his thumbs drove into the sides of his vest.

It was time to go, Grete. Otherwise I would have laughed at these people, right in their faces again, because my good cheer was lodged at the top of my throat. I said that I had already eaten breakfast before I came, and that I wanted to go to Miss Dahlmann if they would be so kind as to show me the way. They had probably not hoped to be rid of me that quickly. They suddenly became nice to me because of this unexpected surprise. They insisted on providing a Negro to lead me, which I summarily accepted. There is nothing like good recommendations for your compatriots in foreign lands—no one could possibly ruin that!!

Miss Dahlmann is some years older than I and somewhat stiff and "English," but she was good-hearted enough to be helpful to me. So I eventually stayed with the woman who was hosting her, and we both ate. She is my only companion here; even if her company is not exactly warm, it is not disagreeable. She looks at life with a lot more detachment than I do, and that's how I guess she manages to cope with being a guest at the Goldschmidts'. I took many useful—either intentional or involuntary—pieces of advice, and I believe I will leave more knowledgeable about local ways than when I came.

Petrópolis itself is, in my opinion, a miserable nest. The main amusement of the visitors consists in going to the omnibus stop every afternoon and gaping at the other visitors arriving. The palace of the emperor is a long, spacious, but terribly boring, building—there is nothing really to look at, just many windows. I am bringing an image of it engraved on a glass paperweight. I am also bringing a couple of small vases on which is written "Lembrança de Petrópolis [Souvenir of Petrópolis]." These things are, however, not that interesting since they all come from Europe and are then engraved over here. I very much admire the wood turning and wood engraving of a German man who has a little house here, a warm little man with an equally warm and numerous family. Sometimes I go there in order to chat for an hour. I also bought a splendid tobacco case which was finished with breadfruit and is crowned with the etching of an Indian on top.

The rest of the Germans living here are just uneducated peasants. They have kept their German language and some German vices, but, in general, they have indeed been influenced by the customs of the country. For quite some time, Petrópolis has no longer been a purely German colony as it was originally.[53] Many colonists from various countries live here, and you hear all sorts of languages. The languages that I like the best are Negro-Portuguese pidgin and low German: "Looky there if it ain't rainin'"—"Wait a sec a lil' bit"—"I cain't yet do it"—such are the sorts of things you hear on the street.

The location is terrific, that must be said! High in the mountains, nestled between incalculable swaths of trees, it offers amazing walks on well-paved roads through the woods such as are generally difficult to find in Brazil. This is because the first roadway into the forest is difficult to make and everything grows so quickly with undergrowth and vines.

53. Although first claimed as a pleasant retreat during the 1820s by Emperor D. Pedro I, who purchased the land there in 1830, Petrópolis was formally founded in 1843 as the "imperial city" by his son, Emperor D. Pedro II. It grew up around a summer palace that he ordered built after sponsoring the immigration of German-speaking colonists from the Rhineland to settle in and around the city. It was their descendants whom Ina pejoratively dismissed as "peasants." Hence numerous homes in the city, especially those rented by Brazilian summer visitors, reflected the marriage of German architecture to Mediterranean tile roofs. By Ina's time, the "German Hotel" where she first stayed was just one of many catering to foreigners who belonged to Rio de Janeiro's European communities.

I am going to stay here for another month, and then I will seek my fortune in Rio in order to get to know the city a little better. I now have better nerves and more courage! A thousand greetings from

Your old Ulla

Recently Miss Dahlmann and I met the empress, who was out with a lady from the court. On Sunday we saw the emperor, the princess, and her husband, the Duke of Eu, as well as the three small princes, all together going for a ride in the same carriage.[54]

54. Ina refers to the emperor's daughter, Princess Isabel, and her husband, the French count d'Eu (Gaston de Orléans), and their children, the three small princes. The grandson of Louis Philippe, deposed king of France (1830–48), the Conde d'Eu was not a duke.

Rio de Janeiro

February 8, 1882

My dearest Gretchen!

There I was again in the colorful, southern city and right in the middle of its bustling life! Gretel—Rio is beautiful, one must admit, incredibly beautiful and fantastic, especially looking out over the bay as I did during my arrival and now again during my return from Petrópolis.

The city unfolds like a fairy-tale before my neglected north German eyes. The city juts out like a terrace from Brazil's coastal mountains into the bay, colorful and glorious, a unique sea of color and light. It is only interrupted—or, rather, enhanced—by the thin palm trees and the large-leafed banana trees sprinkled about everywhere. There is nothing to remind us of our monotonous red walls or uniform gray paint—everything is white or colorful and swimming in Brazil's saturated sunlight. Indeed, the small forts on the little islands in front of the inner bay do not look at all like gloomy defense fortresses hiding among palm trees and colors, but, rather, like charming little idylls. One has to force oneself to believe that they are real. Here as well, one can find the "flower island," the first asylum for immigrants. I do not envy the fate of the people on this island, but nevertheless, the place reminds me of the idyll in Dranmor's *Requiem*:

> I know a beautiful island, as if lost
> In the still ocean, covered with forest,
> Stretched out in the mild rays of the sun,
> Like an asylum made for poets.
> An Eden breathing with tropic glow,
> An island, like a gathering of wild roses
> Surfacing from dreamy waves
> For sad people, for the homeless.[55]

And at first glance, the city looks the same from the inside as it does from outside: fantastic, southernly, exotic, and wonderfully charming. And yet, aside from the deafening noise, there are aspects of the place that one would

55. Dranmor's (pseud. of Ferdinand von Schmid) *Requiem* was published in Munich in 1869. Ina later authoritatively quoted the observations of this Swiss romantic poet on Brazil.

gladly do without: dirt and chaos! The streets are narrow and badly paved. I once drove in a coach on the streets, and let me assure you, never again! The sidewalk is just as dirty as the main road. The houses do look merry with their three, four, and sometimes even more, different colors, but mostly they are not clean, and much of the wood is warped from the roof to the door threshold. Everything seems to us North Germans, who have been raised strictly, to be put together haphazardly. And the people are so—yes, I don't exactly know how to describe it—I believe "undisciplined" would be the right word.

Here you can see a group of Negroes smoking and spitting, there you see a Negro woman squatting in the doors of the shops and picking over coffee beans. The sidewalk is often overrun with black men and women, mulattoes with their tables and baskets filled with oranges, bananas, coconuts, firecrackers, and all sorts of other trifles. They would perhaps attract the European shopper, if only because of the exotic nature of the first impression. But then a glance at the area surrounding their carts would repulse him: apple peels, matches, paper rags, cigar butts, along with all sorts of rubbish, compete for preeminence, and the train (!) of the vendor's muslin dress gets dragged through it all. In many shops of the legitimate business district, even in some shops in the more elegant area of the city, I saw straw, packing paper, twine, broken devices, and other things lying around on the floor. Nobody seemed to consider this unusual. The Brazilian encounters this sort of disorder with a childlike harmlessness that is almost touching. I do believe, Grete, that we Europeans could eventually get used to looking at other people's dirtiness without any problems, even if we ourselves cannot tolerate the dirt.

I haven't seen many beautiful shops, and, above all, nothing that would be characteristic of this country. One shop does have beautiful items made from untinted feathers of the local, gorgeously colored birds. The available fabrics for balls are delightful! Whatever you buy other than that, however, is almost exclusively European. There is hardly an item in the shops that has not seen the Atlantic Ocean, other than the country's natural resources. Clothing fabric, boots, linen, woolen goods, furniture, lighting fixtures, kitchen appliances, books, even the paper and the needles come from Europe. Even the calico fabric comes here, to the land of wool, from France and Germany. They send the raw material there that they themselves know how to manufacture only insufficiently and just in a few factories.[56] And when they want to eat white cane sugar [refined sugar], the country of the sugar cane imports it from

56. Although Brazil had a growing cotton textile industry by the 1880s, it was not until after World War I that the country produced first-quality cotton or woolen clothes.

the country of beets. Some things here are amazing! In the Rua d'Ouvidor, something of a hybrid between a shopping street and a promenade, there are large shops with elegant ladies' apparel. It all comes from Paris and everything is horribly expensive. And yet, the rich Brazilians buy these articles with the greatest pleasure at the highest prices specifically for the "season," that is, for the performances of an Italian opera company set up here. All of the ladies appear at these performances in the loges in well-cut ballroom gowns. There are few private parties outside the borders of the diplomatic corps, and the emperor does not appear with pomp, something that partly stems from his well-known personal simplicity, partly from the low funding available to the Civil List of Brazil's rulers. The only theater performances take place at the princess's house. The large imperial palace is in São Christovão, a city on the outskirts of Rio. It is an imposing, dreary building. The palace does nevertheless contain some gorgeously decorated rooms, but it is located in a very ugly area. If I were the emperor of Brazil, I would have built a graceful, airy mansion in Botafogo, another delightful city on the other side of the outskirts of Rio. I would have left São Christovão to its neighborhood of slaughterhouses and its hundreds of thousands of crows![57]

Botafogo is charming. The mansions with their gardens are formed like a crown around the bay of the same name. Behind them the mighty Corcovado [Hunchback Mountain] towers high; in front of the bay, one can see the strange Pão de Açucar [Sugar Loaf], the cone sugar mountain. The glory of the flowers in this outlying city where only elegant, rich people live is enchanting! The abundant vines of lush verdure crawl over the walls. In these vines one may find large, beaming, dark red, purple, yellow, or white flowers. Mrs. Brassen, in her nice book, *A Voyage in the Sunbeam*, echoed my senti-

57. The royal residence at São Cristovão dates to 1808 and the very arrival of the Portuguese court in Brazil, when Regent D. João appropriated the palace from a local nobleman in order to live there with his sons. His estranged Spanish wife, D. Carlota Joaquina, took up residence with their daughters in Botafogo, on the city's southernmost periphery (now the location of a beautiful marina). By 1881, the palace at São Cristovão had become the National Museum, and its environs inscribed the city's original factory and working-class district. Today, the Quinta da Boa Vista, surrounding the imperial palace in São Cristovão, is a beautiful public park where families go on Sundays. The former palace remained the National Museum, where tourists could still see the filigreed wallpaper that Ina must have admired as "some gorgeously decorated rooms." Tragically, 90 percent of the National Museum's collections was destroyed by a fire on the night of September 2, 2018, amounting to an unprecedented loss of Brazil's cultural patrimony. Some of the 2016 Olympic Games were played in the Quinta da Boa Vista locale. Adjacent to the park is historic Maracanã Stadium, which seats nearly 178,000 soccer spectators, with standing room for 42,000 more—the largest in South America.

ments exactly when she said that the colors of the flowers seem to be more luscious in Brazil than anywhere else in the world.[58] Even the white seems to be more intense. One really has that impression here, and inasmuch as nature is allowed to speak here, everything is enchanting!

The Laranjeiras mountain, the Santa Teresa mountain—in short, all the hills of the city—are only occupied by mansions. Many foreign merchants live on the Santa Teresa mountain, and they have their shops down below in the city.

Since I have tried in vain to find some sort of employment here in Rio, I took the opportunity to explore the city more thoroughly. There is not that much to see. The churches all look alike, and none have particularly interesting works of art. The museum (many people even have no idea about its existence, and only very few visit it) is not bad. There is a fabulous collection of partly stuffed, very rare birds. The Academy of Arts, which houses a painting and statue collection, is very much still undergoing growing pains, especially regarding the statue collection. However, there are some interesting paintings by native artists. I liked them very much because of their colors and their lively composition. I am including a photograph of one of the paintings representing "the first mass in Brazil." I only regret that I did not acquire some of the others available, especially a colossal battle painting by Meireles.[59] On the whole, however, it is remarkable how little sense the Brazilians have for the plastic arts. It is admittedly not that surprising, since the declamatory arts must, because of the Brazilians' nature, attract them more than the plastic arts. The Brazilian is a born speaker. He declaims as soon as he has to utter a somewhat long sentence, and every one of them loves music passionately—especially Italian composers, then French operettas, and, finally, Meyerbeer.[60]

The Brazilians value sculpture and architecture even less than they value painting. The city has absolutely no architectural decorations on buildings, bridges, or gates. There are no magnificent buildings, even when one takes into account the rather simple financial mint. I have only been able to discover two monuments, and on top of that, one of them represents a saint. The

58. Ina refers to Lady Anna Brassey's *A Voyage in the "Sunbeam," Our Home on the Ocean for Eleven Months* (London: Longmans, Green, 1878).

59. Both paintings were by Vitor Meireles (1832–1903). The *Primeira missa no Brasil* (1861) depicts the mass celebrated at Porto Seguro (Bahia) by the naval expedition of Pedro Álvares Cabral that "found" Brazil on April 22, 1500. The "battle" pertained to the recently completed *Batalha de Guararapes* (1879), a painting that acquired iconic significance for the First Republic. It depicts the 1649 military victory at Guararapes, by Pernambucan militias over the occupying Dutch forces, a victory marking the emergence of Brazilian nationalism.

60. Giacomo Meyerbeer (1791–1866) was the originator of French Grand Opera.

lack of monuments is probably partially due to the fact that the country has had only a very short history since its independence, and it has therefore only few historical memories. The monument other than the monument of the saint (I even believe it is São Francisco) glorifies the most important moment of Brazil's history. It represents the first emperor, Dom Pedro I, the father of the current emperor, on his horse, just as he is galloping by with the constitutional charter in his hand. The statue was made by a French artist. It is splendidly and freshly conceived and graced with precisely the right dose of pathos that would secure success with the Brazilians. In bas-relief, the pedestal bears allegorical representations of the four main rivers of the country: the Amazon, São Francisco, Orinoco, and Madeira.[61]

Of course, I have also visited the gardens of Rio. I went to the very graceful Jardim Público, which is located close to the middle of the city and where German musicians recently performed a Mendelssohn duet. They also played in another garden, a new one that is well located in the middle of the city, and, "last but not least," in the famous Botanical Garden with its even more famous street lined with palm trees [the Alameda das Palmeiras]. Gretel, one could even claim that this street is interesting and well worth seeing for foreigners, but I myself do not find the long, bare trunks all that beautiful. Besides, this famous street is unbearably devoid of shadows.[62] This judgment is something that I impart to you only under the most profound seal of secrecy. Otherwise, the traditional admirers of this street will stone me, even if only with *biscoitos* no. 3! The street is strange and thus beautiful as well—*basta* [enough]! I will try to get used to this way of thinking, and, from now on, I will look at the palm tree as the street-lining tree par excellence. Will I be able to do this really, though?

Your rebellious Ulla

61. The bronze statue of Pedro I, executed by Louis Rochet between 1855 and 1862, commemorated independence in 1822 and was Brazil's first civic monument. Rochet conducted anthropological and zoological research for the statue's granite pedestal, whose sculptures of native fauna and indigenous groups symbolize Brazil's four great rivers—the fourth being the Paraná, not the Orinoco, as Ina indicated. See fig. 17.

62. Ina refers to the showcase feature of Rio's Botanical Garden—the much-admired "Corridor of the Palms" (Alameda das Palmeiras), originally planted as a single tree by D. João VI in 1809, a year after he inaugurated the Jardim Botânico. The garden, at 141 hectares (350 acres), contains over seven thousand plants. Today it still boasts imperial palms, and they exceed thirty meters (one hundred feet) in height. Descendants of the original trees, they were grown from seeds salvaged after a twentieth-century fire destroyed an earlier generation of the palms. See fig. 19.

Rio de Janeiro

February 12, 1882

Dearest Grete!

I have to write to you again. Just think, since the day before yesterday, I have been engaged here in a *colégio*! A colégio is a high school for women, that is, a boarding school. My task is to induct the daughters of this country through four grades into the secrets of the German and English languages and to give an immense number of piano lessons. Oh Grete! These two languages, especially the German language, will probably remain a book with seven seals for them. It is odd how little they learn under my tutelage. I have not yet been able to find out whether or not this is my fault or theirs. Perhaps it is the racial difference between the Romance and the German, as they can learn French half in their sleep. Furthermore, the French teachers fare better with their students. I had half a mind to take out the Bormann, but then I left it alone as I knew that I would find too many reproaches for myself as well.

Since there are too few classrooms, I usually hold my classes in the same room with another teacher. While Portuguese poems are being declaimed on one side of the room, I am trying to explain the complexities of German declensions to my inattentive "Donas" on the other side. The three articles with their four cases are (not to mention the plural), in all their twelve-part obscurities, so unwelcome to them that I really feel that our *der*, *die*, and *das* is regarded by the entire sickly-yellow community as an insidious invention that has only been manufactured to spite schoolchildren. Just recently, when I corrected one of the little black-eyed crabs—"The umbrella is behind the [*der*] door"—she threw her book onto the table with tears of anger welling up and screamed in fierce rage: "What! It has always been the [*die*] door, and now it is suddenly the [*der*] door?!"

Grete, I was utterly nonplussed and did not know what to do at first. But scenes such as this happen often here. The better families don't let their children attend the colégios, which means that this community is typically the least well behaved and the most rowdy that one could possibly set eyes upon. They often rant and rage until their faces are as brown as cherries. At this point, our young French teacher, Mademoiselle Lerôt, always locks them in an empty closet until they are quiet. We rarely see the principal, actually only at mealtimes. She is the only one who possesses authority with the wild band, perhaps because she shows herself so seldom. She is always sitting in nice clothes in her living room. She receives the parents of her pupils, and she only gives one reading class for every grade. She doesn't like it when we ask her for assistance in school matters, and thus I have no other choice than to help myself, as does Mlle. Lerôt.

I haven't yet been able to learn anything about the curriculum or even a schedule, and everything here seems to me like raging chaos for the time being. Up until now, despite my best efforts, I still haven't been able to ascertain the number of students I have for piano lessons. When I sit down at the piano at six thirty in the morning, one student after another appears with her music every half hour until ten, as if they were being spit out by some mechanical clock. I take note of them one after the other and, with effort and trickery, I will eventually set up some sort of schedule.

For the moment, they are quite fond of me, and the reason for this, as Mlle. Lerôt tells me, is that I dress well (apparently one can sometimes still win over the hearts of children in this way!), and I "don't look like the other Germans." This last comment is without any doubt meant as a compliment; nonetheless, it made me quite angry. But how can one expect considerateness from children if adults themselves are not ashamed to commit such lapses of tact? Today Madame was talking in the music room with a Brazilian lady and a mother of one of the pupils. The Brazilian woman said quite loud in Portuguese: "Is she German? Oh, she doesn't look at all the German type, and she is well dressed!" Denying me the category of the "German type" was for myself, a rigid German, as you can well imagine, extremely painful and, at the same time, quite astonishing, given my blond hair. I ask myself what sort of garments my German predecessors and other colleagues must have worn if the apparel of the German ladies excited such disapproval from the Brazilian women? By the way, you can find this contempt of things German everywhere here. The most drastic example that I have yet experienced occurred at a hair stylist's, where I went just to clean up my recently cut hair. I had no idea that there was something conspicuous about this. But the Brazilian woman never walks on the street alone and under no circumstances would she get a haircut outside of her house.[63] The boy with the scissors thought at first that I was French, since I told him what I wanted in French. Then he asked me if I

63. Merchants catered to respectable, upper-middle-class and upper-class women, taking their wares to the women's homes, so strong was the prejudice against their venturing into the streets.

was Russian, and when he finally went through all of the countries, half to my delight and half to my dismay, he finally asked me: "Mais enfin vous n'êtes pas allemande?" [But then you're not German, are you?] "Et pourquoi non?" [And why not?] I said, inwardly seething. "Ah bah," he said with contempt, "that's obvious: Germans are always badly dressed and are never chic."

"*Les allemandes* [the Germans] thank you very much," I thought. Then I left, swearing eternal enmity to the place.

But now somebody is ringing the bell for teatime. O this colégio—tea! Right now I'm taking advantage of the immense heat so that, instead of tea, I can make myself *cajuda*, a lemonade made from cashews that is enjoyed here frequently and is quite refreshing.[64] The second bell—I've got to go!

Your Ulla

64. Ina refers to the drink made from the juice of the cashew fruit, not the nut, today called *suco de cajú*.

Rio de Janeiro

February 17, 1882

Grete, have you ever been to the dentist to have one of your molars pulled? Perhaps. But has it ever happened to you that someone threw something hard on your carefully guarded cheek where it exploded and then dispatched a small flood of patchouli-scented water into your throat? No? Then you do not know how angry you can get. Don't deny it! You don't know! I, for my part, have now received such an unexpected awareness of the amount of anger that I possess through the aforementioned procedure that I was completely humbled in my own good opinion of myself.

I made my discovery in the Rua dos Ourives [Street of the Goldsmiths]. The first effect of this discovery was, as I said earlier, to rob me of the beautiful illusion that I had concerning the mildness of my disposition in a single blow. Then "paff!" A second hard something, followed by a flood of water that sought out the other side of my mouth, numbed my self-accusations, and my rage welled up even more vehemently inside of me. . . . "Piff!" It whizzed by my nose and exploded on the wall next to me—I wanted to bend over in order to confirm the nature of these horrible small balls—"puff"! It exploded with a dull thud onto my neck and ran down my back.

Beside myself with rage, I stood still and looked around myself, fully forgetting my toothache. Around me I saw such impertinently cheerful faces, faces seen through the eyes of a weak, angrily sputtering countenance: elegant gentleman, dirty mulatto boys, clerks, loiterers, even the ladies on the balconies. They all turned into just as many grinning devils, and all of them took aim at me with these accursed watery bullets, which were small and hard. It was as if it had all been planned against me, a wretched person, afflicted with a toothache. I pressed myself automatically against a house so that I could at least be safe from behind. . . . Sssrrr the liquid flowed in a well-calculated gush onto my hat (there was a real feather on it!), flooded the rim and sought a way out in my collar.

I was completely numbed. What was this? What did it mean? Was I really awake and was I really on one of the best streets of Rio, or was all of this a crazy dream?

Then a young, smiling Brazilian woman leaned out of the window where I was standing rooted to the spot. I turned to her and wanted to speak to her, but she lifted up her hand in which was gleaming a small, shiny bottle—"huist,"

"huist"—and for a moment both of my eyes were disabled. That was too much! I was beside myself. An impotent range and simultaneously an unbelievable cowardice in front of all these mysterious enemies gripped me, and I completed the rest of my journey as if the Evil One himself were following me.

My entire body was shaking with rage and dripping with every movement when I arrived at my destination. I broke down in tears and sank onto a sofa in the waiting room of Dr. Müller, who had been treating me for one week in his dentistry practice.

"But my dear lady, what is the matter," he called from the adjacent room. And when he walked in and saw me dripping thus, his face twisted into a variation of one of those expressions of cheerfulness mentioned above, and I saw how difficult it was for him not to laugh out loud.

"Yes, my God!" I exclaimed, beside myself with rage. "What is going on here, has everyone gone mad in Rio?"

Then the doctor let loose his laughter, took me by the hand, led me to the calendar on the wall and pointed to a line on the month of February: *Carnaval.*[65] I read the word and sank, giving a dull sigh, into the nearest chair.

The doctor began to pick things off of me. "What are you doing?" I asked feebly.

"I am removing at least a few pieces of the wax."

"Pieces of wax?" I replied, just as feeble, but surprised.

"Well, you have, as it seems to me, gotten a proper dose of the things, wax eggs filled with water. Rio will now be continuously filled with these things until Ash Wednesday."

Until Ash Wednesday! That was still eleven days away! With a silent horror I estimated the potential amount of patchouli water and wax egg shells—not even taking into account the water buckets that could make their way into my wardrobe in the next eleven days. I angrily crushed the wax of half an eggshell that I just pulled out of my dripping left sleeve.

"Then your tooth is pretty much safe for today?" smiled the doctor.

"No, quite the contrary," I called with a renewal of my previous "energy"—"I have to take out my rage on something, even if it is directed toward myself; rip it out! Rip it out!" And thus I became poorer by one wisdom tooth.

65. The event is pre-Lenten *carnaval*, the "profane" celebration that precedes the beginning of the "sacred" observance of Lent. Carnaval officially begins on the Saturday before Ash Wednesday and ends at midnight on Shrove Tuesday ("Fat Tuesday"), four days later—with Ash Wednesday opening the six weeks of Lent.

When I came back to the colégio and told of my adventure, the small band fell into terrible excitement—"Laranjinhas, laranjinhas!" was the common battle cry. The Brazilians call these horrid little wax bullets *laranjinhas*, that is, little oranges. In my opinion, however, they bear not the slightest resemblance to oranges. Rather they have the form and size of chicken eggs, and the children pour them themselves, using a wooden mold. Dozens of such molds appeared all at once, as if by magic, in our honorable colégio, and before we teachers knew it, the water battle was in full swing. Not only did they bombard one another with laranjinhas during the break, but even during class time they sprayed their neighbors with water in their ears and clothes using *bisnagas*, which had been smuggled in by God knows whom. One could not even conceive of holding a calm, collected lesson. The bisnagas are little bottles just like our colorful little bottles, and people fill them with all types of perfumes, even with the most sophisticated sorts.[66] On Sunday, however, when the children had nothing to do, they turned completely savage and drenched one another from head to foot with water from large stone jars and washing bowls. The entire bedroom was swimming, and Mlle. Lerôt and I stood helplessly before the water-intoxicated gathering that sprang around like savages and screamed until, luckily, Madame came and made an end to the affair. Since then we have had calm in the house.

Outside, however, this tasteful carnival game continued to go on. Every day, I cursed the fate that drove me to the Rua dos Ourives. I contemplated for hours at a time how I could put together the most watertight costumes possible. The Brazilians, however, are happy during this time, completely "outside the little house." One can see young, rich Brazilians walking in the street only in order to pursue this watery "amusement." A Negro boy trails behind them, holding laranjinhas and bisnagas at the ready in a large, mighty basket. Thus do these individuals waste hundreds of francs. Although it keeps being forbidden every year, every year it continues to happen. The Negro women stand naively on the street corners holding huge tables full of laranjinhas for sale. On the horse tramway, everyone fears everyone else. And just when people begin to treat their neighbors with a little more trust, the next moment someone winces horribly, as the man standing behind him has poured an entire bottle of water into his collar with a truly devilish pleasure. But you can't get

66. The *bisnaga* operated like a large perfume atomizer and represented a "civilized" improvement on the cruder *seringas* (syringes) that shot all kinds of repulsive liquids onto unsuspecting victims, often from windows or balconies.

annoyed, because if they see that, then you are truly lost. And the more you attempt to protect yourself in your clothing, the wetter you become. Now, thankfully, the affair is coming to an end, since yesterday was the great carnival parade, and today is the masked ball that ends the festivities.[67]

I watched the parade in the Rua d'Ouvidor from the balcony of a family whose members are friends with Madame, and I can't say anything other than it was completely brilliant. Many of the floats whose materials they ordered partly from Lisbon and partly from Paris were even quite funny. One of them was entitled "The True Image of Hell," in which life-size straw puppets of monks were burnt, priests were beaten, and nuns were being broken on the wheel. And this in a Catholic country! But the Brazilian is not as pious as his predecessors. Another float was greeted with jubilation. There was a hole in the roof of a little house on the float, and a mask looking deceptively similar to the local telegraph director peeped out at regular intervals every couple minutes. He attempted to cut the telephone wires above the house, which he had, in fact, actually ordered his subordinates to do. After these display floats, there was a long line of coaches with masks, but these were only gentlemen and ladies from the theater and the demimonde. Because nobody was allowed to throw anything at the procession, one could watch it calmly. And yet, I still wasn't able to get rid of the goose bumps that had been brought on because of the creepy stories told by a Brazilian standing next to me. One was about a German teacher who, because he wore neck protection during carnival time a couple of years ago—thereby throwing down the gauntlet to the locals—had eventually been caught by two sturdy Negroes and dragged into a bathtub filled with water, where he caught cholera. The other story was about an Englishman who had caught yellow fever and died from the bisnagas and laranjinhas. When he was about to begin the third story, which was supposedly about a Russian, I asked him to spare me.

Now! Good night, my Gretel! It is frightfully hot here, so much that the light bends before me. But I can bear it, since I seldom find it oppressive. The high atmospheric humidity makes the heat milder. The worst time will soon be over, and with this, the time of yellow fever, which nevertheless every year after this wild carnival time experiences another upsurge. About one hun-

67. The masked ball—borrowed from Venetian Carnival—as the affair of the upper and middle classes, took place in private homes and posed an elegant contrast to the raucous "street carnival" (*entrudo*) monopolized by the popular classes and unsuccessfully prohibited by the authorities.

dred people die just from yellow fever every week. It doesn't seem to want me, Gretel; otherwise I would have long since caught it given my terrible nourishment right now, especially since it tends to take "the whitest skin" first: Europeans, and especially English and Germans, are the most exposed, and only last of all do the Negroes catch it.

By the way, apropos of nourishment, Grete! The time has come when I have developed a "passion for dried mutton." At least it is not so fatty, and because of this, it is best enjoyed in hot weather. I only eat with full appetite, however, when the Carsons invite me to a good English beef [original in English], which they do as often as I can get away. They are extremely, movingly, good to me, Grete, and much of the courage that I have in this foreign country I owe to their friendly reception; *God bless them!* [original in English].

But Mademoiselle is getting impatient, I have to finish. I kiss you, my Gretel.

Your Ulla

Rio de Janeiro

February 21, 1882

O Gretel, this colégio—it's overwhelming me! I must be a quite miserable teacher! They don't learn anything with me, they learn nothing at all. I wonder if there are school inspectors here—I would end up disgracing myself. I am so poorly suited to superficial whitewash. As soon as I begin to go more in-depth, though, it gets entirely out of control. I am completely in despair! And then there is the discipline! The mere word makes me red with shame. Imagine the following scenario. Recently, I entered the classroom and I found the place noisy and agitated, and in my helplessness I made a despairing gesture toward Bormann. As soon as I was able to calm them down enough to be heard, I gave the commands: "Stand up—Sit down!" five times in a row, which never ceases to shame a classroom in Germany. Yet here—*o sancta simplicitas*! After I had made clear to them—and that only with difficulty—what I was demanding from them, the children were so far away from looking at it as a punishment that they believed I was trying to make some funny joke. Finally, they started hopping around by themselves like a pendulum, back and forth, and they were having as much fun as kings. Grete, from this moment onward I have dispensed with Bormann in Brazil! I have finally understood something. If pedagogy is to be introduced here, it must be Brazilian and not German-Brazilian in conception. Whatever it presupposes, it must have the character of the people, it must be adapted to the domestic relations of these people. Brazilian children should not even be educated by Germans; it is a waste of time. The foreign twig that is being grafted onto the youth is not working! What is happening with me and the children here is analogous to what I wrote to you about São Francisco in relation to the plants. We do not understand one another, we speak externally and mentally a foreign language with one another, and especially this last point makes my existence here into something terribly uncomfortable.

Furthermore, my external "comfortableness" leaves much to be desired. My "room" is a windowless alcove that branches off from the pupils' room and only receives air and light through the door to their room! Its entire furnishing consists of a bed (it is an inexpensive version of the one in São Francisco), a washstand, and a chair. I own neither a closet nor a chest of drawers. My suitcase serves as a container for my linen, and for my better clothes I am still hoping to get a chest of drawers by flattering Mlle. Lerôt, a gift for which the children would also be grateful. I also write in the room of the Frenchwoman, the person in this house with whom I most sympathize despite the age-old hostility between our nations. Her room is not any better than mine, but she has a table and a little window above, in the ceiling, while I almost suffocate in my dark hole. There are many such holes in every Brazilian house. In addition to that, we both suffer horribly in this house on account of the *baratas* [cockroaches], disgusting beetles, as big as May beetles and with a stench as foul as the plague! The *barata* is a common affliction of this country, but so many in one house—hundreds or thousands—I have not yet seen. In the evening, when I go to the bedroom with the children, the floor is teeming with these disgusting animals, and we immediately hunt them down with boots and all hard objects within easy reach. Hundreds run away from us, but hundreds of corpses remain on the battlefield and are then disposed of. Do not believe, Grete, that this is an exaggeration. Apparently, it is really this bad in old houses, and other travelers through Brazil could confirm similar stories. I won't even mention the mosquitoes, the ants, the lizards, and the other vermin. These are nothing compared to the *baratas*, which, by the way, eat and ruin everything that they possibly can. Just in these last few nights they managed to eat my Goethe right out of its book binding!

My enthusiasm for Rio has rather cooled off in general. Life here in the colégio is not very stimulating, and wandering through the streets is like torture because of the extreme "politeness" of the men. They are not used to seeing ladies alone on the street, accustomed as they are to the behavior of their own women, and even when they know that foreigners here must claim this freedom, they nevertheless seem justified to themselves to speak to European ladies and pester them when they are alone. "Comment ça va-t-il, Mademoiselle?" [How do you do, Mademoiselle?] "Mais, ou allez-vous si vite, mon enfant?" [But where are you going so quickly, my child?] Finally, I have acquired the habit of simply ignoring such manners of speech without crying. What will you say to this, I wonder? Just a short time ago, I was leaving a glove shop, when a long, thin Brazilian placed himself before me and with the most shameless facial expression gave forth a smirk from under his jaw, saying: "Pas décidement jolie, mais gentille, très gentille" [Not exactly pretty, but sweet, very sweet]. I fled angrily from the scene, something that seemed to amuse him greatly.

Oh Grete, if only there were some sympathetic soul here for me! Mademoiselle Lerôt, Miss Dahlmann, yes, they are friendly and dear—but I would like to have a real friend—a real one, Grete! Oh, my dear, if you were here—

but no, I don't even want to utter the wish! You stay over there, and (I am whispering this secretly into your ear) I will return again—as soon as I have the money for the trip. For the moment, there is a great ebb in my financial resources, and my colégio wages are not going to bring in a large flood of wealth. So I just have to sit still; the ticket alone for the ship to Hamburg costs thirty pounds!

The 22nd

Today, I visited the pastor of the German congregation living here, and I visited the German consulate. Both were very nice, and the consul, who is a sophisticated man and "appreciates" the Brazilians according to their merits, recommended that I go to the Province of São Paulo, if I could get anything over there. My current employment was not a good position for me, and I would have other colleagues in São Paulo. I took that to heart and began to study zealously the *Jornal do Comércio* wherever I could get a glimpse of it. Amidst announcements concerning runaways, and between offers selling slaves, *professoras* were being sought as well with numerous capabilities and talents. By the way, I learned here that only those who are more in demand are called *professora*. Otherwise they are referred to as *mestra* [teacher], designating a position lower in status. It is truly lucky that there are no contracts here nor do they hold you to a period of giving notice. If you have to be ready at any time to be free on any random day, then you can just pack up and go by yourself if it becomes too unbearable. Adieu, my treasure. Recommend me to the benevolence of all nine muses so that they let me make my way to São Paulo!

Your Ulla

Rio de Janeiro

March 2, 1882

In all haste, just a couple of words, my dear Gretel! I have been contracted in São Paulo, and indeed, just consider my luck: I am going to the city of São Paulo to a very nice family, so it seems. Consul Haupt was so very nice as to have an advertisement printed for me in the *Jornal do Comércio*, and he must have printed my name in boldface type, because a Mr. Costa came from São Paulo just in order to engage this miraculous creature of a *professora* (*mestra* in the vernacular).[68] So tomorrow I am going to the "intellectual capital of Brazil," as the residents of São Paulo name their city with pride and fondness.

Madame was very much annoyed when I told her that I wanted to leave. She hardly said goodbye to me, but all of the people who wish me well are urging me to take the position.

Do you know what has become clear to me just now, Gretel? The reason why my German colleagues were not able to receive the approval of their Brazilian sisters in matters concerning their toilette! And I will probably have to do without their approval as well. Just imagine, if it is possible for you to do so, that I just recently asked a French seamstress to complete a calico dress for me that I had to have, and I had to put down on the house table seventy-eight marks in cash to this aristocratic "Madame Victorine" in advance. I turned to stone and I will never go to a Madame Victorine ever again when the things that I have brought with me no longer suffice.[69] Rather, I will make them myself, just as my colleagues here do quite often: I will grab the scissors and needle myself!

The first "success" brought about by this calico dress is that I had to ask Mr. Carson for money in order to reach my new destination. I am writing this to you as an *exemplum tragicum* to the usefulness and benefit of all those who might be tempted when someone offers them a salary of four thousand to five thousand marks. By the way, in my next position I will receive only three thousand marks. But I still have courage; I won't let it get me down. How did that witty Frenchman put it? "Il faut fatiguer l'infortune" [One has to wear down misfortune]!

Your resilient Ulla

68. "Mr. Costa" was Ina's pseudonym for Dr. Martinho ("Martinico") da Silva Prado Júnior (1843–1906), although she identified his wife, Albertina de Morais Pinto, by her real given name—Dona Albertina.

69. Mme. Victorine was a real person. Her dressmaking establishment in Rio de Janeiro continued to be in operation into the first decade of the twentieth century.

São Paulo

March 20, 1882

My one and only Grete!

Today I received a whole pile of nice, friendly letters that were forwarded to me by Mr. Carson. I am surprised that they all managed to arrive! You feel very sorry for me on account of the "horrible colégio," you dear woman, but now this is all thankfully *tempi passati*, as you see, and here in São Paulo I feel as if I were in heaven.

Even the trip here was very interesting, since it took me through a quite variegated landscape. At nine o'clock in the morning Mr. Carson put me in a first-class coupé on the São Paulo Railway—first class, Grete, not out of pride or out of a sudden flood of money (on the contrary, you know about that: Madame Victorine!), but rather because in this country there are only two train classes, and in the second class, only the Negroes of all varieties of color travel. My seat had little in common with our first-class coupés back at home; indeed, it had more in common with our third-class carriages. The car, with its twenty-four seats of braided tube and its eight open windows, which let in the wind, sun, and dust simultaneously, offered a most uncomfortable resting place. There are almost only gentlemen in the car. Furthermore, there are no nonsmoking coupés or coupés for ladies in this country in which I could have taken refuge. As soon as the train started moving, the Brazilians took out a large white sheet with tassles all around it and a hole in the middle through which they put their heads. These things are called *panchos*, and while the light ones are used against dust, the heavy ones are used against rain and cold.[70]

Most of these gentlemen sank very soon behind the giant sheets of the *Jornal do Comércio*, and it did not last long before they remembered—to my horror—their cigarettes. If the trip had been thus far only a moderately agreeable one, it now became a veritable martyrdom. Not because of the smoke. You know, Grete, I am not that squeamish, but for the Brazilians who do smoke, the world around them seems to be nothing other than a large spittoon. The obvious disgust of all the foreigners, open for all to see—yes, even some quite embarrassing scenes in restaurants and on English coastal steamships—have not been able to change anything about this disgusting custom. The Brazilian

70. She means *ponchos*, a term borrowed from Brazil's Spanish-speaking neighbors.

regards continual spitting as something quite harmless. They are well equipped in their houses for this practice, as next to every one of their uncomfortable wicker sofas you can see on both sides the most beautiful, colorful spittoons, always matching one another in pairs. They are so big and bold that I first took them to be flower pots.

I made the attempt to withdraw to a certain extent from my space—which every now and then would increase by two or three smoking, chattering porters—by getting up and surveying the area through the open window. But this idea turned into a pathetic fiasco. A Brazilian train, once it is already on its way, rushes with an unbelievable rapidity, and it wobbles here and there. When one gets one's foot stuck in the (naturally unsecured and tattered) floor mat, then one can count oneself lucky if after three seconds one finds oneself thrown back onto one's seat with only a lump on one's forehead and otherwise healthy limbs. The speed of transportation along with so many inconveniences and so much naiveté has something about it that could best be expressed by the phrase "uneducated civilization." Naturally the notion might at first make one smile, but it is an impression that I have often felt in this country.

In spite of all this I was able to perceive nature around me in its entirety and admire its riches, its grandeur, and its breadth. Everything is larger here than in our own country. There is something everywhere like an overabundance of the given space. It seems to me always as if nature had distributed mountain and valley with such generosity only to fill everything up again. Then nature, as it was pleasing to her, decorated with full hand her work with large-leafed trees and strange fruits, with graceful shrubbery in a constant state of aspiration toward becoming trees, and with large, intensively colored flowers. All of this fantastic decoration seemed to exist for the purpose of letting the comparatively tiny race of men experience the powerful sublimity of nature as less oppressive. Mountain and valley continually alternated, and we passed through thirteen tunnels, of which the longest took four minutes of travel time.

Dr. Costa (naturally, "Doctor") picked me up here in the train station with the two oldest pupils given to my care.[71] The girl of twelve years, Lavínia, immediately made a very nice, fresh impression upon me. I can probably say that since then I have really managed to win her over. Indeed, Grete, I feel

71. "Dr. Costa" did indeed enjoy the right to be addressed as *doutor*, for he was a graduate of the São Paulo Law Faculty, class of 1866. Subsequently, however, Ina's letters downgraded him to "*Mr.* [Sr.] Costa," conforming to her assumption that he was just one more Brazilian boasting an ersatz degree. In reality, she was attempting to disguise his very prominent identity.

here as if I were in heaven—the colégio lies behind me like a gloomy dream. My colleagues nevertheless shake their heads when they see my enthusiasm. For they claim that the Costa children's misbehavior is so notorious in the whole city that they were unable to find a governess here.[72] For the moment, however, I am not paying attention to it, and I am happy that I am here and can associate with colleagues and other people.

There are quite a few Germans here in São Paulo. They are usually craftsmen, however, and I tend to frequent only the house of the German pharmacist whom I had first sought out in his capacity as consul.[73] These are magnificent people, Gretel! Extremely educated and yet simple, smart, sympathetic, and hospitable. Already many German travelers to Brazil have experienced a couple of happy, invigorating hours or days in their house, and even princely guests have felt comfortable in the friendly house of the Schaumanns. I was there Sunday afternoon and made the acquaintance of two very nice colleagues, Miss Meyer and Miss Harras, about whom I will probably be talking more often to you. In addition to that I also made the acquaintance of a third, older colleague, one who had already been educating the cousins of my students for years. So you see, it appears to be much better here than my previous Brazilian experiences. I am among people here and not so dreadfully alone!

At the Schaumanns, one can meet people from all countries of the world, so that here one can actually speak of genuine entertainment. Just recently, an old, eccentric Danish engineer—who was in previous days a captain—came by one evening, as did a French music teacher, a German doctor, and an English engineer. The last was a very nice person who only wanted to talk to me and was delighted by my English, which he found very good. His name is Mr. Hall and he has lived for half a year here in São Paulo, where he runs a big, English machine factory. He looks like—no, not quite! I had believed I had seen a similarity, but, in fact, he doesn't resemble anyone. Ah, Gretel, I am so happy to be here, so very happy!

Your happy Ulla

72. The gossip that Ina heard has been independently confirmed: Martinho da Silva Prado Júnior sought a governess in Rio de Janeiro because the reputation of his children for bad behavior was so notorious that no governess from São Paulo would work for him.

73. Ina refers to the real Gustav Schaumann, owner of a pharmacy and the German vice-consul. His son, Henrique Schaumann, who became a naturalized Brazilian citizen, had returned from Göttingen in 1877 with a degree in chemistry. Eventually, he assumed responsibility for the pharmacy and was elected to the city council.

São Paulo

April 5, 1882

My dear, sweet-hearted Gretel!

It is really true: São Paulo is the best place for governesses in Brazil, the city as well as the entire province, because here the little men and women—that is, the younger generation—flirt with "knowledge" and prefer to dabble with scholarly pursuits and philosophy. This is a university city! Nevertheless, you shouldn't imagine this to be a Bonn or a Heidelberg, especially because this Academia cultivates only one faculty in particular, namely the faculty of law. Further inland in the province, some place with "fathers" in its name (the exact name of the place is escaping me), they train priests. Here, they train lawyers, and in Rio de Janeiro they train the disciples of Asclepius, the "doctors" par excellence.[74]

The Brazilians make excellent lawyers inasmuch as they can thereby make use of their declamatory talent. They speak gladly, even if they say nothing; the pathos that they spend on only one speech could easily provide ample furnishing for ten of ours. And yet, they don't display any actual enthusiasm nor individuality—because they all speak in the same traditional tone of voice, which appears to remain the same in all situations. Everything is exterior, everything half-educated and mere gesture. This pompous phrasing, this pretentious pathos is in itself always rather suspicious and almost like acting. Once you really want to probe deeper and ask them about something, they cannot give you a proper account of anything.

There are people who stand at the head of the Republican Party, and they know neither the history nor the Constitution of their own country, let alone those of other nations.[75] Then there are others who claim to align themselves

74. The reference is to the Faculdade de Direito de São Paulo, or the São Paulo Law Faculty, founded in 1828. Brazil had no real universities until the 1930s, although schools of medicine (Rio de Janeiro and Salvador) and engineering (Rio de Janeiro and Salvador) were founded in the first half of the nineteenth century. Prior to the arrival of the Portuguese Court in 1808, Catholic seminaries were the only institutions of higher learning, such as the monastery and seminary in Itú, São Paulo, known as the Convento e Seminário de N.S. do Carmo, founded in the mid-eighteenth century, whose name escaped von Binzer.

75. The Republican Party of São Paulo, founded in 1873, was preceded by the Republican Manifesto of 1869. The party opposed a monarchical form of government but remained silent on the issue of slavery. Ina's employer, Martinho da Silva Prado Júnior (Mr. Costa), had joined the party by the mid-1870s. By 1882, he had begun to invest in coffee plantations using a workforce of mostly free laborers. However, his household staff in São Paulo was largely composed of slaves.

with the philosophical system of the ingenious Comte, and they haven't even comprehended his most basic doctrines.[76] They make judgments about the languages of foreign nations and cannot even explain any rules about their own language. They have to have all of the new technological inventions immediately, but the engineers all come from Europe to set everything up, and when they are gone again and something goes wrong with the machinery, then the local engineer will certainly be incapable of repairing it. Meticulousness is nowhere to be seen, and even when they externally seem to seek a connection to the German concept of education in all areas of knowledge—as long as they cannot assimilate at the same time German diligence and seriousness, German perseverance and conscientiousness—then it is always going to remain a pantomime. They do not emulate us in our interiority, and this feeling continually imposes itself upon me. The Brazilians themselves instinctively confirm the rightness of this feeling inasmuch as they always tend with their hearts toward the French and other Romance peoples, even if German spirit and English energy impress them more. But I know that I am preaching—so let's change the subject quickly to something else.

My current "education-subjects" [her students] are indeed true exemplars of rebelliousness, and only in Lavínia's case has this tendency peculiar to the family weakened and transformed into an agreeable freshness. With the boys I have a more difficult job. More than once during the lessons, the brothers had one another by the collars before I even knew what was happening. One of the brothers need only give the wrong answer, then the other throws in a lively, cheeky correction, for which the other one then strikes him with the ruler faster than lightning—then we have a pretty scuffle and it is for me no trifling matter to put to rest this fraternal quarrel as quickly as possible. Just recently, I pulled myself together and simply sat the smaller one by the door; I find this strategy actually rather effective. But I will try to persevere here; one must strive to improve such poor, badly raised children. Don't you also think so, my sweet Grete? I would definitely not like to leave yet again.

76. The ideas of Swiss-French political philosopher Auguste Comte (1798–1857) exerted a powerful ideological influence by the 1880s, but his positivism had been significantly modified to fit Brazilian circumstances. Brazil's junior officer corps and many younger civilian politicians or professionals (especially engineers) were its major adherents, attracted by the ideological emphasis on secularization, technology, and "progress"—implying the abolition of slavery. In 1881 the more orthodox faction of positivists founded a Brazilian Positivist Church after breaking ties with the French Positivist Church, based in Paris. Brazil's flag still bears the positivist motto, "Order and Progress" (*Ordem e Progresso*), adopted soon after the proclamation of a republic in 1889.

Yesterday, coincidentally, I met Mr. Hall when I was on my way to Miss Meyer's place, and he accompanied me right up to the house. You know, Grete, he is really very attentive, not at all like the Brazilians, almost like a German. He has such penetrating big blue eyes and looks so masculine. He asked me if I didn't go on Sundays to the Anglican church, for there is no German church here. I had indeed not been to the English church, but it is true, I should have done so. It is not right that I have not visited up until now. Next Sunday I will definitely go. One thousand kisses to you from

Your Ulla

P.S.: I am sending with this letter two translations into German of a Brazilian poem by Gonçalves Dias (written in Europe). The poem itself claims to exhibit a national folkloric element, if one could speak of such a thing in this country, where there is no actual "people."[77] Indeed, I cannot yet find anyone who can tell me the text of the national anthem.[78] One translation is by Mr. Schaumann and is almost literally translated; the other, more liberal, by our honorable Dranmor. You will be able to recognize the poet immediately. I am putting the more literal translation first:

Song of the Exiled

My homeland has palms
And there the *sabiá* sings,

77. "Canção do Exílio" ("Song from Exile"), by the Romantic poet Antonio Gonçalves Dias (1823–64), appeared in his collection entitled *Primeiros Cantos* (1846). A nationalistic celebration of nature, the poem immortalized the *sabiá* (a thrush) as a songbird synonymous with Brazil, while part of the larger corpus of the *Cantos* reversed the image of the Indian as "savage" and humanized indigenous warrior heroes. Verses from "Song from Exile" have been memorized by millions of Brazilian school children for a century and a half as an expression of their love of country and the longing from abroad known as *saudades.* More recently, the *sabiá* has been celebrated by Antonio Carlos ("Tom") Jobim and Chico Buarque de Holanda in their song of the same name.

78. During the period of the Brazilian Empire (1822–89), Brazilians sang three anthems—to independence, the flag, and the *pátria.* Ina may have listened to the "Anthem to the Independence of Brazil," whose music was composed by Emperor D. Pedro I. The lyrics, written by journalist-poet-politico Evaristo Ferreira da Veiga, were not easily accessible to the average person, probably explaining why Ina could not find someone to tell her the "text." In 1890, Brazil adopted an official national anthem for the Republic after holding a competition. In 1922, on the centenary of independence, new lyrics by Joaquim Osório Duque Estrada were adopted. Even today, Brazilians complain that the lyrics to their national anthem make it difficult to memorize.

The birds chirp differently here.
They chirp differently there.

Our sky has more stars
And more life our forests
And more love our life
And more flowers our fields.

There in the evening, when alone,
How much sweeter I dreamt there!
O, my homeland has palms,
And there sings the *sabiá*.

Full joy offers my homeland,
As I have not yet seen here
And at evening, when alone—
How much sweeter I dreamt there!
Yes, my homeland has palms,
And there sings the *sabiá*.

May God not will that I would die
Without ever seeing it again.
Far from the happiness of the homeland,
(O, I find it only there!)
Far from the homeland's palms
And the song of the *sabiá*.

And now the translation by the poet:

Song from Exile[79]

Palms decorate my homeland,
There so intimate,
Where from green leafy crowns
The *sabiá* greets us.

79. This translation by Dranmor (Ferdinand von Schmid) is presumably taken from his literary journal article about Brazil: "Lied aus der Verbannung," *Das Magazin für die Literatur des In- und Auslandes*, no. 99 (1881): 270.

Show me sweet forest shadows,
Meadows, equal to ours,
Stars, as they shine down
Onto love's magical realm.

In the gloomy winter nights,
O, how do I think with grief
Of the land of the palm groves
And the singer's *sabiá*.

For it gleams in beautiful abundance
As never I elsewhere saw,
And in all dream images
Close it is to my longing
With the whispering of its palms
With the greeting of the *sabiá*.

Let, O God, me die only then
When my land I see again,
And the homeland would make me happy
As it has never happened here,
As the palms foretell
And the call of the *sabiá*.

São Paulo

April 21, 1882

Today something happened in our house about which Mr. Costa and his wife were very annoyed, which I, however, could not help but find very funny.

We had a slave in the house, a strong young lad of about twenty-five years, who at this time, when nobody buys new slaves anymore and no new ones are growing up, was very valuable to his master. This good lad was then sent downtown the day before yesterday to get something, but he did not show up later. At first they believed that something bad had happened to him and they ordered a search for him, but nothing came up. Then they assumed he had run away, and Mr. Costa let this be printed immediately in the newspaper. Yesterday morning, he suddenly received a message from the local "Society for the Abolition of Slavery," to the effect that the slave Tibério had reported to the bureau of the society in order to be bought free. He had deposited two hundred mil-réis (about four hundred marks), which they were offering to Mr. Costa now as a purchase price. They were going to hold the black man there until there was a decision. Mr. Costa swore and raged like a savage man in the house. He called himself an ass for the fact that he did not send the slave much earlier to the plantation, and, finally, put up a counter offer of two thousand marks. This morning, they had an appointment with a doctor and another specialist who were to decide about the value of this human merchandise. If our good warden was already in a rage yesterday, today he came back as if possessed by the devil. He cursed and clamored so that the walls shook. What, then, had they done? In the amount of time from yesterday to today, they had given Tibério such a great quantity of a laxative that the once strong lad appeared at the meeting naturally to be a miserable knee-knocking creature. The doctor and the specialist could obviously not evaluate him as being worth more than two hundred mil-réis. What do you think of that? Yes, it's not honest work, but there is, then again, a rather good bit of humor to the whole situation.[80]

80. The plantation where Martinico would have sent Tibério was Fazenda Albertina, his very large property in Ribeirão Preto, purchased in 1877 to mark his debut as an investor in the coffee export sector. Two hundred mil-réis (US$88) was definitely a low price for a healthy male slave age twenty-five. His value, assuming good health, was closer to one conto (US$440), meaning Martinico's counteroffer of two thousand marks (one conto), appeared pegged to the market price. However, a sympathetic judge in São Paulo probably would have set Tibério's price much lower—even without the doctor's report that he was not in good health.

Actually, people are talking quite a bit right now about the emancipation of slaves. The matter seems to have suddenly gathered momentum. Every year, the state earmarks funds in its budget in order to buy slaves. In the provinces, emancipation societies are being established, and many slaves are being freed through private initiatives.[81]

This movement is certainly quite pretty, but the whole process is managing to excite a great stir! You would hardly believe the amount of dirt that comes out of such a thing. The German newspaper provides every now and then interesting highlights drawn from these affairs. In the province of Espírito Santo some time ago, two slaves age sixty-nine and seventy were bought from their masters for one thousand marks (five hundred mil-réis) each, using state funds. But who benefited from the matter? The two old, used-up slaves, who would have soon been freed by death at any rate and who now had to beg for their bread—or their masters? In the case of another slaveholder, a seventy-two-year-old slave woman got married to a seventy-five-year-old free man. However, since those slaves who are married to free people are always considered first among those to be bought free, the master asked for two thousand marks (one conto) from the emancipation funds for the seventy-two-year-old slave—and got them![82] In Tatuí there was a slave who was in the final stages of tuberculosis and who was bought free by the state's emancipation funds for the sum of one conto and five hundred mil-réis (three thousand marks). But these and similar such stories of bribery and corruption are nothing compared to the discovery that the Negroes who had long since died were put into the lists as having been bought free with the emancipation funds. Their former masters had naturally pocketed the money

81. Correctly, Ina perceived that in 1882 abolitionism was beginning to gain traction as a national movement. São Paulo then was leading the nation in abolitionist militancy, given that the failure of the 1871 Law of the Free Womb to emancipate large numbers of slaves had become manifest to all. Imperial financing of the national emancipation fund proved woefully inadequate, and private manumission societies were being formed to take up the breach—at least in the cities.

82. The national emancipation fund set priority categories for slaves to be manumitted, privileging the elderly or married slaves (where one partner was free) as first priorities. The situation of elderly slaves was subsequently mitigated—at least theoretically—in 1885, when the Sexagenarian (Saraiva-Cotegipe) Law was adopted on September 28. Although it declared all slaves over the age of sixty to be free, this law carried the condition that they had to serve their current owners for three more years, showing them proper deference—on pain of revocation of their free status. Thus even this group would have to wait at least until September 28, 1888, for freedom—except that adoption of the plenary Golden Law of May 13, 1888, freed all slaves unconditionally, without compensating their owners.

for themselves. At this point, they then let the slaves, after a certain amount of time had passed, die for a second time, and this time for good!

On the other hand, there is also a lot of true nobility to be recorded, and daily you can see whole columns in the newspapers filled with the names of slave owners who have voluntarily let their slaves go. One ought not to attach too small a value to these events, and even if I can now hear in my mind your "Well, that's just natural!"—I must nevertheless say to myself that, although I would have thought the same way in Europe, I nevertheless simultaneously recognize that one may be of another opinion here in Brazil. First, the slaves are—even if it is not human to think this way in spite of everything—a lawfully acquired piece of property like any other. Secondly, "all slaves are suddenly set free" means nothing else to most plantation owners than "You are ruined." For it is quite difficult to imagine finding replacements for eighty to a hundred or two hundred obedient slaves—especially in Brazil, where there is no free working class.[83] It is especially difficult for Europeans to have a picture of these remote plantations—above all, when you have not even seen what free labor is in a land of slaves, and when you live in a country like Germany, where the available human resources exceed demand. I can, then, understand the phenomenon for myself, and I find it completely justified when otherwise humane plantation owners refuse to give up their entire fortune—the product of slaves—without a struggle, and, above all, without procrastination and a grace period. I do not believe that any European with my experiences would think differently than I, and you should not believe on that account, my Gretel, that your Ulla has developed here into a hard-hearted enthusiast for slavery.

On the contrary, she is as tenderhearted as ever and has even recently crafted—a lyric poem! That is certainly consoling!

Your Ulla

Before me stand a couple of terrific roses that Mr. Hall gave me yesterday. I met him just recently, by coincidence, and he had just brought them over—by coincidence.

83. Implicit in Ina's reasoning is the absence of a wage economy—meaning a monetized economy—a circumstance following from the historically massive reliance on slave labor and, increasingly, on a "free," but subjugated, peasantry that worked without wages (sharecropping). In São Paulo, the abolition of slavery and the consequent channeling of investments into commerce and nascent industry would monetize the state's economy during the 1890s for the first time. Abolition in 1888 would simultaneously release the floodgates of European immigration.

São Paulo

May 5, 1882

My dearest Gretel!

In your last letter, you "smiled a comment" about the pretentious name of my little student: Lavínia! Yes, but that is just the beginning of an entire gallery from Antiquity that I have under my pedagogical teaching rod. The oldest boy is named Caius Gracchus; my third pupil, Plinius; he was supposed to have been named Tiberius, Lavínia told me, but this name was rejected on account of its being especially "Negro-like." After him, there is a pair of Roman girls: Clélia and Cornélia, whom I still hope to see once with clean faces, if one may even really demand such a thing from tried and true, died-in-the-wool republican children. For the names of the children constitute a sort of political commitment on the part of Mr. Costa.[84] I can follow him right up until Cornélia—but whatever on earth could have made him name his youngest child Vercingetorix is an incomprehensible riddle to me! Is it possible for him to be ignorant of the feelings of the respectable old Gallic warrior for his favorite nation, the Romans?[85] Or was it that he wanted to ensure the existence of the two necessary enemy parties when the children play at being soldiers? This is unlikely, because, first, Brazilian children never play at being soldiers. Furthermore, his cousins would have been able to help him balance things

84. Clélia (Latin, Cloelia; French, Clelie) was a heroic virgin who in 508 BCE escaped the Etruscan king Porsena, whose support was associated with the city republic of Rome. Cornélia was the daughter of the hero of the Second Punic War (ca. 190–ca. 100 BCE), Publicus Cornelio Scipio Africanus, and a prototype of a virtuous Roman woman. These numerous Roman names prompted Ina to refer to the children in her letters as "the Romans" or "my Romans" as well as "my antique pupils."

85. The plethora of Roman names inspired publisher Fernando Gasparian to modify the title of Ina's book by inserting a prefix to her original title: *Os meus romanos* (My Romans). In birth order, the mostly Roman-named children were Lavínia (b. 1870), Caio Graco (b. 1872), Plínio (b. 1873), Maria Evangelina (b. 1874), Clélia (b. 1876), Cornélia (b. 1878), Julieta (b. 1879), and Vercingetorix (b. 1881). After Ina left the employ of the Silva Prados, four more children were born: Cássio (1883), Corina (1885), Fábio (1887), and Cícero (1888). All twelve used the Silva Prado surname. Vercingetorix was named after a Gallic chieftain defeated by Julius Caesar in 52 BCE, but this proved to be only his nickname. He was christened Martinho da Silva Prado Neto (*Neto* means grandson). The only male offspring not to receive a Roman name, Vercingetorix perpetuated the dynastic nomenclature by his baptismal name.

out, since they had already rejected the customary João, Luiz, or Carlos in favor of names such as Themistocles and Pericles.

The big and small female cousins ended up more peaceful. There is no Sappho or Aspasia to compete with our Roman girls, and yet they still manage to confuse our poor European intelligence all the more amply with the overwhelming uniformity of their names: Dona L, Dona Maria Salomé, Dona Maria Magdalena, Dona Maria da Glória, Dona Maria da Conceição, Dona Maria da Cruz—and so on gracefully ad infinitum. And then to see with what certainty the Brazilians can differentiate among all these names, and when possible, even know: Dona Maria Magdalena, daughter of Dona Maria das Dores, and so forth! There is a certain uncivilized aspect to this preference for given names; it reminds one of Adam and Eve, who also had no last names. And yet it would be so much easier to tell all these Marias apart if one simply appended their last name to them as opposed to the given name of the mother, since the given names of those named above consist only of two and three names![86] It also shocks me again and again to hear the youngest boy calling an old women "Dona Gabriela," for example, or an old, white-haired grandfather "Senhor Carlos." I then praise the titles in our own customs! When somebody is named "Mrs. Councillor" or "Mrs. Senior Bailiff," or "Mrs. Superintendent," at least you know that no one is talking about a seventeen-year-old girl. Here, one never knows how high or how low on the scale of years one ought to judge such a "Dona."[87] If you tried to address a lady as

86. Ina appears not to have apprehended that the second name to which "Maria" was appended usually proved operational: Maria Aparecida would be called "Aparecida," even "Cida"; Maria da Conceição would be "Conceição," and so forth. Moreover, Ina failed to perceive the pivotal importance of given names over family names, especially for females. That emphasis still survives today, but made more sense in the 1880s, given the relatively small pool of family names and the elite propensity for marrying cousins. Within a given extended family, redundancies, even among individuals bearing multiple family names, meant that given names plus the referent of a parent's name—or, alternatively, nicknames—provided highly practical ways to discriminate among those with the same family nomenclatures. Thus, Martinico Prado (Martinho da Silva Prado Júnior) was distinguished from his father, Martinho da Silva Prado, due to a universally operational nickname.

87. The title *Dona* derived from social distinctions of nobility—specifically, the lowest rung on the ladder of nobility applying to a gentlewoman. Well entrenched by the 1880s as a title of address for middle- and upper-class women, it did not come to be applied to women of all social classes until the twentieth century. *Senhora* never functioned as a title or an honorific, as its cognate does in Spanish, which explains Ina's initial expectation that it should. Instead, *Senhora* stood alone as a form of address—as in "madam" or "miss." The one exception was "Senhora Dona Albertina Morais Pinto da Silva Prado" (wife of Martinico Prado), the deliberate redundancy reserved for a woman of wealth and respected lineage.

"Senhora Maria," for example, then you would greatly insult her, as in polite society Senhora is only allowed without a name following it. And it is only used with a given name for the lower class of freed women—for free mulattas, for example.

We German governesses and probably other [female] foreigners usually have the fortune to be addressed in shops and in other places with the salutation *Madama* [Madam]—an odious, ugly word, however, that appears even more insufferable as one must admit that Brazilian arrogance invented it specifically to differentiate the *estrangeiras* [foreigner women] (always pronounce it with due contempt, if you please) from the *brasileiras* [Brazilian women].

The servants in every family call the lady of the house *Sinhá*,* the gentlemen of the house *Sinhô*, the eldest daughter always *Sinhazinha*, the eldest son *Nhonhô*; the latter two designations are also, among the siblings, customary. For the rest of the children come still other names: Nhonhozinho, Nhanhá, Sinhara, Nenê, and, rather commonly, Bebê and similar appellations, each one always uglier than the last. One imagines a row of siblings as follows: Sinhazinha, Nhonhô, Nhanhá, Sinhara, Nhenê, Nhonhosinho, Bebê—to our ears this is the height of tastelessness, but in Brazil, these names occur in virtually every family. They often prefer to shorten the names of girls called Maricota to "Cocotte"!

Countless people here go by so-called *apelidos*, short handles or nicknames. This custom can be also found in Upper Bavaria and Tyrol, but there the nicknames are still always real names, whereas here they are often completely inexplicable nonsense. In [Fazenda] São Francisco, there was a Portuguese man who tilled the earth, and he was never called anything other than "John-with-the-Hat" [João de Chapéu]. Even Dr. Rameiro spoke of him like this with the most indifferent face, and I am convinced that his name was written down in this manner in the daybooks. Once, when the doctor rode to a small neighboring city and asked for the house of a Senhor Carlos de Oliveira, nobody understood whom he was referring to. Then, when he luckily

*The *nh* is pronounced like an *ny*—that is, it corresponds to the Spanish *ñ* or French *gn*. Editor's note: Ina confused the initial sound of *nh* with that of an initial *r* (an *rh* sound), mistakenly writing "Rhonho" for "Nhonhô." She also misheard *Sinhara* as *Senhara* and *Nenê* as *Nunu*, suggesting that her ear was not finely tuned. These forms of address originated among African slaves, reflecting their imperfect pronunciation of Portuguese, and then were incorporated into the vernacular speech of the slave owners' family members.

remembered his dumb *apelidos*—Nhonhô Padre (Little Gentleman Father)—they immediately gave directions as to where he was.[88]

On the other hand, it seems as if the Brazilians' names cannot be flashy enough, and they put them together in as many different permutations as possible. Do you recall how we obsequiously honored the little Brazilian woman in the boardinghouse, or rather, her amazingly showy name? Julieta Olímpia Leite da Costa Pinto! What would an Anna Schulze be in comparison to that, or how would one feel knowing that there were other people named Meier! But, but—the illusions are disappearing! Imagine that Leite is milk, Costa is cost [coast], Pinto is chick, and then you will perhaps be reconciled, as I was, with Schulze, Müller, and maybe even Meier. And probably 50 percent of the population has precisely one of these names—Costa, Pinto, Leite—in some way or another. Chaves means key, Machado means axe, and then Leitão means in pitiless German: piglet! Yes, the Marquis de la Marlinière is right: "The German language is a skimpy language, an awkward language"! Most of our names, even with our exasperating consonants, just peter out at the end, paltry and unremarked! How much better to finish in a lovely vowel, an *a* or an *o* or even an *oa*!

Yes, if it were as easy in our good old native Germany as it is here to wangle a beautiful name, I bet that the so-called collective names would soon die out, and how the House of "Cohen" would breathe a sigh of relief![89] *Here*, if someone's name doesn't suit him, or if it gives occasion to mix-ups, then he just adds another name, puts it in the newspaper, and *basta*. Miss Meyer lives here in a family in which the master of the house and his two full brothers have completely different names.[90] One sees that they take the good where they find it. There are people in this country who call themselves Montmorency,

88. Ina overlooked that Brazilians did—and still do—employ standard nicknames precisely corresponding to given names, such as Joca (João), Tonho or Toínho (Antonio), Zé (José), Chico (Francisco), Lota (Carlota), Bia (Bianca and Beatriz), Dora (Auxiliadora), Cida (Aparecida), etc.

89. Ina sympathetically refers to the position of Jews in Germany who sought to change their names in efforts to assimilate to a German nationality. Despite constitutional guarantees of religious equality, in the 1880s their petitions for name changes were encountering bureaucratic refusals, especially in Prussia. That she was aware of this issue demonstrated how remarkable her efforts to keep abreast of current affairs in Germany proved to be.

90. Ina's frustration stems from the fact that no strict naming rules existed (unlike in Spanish) and that siblings often had different surnames because each person decided what his/her adult name should be, some brothers favoring a name from the father's side and others from the mother's. Men even changed surnames in adulthood after a number of years passed.

Medina-Coeli, and so on; and there are also numerous Pedro de Alcântaras, which, as you know, is the dynastic name of the emperor.[91] Over the last decade, some German names have also found favor in the eyes of the Brazilians. According to one publication, someone who was unhappy with his name wanted to name himself Habsburgio, which in and of itself would leave me cold. If only some German researcher doesn't suddenly get wind of the existence of this name in Brazil and then, in the enthusiastic joy of discovery, doesn't suddenly project a line of Habsburg émigrés with all sorts of intricate dates and numbers into his history books. Well, I'll keep the newspaper clipping until you have the examination happily behind you.

By the way, the other day I was duly peeved at this whole naming nonsense when an individual of low repute was detained for disturbing the peace and gave his name as João Leão Bismarckio.* If the emperor wants to put up with all the pseudo–Pedro de Alcântaras in his country and the slave baron permits his recently emancipated slave to attach himself to his own last name, then we say: "De gustibus non est disputandum." [There's no accounting for taste.] But I think that we Germans nevertheless consider our names to be more sacred, and one ought not to tolerate such a thing, even in a foreign country.

I have now worked myself into such a lather that I can't find my way on the path to a transition [to another topic]. You won't even mind, dear Grete, if I just take a leap. At any rate this is what counts as modern nowadays, as our writers often make true *saltos mortales* [somersaults] when the narrative is not moving itself along. I find that convenient, therefore. . . . Just imagine that a young Brazilian man recently asked me to dance with the words, "Does Your Excellency already have a partner?" His younger brother was sitting on one side next to me; on the other side, there was a cello leaning against the chair—which left me as the person he was designating "Your Excellency." The man looked too ingenuous to be teasing me, so Your Excellency danced. But the affair amused me so much that at the first opportunity I told it to Lavínia's

91. In addition to the current emperor, "Pedro Alcântara" was the name given by Pedro I to all of his numerous illegitimate sons between 1817 and 1831. Hence, by 1881, the latter's descendants swelled the ranks of individuals bearing that name, often as members of elite social networks.

**Deutsche Allgemeine Zeitung für Brasilien*, June 30, 1883. Editor's note: Why the article's date is later than this letter's date can only be explained by Ina's having added this example while she worked through the letter format of her book (published in 1887). The Brazilian newspaper's date also suggests that she continued living in Brazil in 1883, apparently drafting her book of letters there—subsequent to her concluding letter of "January 1883."

mother, laughingly—then I really looked ridiculous! After all, she told me that the merest courtesy required it. (Please don't even try to imagine the complication of the matter; it could go to your head.) And that "Vossa Excelência" sounds definitely much nicer than the simple "a Senhora." I couldn't object to any of this, and I, "gulping," took my leave with this lesson.[92]

The mode of addresses and titles is a pure matter of study, and in my opinion, it is much more complicated than in our country. I've already told you about how one ought to call ladies. The men are all called Senhor. In Portuguese, the *Don*, where it is spelled *Dom*, is used only for princes. But you can use the Senhor freely—that is, for everyone who is not a slave, even the barefoot tiller of the earth—although in such cases they have a particular way of pronouncing the word very short so that it sounds almost like *sior*.[93] They speak in this way so that people comprehend the distance. And in sentences, the address would mostly be *o Senhor* and *a Senhora*: "Would you [*o Senhor*] loan me this book?" "Would you [*a Senhora*] like a glass of water?"

Você is like our *du*. One speaks to slaves and children in such a way, whereas children address their parents as father and mother or with [*o*] *Senhor* and [*a*] *Senhora*, but only rarely as *Papa* and *Mama*. So somewhere between *Você* and *Senhor* or *Senhora* is *Vossa Mercê*, which you would find translated in Ollendorff as "your grace."[94] It means, however, not nearly as much as "your grace," and comes closest to our *Sie*. It is, for the most part, not customary. Somewhat more deferential than the simple *Senhor* is *Vossa Senhoria*, and recently our distinguished countryman Gruber, who through his activity and his connections has a bit of political influence, told me a nice, short story about name escalation.

He was dealing with a quite simple Brazilian from the countryside (one calls these people *caipira*) because of a vote and had addressed him simply as

92. Ina is still straining to bend *a Senhora* into a title of address (as in "Señora Albertina") when she should say, "Dona Albertina." "You" in the formal third person is *a Senhora*. Dona Albertina tried to explain this when she endorsed the alternate form of a title of address, somewhat mocking Ina to justify "Your Excellency" as very polite. *Dom* was used more widely than Ina understood, as in respectfully addressing elderly individuals or senior ecclesiastics.

93. Today, *Senhor* has mutated to "Seu" in informal contexts, the elided title of address passing into the vernacular speech of all social classes—as in "Sr. Luís," pronounced "Seu Luís."

94. Ina refers to Heinrich Gottfried Ollendorff (1803–65), a German linguist who by 1830 had settled in Paris and who was celebrated for his "Ollendorff method," a new approach to teaching foreign languages quickly. Of his many pedagogical books, she may have read *Nouvelle méthode pour apprendre à lire, à écrire et à parler l'allemand*, 2 vols. (1836).

você. But when the man on his part called him *Vossa Mercê*, Gruber didn't want to reveal a lack of politeness and so took up the same form of address. Then, however, our good *caipira* [hick] jumped over to *Senhor* and then to *Vossa Senhoria*. Mr. Gruber continued to follow him in this direction. But when the man then immediately slipped one level higher and climbed to *Vossa Excelência*, our countryman said, smiling, "Well, my good man, we can now stop. After all, we can't call one another '*Vossa Majestade*' [Your Majesty]!"

Send the next person who claims to hate titles over here, Grete. Here, he would learn to bless all of our native titles which are so often the target of scorn in other foreign countries. The aristocratic nobility is the most incredible thing in this country. There are among them people who work as barefooted ploughmen who came, for example, from Portugal. But the barons, marquises, and viscounts from Dom Pedro's nobility factory bring in quite a pretty penny to the state. It's just a shame that such an expensively acquired marquis title—or a viscount—bought with cash has to be buried with the happy buyer![95] Dom Pedro does not trust his hot-blooded people. The father can be a baron and the son a beggar—nothing of this sort is handed down hereditarily. But what could such an aristocracy mean for the country! Only seldom and out of rare honor, and only when the emperor would truly like to honor the person in question, is the *von* or the title simply added to the name of the person. Normally, it is almost always bound with a place name. Most of these place names are taken from the old native Guaraní language, to which innumerable places here in Brazil owe their names.[96] For example, there is a Marquis de Itanhaem—that is, "of the stone mortar"; a Viscount de Suassuna—that is, "of the black deer"; a Viscount of Uruguay—that is, "of the river of the hen-tail"; a Viscount do Muritiba—that is, "of the place where there is flying"; a baron of Cambatí—that is, of "the black ape"; a Viscount de Iroumitata—that is, of "bring me fire," and so on. Some names are also naturally Portuguese, and then the emperor sometimes has his fun with them.

95. Ina is referring to the fact that the 1824 Constitution prohibited the heritability of noble titles. And she identifies the well-known practice that individuals paid the crown to receive their noble titles, especially in the 1880s, when granting them hit an all-time fever pitch.

96. Ina might have mentioned earlier the importance of place names as variant nicknames, especially for elite men—such as "Joca da Maravalha" (Joca of Fazenda Maravalha). Also, Tupi-Guaraní names became very popular in the nineteenth century because of Romanticism and the nationalistic motive of discriminating Brazilian names from those of the former Portuguese colonizer. Thus holders of noble titles and wealthy landowners frequently dropped their Portuguese family names altogether, adopting indigenous nomenclature or noble titles.

A Baron "Big Mogul" [*barão de Grande Mogul*], which he has invented, is not even the worst of the lot. There are even some applicants who have paid enough, but whom the creative mockery of the imperial title-producer has scared away.

And yet, dear Grete—one has to howl with the wolves: if you write to me again, please address the letter to *Ilustríssima e Excelentíssima Senhora Dona Ulla von Eck.*[97]

That is the least that would be appropriate; otherwise you would find me far too simple. With that, I remain,

Your Ulla

97. It was still quite common, into the 1970s, to use the honorifics "Ilustríssimo Sr." and "Ilustríssima Sra." in addressing envelopes sent through the national mails.

São Paulo

May 29, 1882

My dear, good Grete!

My antique pupils are really quite mischievous, and I need all my possible pedagogical finesse in order to deal with them. In particular, I can never let both of the young boys work alone in the classroom downstairs when Lavínia is having her piano lesson upstairs. It always seems to me like the story of the wolf, the goat, and the heads of cabbage, each of which a ferryman has to take individually over a river. The ferryman cannot leave the goat and the cabbage or the wolf and the goat alone together. Just recently, Caius Gracchus—his father always calls him in a declamatory style, "Gracho"—the stronger, although less talented, of the two brothers, simply shoved his brother out of the lower ground floor window. The other brother stood clamoring in front of it, throwing sand and stones inside—you can imagine the state of the classroom afterwards!

The parents pay absolutely no attention to what the children are doing, and perhaps that belongs to Mr. Costa's republican "system." The three older brothers are trusted entirely to my intellectual care, and the younger Romans are taken care of by the Negro women as well, or as poorly, as befits them. Just recently I saw the little two-year-old Mucius [Vercingetorix], completely naked, running around the garden after he had taken a bath. I seldom see the mother of the Gracchi, nor the brave swimmer Clélia, other than in the beginning stages of their toilette. Even though the Brazilian women, on the street and at "functions," are what the English would call "dressy," at home they are quite primitive when they put themselves together. Even the most elegant and richest Brazilian women go around at home in the most simple calico dress without any fringes, and a big jacket, just as they let their braids hang down. In the hot months this is rather pleasant and refreshing, but in the cooler months it is absolutely nothing more than laziness. For in these months, tight clothes are quite bearable—yes, even desirable. But either the wool clothes continue to hang in the closet, or they don't even have any. At home, they wear calico; on the street, they wear more refined linens and often silk. They think that wool clothes are not clean because they can't be washed every eight days! You know, Grete, these Brazilians have a wondrous sort of cleanliness and order in and of itself. They bathe often. Most of them do so every day, and yet many children and adults are not quite so "without a doubt" around the ears and the neck. They change undergarments and clothes very often, but how often it is all threadbare and untidy! There is a little bit of huffishness on this point between natives and foreigners. Many of the Brazilians' habits excite, and rightly so, reluctance on the part of foreigners, even when it is not as bad as Mr. Zöllner makes it out to be. But in return the Brazilians avenge themselves with the anecdote of the German who, when his host asked him on the second day of his nice little trip if he wanted to take a bath, as he did on the first day, responded with utter indignation: No, he was not such a little pig as to require a bath every day. And on top of this anecdote, the Brazilians naturally follow it up with other, sometimes more bawdy, stories about the German and the English. Well, such disputes are not fruitful and, above all, will not actually change anything about the qualities that are native to these people and that have arisen because of the climate.[98]

Personally, I especially suffer because of the customs surrounding footwear in this country. None of the boots in the house, except for my own, are polished, and you have no idea what manipulations, tricks, and efforts had to be undertaken in order to get the household to use my polishing materials appropriately and to educate a Negro woman about how it ought to be done. Indeed, this last attempt has only succeeded with a high degree of imperfection up until this very day. Mr. Costa lets his boots be smeared with lacquer, which is quite easy. Indeed, they prefer this process to polishing for this very reason. Madame wears slippers in the house; on the street, elegant half-boots or bronze shoes. The ladies here don't need practical, solid shoes, since they simply don't go out if the weather is bad. The children go around with threadbare footwear until it sort of falls off their feet in rags, which happens with Plínio, for example, every fourteen days. It is foreign to the Brazilians to have their shoes repaired. They just wear them until they become useless, then they are thrown away and replaced with something new. There are also no real shoemakers here, but

98. Ina refers to the German occupant of the chair in astrophysics at Leipzig University, Johann Karl Friedrich Zöllner (1834–82), who had died a month earlier. "Zöllner's Illusion" was an optical one, in which parallel lines appeared to be diagonal. However, any specific comment he made regarding Brazilians, perhaps as students at his university, remains undiscovered. Stories about the practice of daily bathing, which Brazilians claim (and Gilberto Freyre demonstrated) derived from the indigenous population, continue to be proverbial. Indeed, even today, there are many funny stories about Brazilians who arrive in student digs in Germany only to discover to their horror that hot water is limited, dictating a standard practice of bathing only once a week!

rather, shops with finished goods, usually from France, so that it is very difficult for foreigners to get something repaired—unless you entrust the matter to the Italian cobblers who are walking around, who patch together boots in front of your door, just as the pot cobblers repair our pots in Germany.

The craftsmen class is practically nonexistent here, and above all, you will hardly be able to find a Brazilian craftsman. The few that are around are usually Germans, Portuguese, and Italians. The lack of craftsmen makes life here more expensive. One can buy finished goods here, but then one does not have the possibility to keep them by having them repaired or reworked. I think that diligent craftsmen would find a much more receptive environment here than an immigrating countryman who doesn't know the climate, the topography, the channels of trade, and so forth, and who would find rather unfavorable conditions on account of the emancipation of slaves, and whose revenue would be made more difficult by the already prevalent overproduction of the main export, coffee. Whatever the craftsman produces, however, always has a market, and diligent, competent people will always manage to make something of this sort work out.

For the first time, I have had the opportunity in these last couple days to actually praise the lack of competent repair people in this country.

Caius and Plínius, namely, each had a velocipede; the former even had a completely modern bicycle that Mr. Costa had ordered for him from England.[99] The Roman boys spent all of their time outside class on these unholy vehicles and had developed such an attachment to them that they even took their meals "from atop the lofty bicycle." Since the parents sat there indifferently, I couldn't protest, but the comfort of my mealtimes was definitely not enhanced by Plínio's threatening three-wheeled proximity. There were even some disconcerting moments that came up upon his return to his place from the small, distracting tours that he would make around the table in between eating. Indeed, after he had collided with my chair in such a manner as to practically send my face into my plate, only then did he receive a reprimand, but the unsettling vehicle remained rightfully intact. Now, however, the horrible thing is fortunately broken, and while I am writing in my room below, at least it is only the huge velocipede that Gracchus has rolling about in the dining room above my head, since it is raining outside. A veritable redemption!

I recently told this to Mr. Hall, and he said that they had among their workers one who could repair the vehicle, and yet, he would "repress" this in-

99. "Velocipede" referred to a very large tricycle.

formation for the sake of my nerves if anyone were to inquire about it. That is nice of him, isn't that so, Gretel? His first name is George. He recently gave me a letter from his sister to read to him, and that's where I saw his name.

But I must come quickly to my conclusion, for Fräulein Harras has arrived. She comes every Monday to me, and Tuesdays we go together to Fräulein Meyer . . . there she is already. She sends a greeting to "my Grete," about whom I have already told her so much.

Your Ulla

São Paulo

June 25, 1882

My dear Grete!

I am writing in an atmosphere of smoke! Take a look at the date above and you will perhaps figure out why. Yesterday was St. John the Baptist Day again (already one year since I wrote you at the time from São Francisco!), and here in this city one understands best what this day means in Brazil!

The saint has been making his presence felt for a couple of days already; every evening there have been fireworks, and people have even been lustily firing their rockets in the full light of the sun. The Brazilians seem to take more delight in the splendid crack of the rocket and its instantaneous light and flash than in their watery carnival sport. That is, the Brazilians keep the contraband of customarily exploding fireworks throughout the entire year, while their water joy [*bisnagas*] is limited to carnival season. Rather often on nice evenings in Rio de Janeiro, we had to flee from the garden into the house because people were playing around close to us and the Brazilian pyrotechnicians were fully indifferent to the direction in which they aimed their rockets, or to the people around whose heads these flashing balls would fly—they just cared that it went off well and crackled and blistered. You can see throughout the entire year the more simple fireworks for sale lying on the merchandise tables of every Negro woman in the cities. Every *muleque* (a mulatto boy corresponding to our "street urchin") who has a couple of réis will certainly buy, in addition to the beloved sweets and cigarettes, a little firework stick or his *cracker*, in order to gladden his heart with the spraying and rattling.[100]

Last night and the night before last, I did not sleep at all. In every street, in every courtyard, in all of the gardens of our neighborhood there was crackling, rattling, chuffing, banging, and whizzing in such an abundance and with such endurance that I think I have an approximate idea of how it sounds to be under intense gunfire. The entire city smells like gunpowder, and my room, which is like a little alcove without direct ventilation, is so completely smoke-filled that, for a couple nights, I will probably not be in danger of forgetting Saint John.

100. This is a British term for a type of firework that explodes with a sharp noise—a "crack."

Yesterday it was even dangerous to go out into the streets. The sport began early in the morning. The students were the worst, of course. They found a particular pleasure walking around in a seemingly harmless fashion, and then suddenly, in front of a person approaching them or even an easily recognizable foreigner, they would let crackle a half-dozen cap bombs at their feet or shove one of those famous little pinwheels under their noses. Earlier, the crowning point of the whole firework activity had been the so-called snakes, fireworks that gyrated around on the ground and that people used in an equally childish and outrageous manner by sending them toward the feet and clothing of women. The fun lasted until finally an all-too-skilled child of the muses set the light calico dress of a mulatto woman on fire, thereby causing the woman significant burn injuries. Then everyone decided that it was frankly about time to put the lid on top of the well—a little late, since the child had already fallen down it, and yet, it seems that one must be grateful for everything here in Brazil regarding such matters.

You can imagine, Gretel, that the Romans had gone completely crazy; I was merely astonished that they had not burned down the house above our heads! That Gracchus had singed his hair and Plínius's finger had gotten lightly charred, such things are clearly self-evident and are not even worth mentioning. Even Lavínia got out of hand a little bit and had inflicted numerous fire damages on a dress.

Last night was the night of fireworks par excellence, and Mr. Costa invited me rather solemnly to stay upstairs after dinner, as they wanted to "make a little fireworks display." Of course—as if up until that point there had been too little of such a thing!

Surprisingly, the police had managed to make a decree that on this evening there would be no fireworks allowed in the streets or from street windows, and, what was more, the prohibition was actually obeyed! Because of this, I believed, in my European simplicity, that Mr. Costa would put on a nice, orderly fireworks show with the help of the Negroes in the little garden behind the house, which can be seen from the dining room: with Bengal fire, straight-candle rockets, softly glowing globes of light and streaming pinwheels, just about as we would imagine such a show at home. I was strengthened in this belief by the presence of ten to twelve guests, and, full of such expectations, I approached one of the higher-up windows. But Grete, I have bad luck with the Brazilians' favorite sports, as . . . ssssssht! It greeted me thus, and terrified, I recoiled from the sparks of a misfired rocket that a skilled devotee of the crackling and whooshing Saint John had aimed incorrectly in a direction that favored our window. Many women and children who had gone up to the window with me jumped back laughing and shrieking. Yes, the whole thing actually elicited a sort of delighted elation, so that I was left nonplussed with my own inner indignation. Is this good humor actually desirable, and are we at home too "disciplined"?!

However, now our fun began as well and, indeed, it consisted—to my great disappointment—in having us make our own fireworks. Such a thing amuses the Brazilians much more than just calmly looking on, and the boys were already squirming with impatience.

Mr. Costa had ordered a large amount of fireworks from Rio just for this evening, and he distributed them liberally among those who were present. Long tubes with sparks and English crackers [original in English] played the main role in the festivities; everyone received as much as he or she wanted. Everyone pushed themselves toward the windows in a thick crowd. Three or four sparkling rods jutted forth from every window, held by the brown hands of ladies wearing multiple rings or by the impatient fingers of small, wild tomboys, which then usually threw the sticks—not yet fully extinguished—down into the courtyard. Then, as quickly as possible, they would grab a new stick or something else to burn. The room eventually was filled with the most disgusting smoke in spite of the open windows, a smoke that was probably produced prodigiously by the flame-spraying sticks and then blown into the room by the evening wind.

A cold-blooded spectator would have found something infinitely amusing in this scene: These beautiful ladies colorfully dressed and gilded in gold with smoldering sticks in their hands, who, turning their faces away and squeezing their eyes shut, were enjoying the smoke of their fireworks. There were also the noisy, excited boys with hot heads, springing around the room as if they were crazy and throwing one cracker after another out the window. No one saw the crackers coming, and their presence was announced solely by the explosion on the stone pavement of the courtyard. And then there was the imperturbable seriousness with which the lord of the house distributed the fireworks. All of this was wrapped in a thick atmosphere of smoke—I confess that I had never in my life ever participated in such "pleasure." After an hour, sixty francs' worth of material had been fired off, the entire upper story of the house had been befouled for the night, and, the next day, two foreign fingers and one Roman one had been burnt. And I hope at least the back door of the house, the clothesline in the courtyard, and the warped garden fence had fun!

Plínio tried to use his burned left hand as a pretext not to write with his right one, and he was most enraged when this didn't appear to make as much sense to me as it did to him. Oh yes, Grete, the Romans are bad, but I will have patience. Mr. Hall also thinks I should try to endure all of this. But, as for Bormann—you see yourself, Grete, that he was not prepared for Brazilian children with a republican education! Well, keep your head up, that's the way it grew!

Your old Ulla

São Paulo

June 28, 1882

Try to imagine, Grete, what sort of a blow just hit me from out of a cheerful sky! I have to leave São Paulo! This is fate's revenge for my flight from the colégio! I will now have to go back to a plantation, and I will be alone again living among snakes and Negroes!

But listen.

I already wrote to you in my last letter about something that you will probably keep in mind when you hear this—namely, that the Romans had been completely out of control during the days of the pyrotechnics. How far it had gone, however, we ourselves did not know. They certainly must have studied "Max and Moritz," as they have so much in common—in a Brazilian way—with these classic characters performing stupid pranks! What, do you think, was their main prank on Saint John the Baptist's Day? They had gone to the main street and had thrown fireworks at the feet of the horses on the tramway and laid cap bombs in the tracks, and, of course, they had amused themselves like young devils, until finally they caused a horse to fall and break one of its legs. Then yesterday the director of the tramway brought suit against their father that he must pay for the horse, but he could keep the annoyance of the matter free of charge. This pleasant intermezzo made the Roman Republican father so angry that he intends to send the boys immediately to the monks to be brought up. Since it would not be worthwhile to retain a governess for Lavínia alone, she will be sent to a colégio. Poor Lavínia! But also poor Ulla, who now must travel again! I liked it otherwise so much here in São Paulo! Now I can truly sigh along with the trumpet player:

> Every year a different plant grows
> In the garden than times past—
> Life would be a dance of fools,
> Were it not so serious!

Oh Grete, I have become with one swoop so discouraged; I could cry forever. I have nothing but unhappiness! Mr. Hall, to whom I told this tonight—I went to Fräulein Meyer, you know, and he met me there coincidentally—thought as well, completely shocked: "It's too bad, yes, this is too bad!" [original in English].

Fräulein Meyer believes she knows of a position for me with the cousins of her own pupils, but that is in the countryside again. So I have to leave São Paulo, which I love so very much! Oh Grete, I'm telling you, I love São Paulo to the point of enthusiasm. I will be unhappy when I am gone, totally miserable! Life is difficult, Grete!

Your very sorrowful Ulla

São Paulo

July 1, 1882

Yes, Gretel—"she has to go to the countryside." But it is thankfully not far; only two hours by train from here to the station for the plantation.[101] It consoles me to some extent that I won't have completely disappeared off the face of the earth. But people have told me that I will find life on the plantation extremely primitive, as it is equipped according to the old style of the countryside. I am halfway scared about this "style," but I am also halfway curious about the true Brazilian country life, about which the many hundreds of people who visit Brazil never get an idea. In this way, we governesses have an advantage over the merchants and other Europeans, as very few of them ever leave the coastal areas, and most of them go back to Europe after ten or twenty years without ever having known in the most paltry manner the countryside or the life of Brazilians. We, on the other hand, who live directly with families, have to participate in all of their vexations.

Well then, off we go to São Sebastião. *Variatio delectat*! [There's nothing like change!] I will write as soon as this new saint permits me.

Your faithful Ulla,
"wandering" instructor

101. Ina would disembark at "The Station," officially the Santa Bárbara d'Oeste Station, ten kilometers distant from the *vila,* or town, of the same name. It was a stop between Campinas and Limeira, on the line called the "*Inglêsa*" (Cia. Paulista de Estradas de Ferro, Ltda.), which ended at Rio Claro. Opening in 1875, "The Station" was 124 km west of São Paulo.

São Sebastião

July 11, 1882

My dear Grete!

It is true, St. Francis was definitely the more elegant of the saints. Here everything is very primitive—and yet, I get along better with the saintly Sebastian! The family here is the most amicable that I have ever known among the natives. They are also the most sensible, and I would almost say European (in spite of the primitive conditions on the plantation, they are not as sluggish and lazy as most of their countrymen).

Among those "European" qualities is the fact that Mr. de Sousa came and picked me up from the train station himself.[102] For the Brazilians have such peculiar ideas about what is fitting that they find it highly inappropriate when a young governess makes her way back from the station to the plantation accompanied by the father of her pupils. On the other hand, they find it very appropriate whenever she travels alone with a Negro coachman or on horseback with a free worker, a so-called *camarada*, as they had just expected a colleague of mine to do on her way from São Paulo![103] Mr. de Sousa was even very attentive and spoke with me on the way. In general, as Fräulein Meyer once claimed in a rather droll manner, we Europeans always consider it politeness on the part of the Brazilian gentlemen when they ignore us. Unfortunately, she is not quite mistaken in this claim, and therefore, I am that much happier that I have managed to end up among sensible people.

We made our way back from the station to the plantation, which in this hot, damp time of year is only possible by riding in a wagon, and we drove almost five hours. Sometimes I thought that we would not arrive safe in São Sebastião—we were going up and down over such steep cliffs, through huge

102. By 1882, The Station's surroundings enjoyed a separate identity as "Vila dos Americanos" (Americans' Town). The "Americans," known as *Confederados*, were émigrés from the defeated Confederate States of America who first purchased land in late 1865. In 1900, "Americana" became the town's official name; in 1924, the "Vila" became a legal county in its own right. Today, "Americana" still celebrates an annual festival honoring Confederate ancestry.

103. *Camarada* referred to a member of a free labor force that was mobile, but temporary and paid in cash—such as the gangs who cleared forests to open land for new plantations.

puddles and other abnormal variants of what one might call a "road." I came to see a massive difference between this area and the province surrounding Rio, especially the road to São Francisco, which was almost as good as an avenue. But it is actually more interesting here, Grete; it has more "local color."

We passed by a long stretch of primeval forest, where the road was rather poor and was actually only made for riding animals. The planters of the area are continually at pains to keep this road open, since it becomes overgrown so easily and, during the damp time of the year, no one can work on it that well. Whenever it has to be fixed and cleared, every *fazendeiro* [owner of a *fazenda*] who uses the road sends a number of slaves to The Station, and they all work their way back together; gradually the participating parties fall by the wayside, either at the plantations for which they work or, if these are not located immediately on the road, wherever the road diverges to their plantations. Our trip through the forest had little in common with a trip through our native beech groves or pine forests, since a forest looks quite different here than it does at home. There is nothing orderly or cultivated, and one cannot go inside or even see through them. Here, one cannot even expect that solemnity that overcomes us so easily in the silent forest cathedrals of our homeland; the whole thing has something more exciting, half fantastic and secret, half nightmarish and fearful. The magic of the primeval forest, that which gives it charm, consists in something other than the impression that our forests make. You shouldn't think that the trees inside are so very thick and stout—at first, the whole thing even makes less of a powerful impression than, for example, one of the big beech groves that can be found in Holstein or Westphalia.

I once brought the entire Vehmic court frightfully into an uproar with my claim that I, the child of a forester, had not yet seen a proper forest in Brazil, being unable to designate as a forest these long, thin, trunks that belonged to various types of wood and that stood apart from one another in the most unequal distances. One has to, as I now know, drive or ride through such a forest in order to get the proper impression of it. Then one sees what the essence of a primeval forest is, which is at the same time that which prevents the individual trunks from becoming massive. The brushwood, almost impenetrable, lies about the trunks, and whoever wants to enter the forest in fact has to go step-by-step clearing the way with his hands. One sees from afar that the trees are not tightly packed. The gray trunks jutting out with the thin folia of their crowns are the only thing that one can see with one's eyes. Nearby one notices that the individual trees are pushed closer together, or at least they seem to be so, because of the fairy-tale-like, lush vines, extending fifteen to twenty meters, which wind up and then hang down, indeed often entwine themselves from one trunk to another. They end up forming a green, trembling wall from which strange, dark purple or red flowers look out with large eyes.

I arrived much more satisfied in São Sebastião than I had thought possible after my departure from São Paulo, and I became even more satisfied when I saw Dona Maria Luísa and my pupils. The former is slightly less than a beauty, as are all the other Brazilian women that I have seen, for she goes around in the obligatory calico dress and with her braids hanging down. There is nevertheless something very refreshing and agreeable about her, and she has raised her little girls well.[104] My oldest pupil, Maricota, is a very dear creature, although her pronounced reticence makes her easily seem somewhat morose, and both of the younger ones are so well-behaved that I almost got an uncanny feeling. We work very well together. I will particularly help Maricota with her English, which will be easier for her than German at any rate, and you know that I love English very much. Mr. Hall always thought that I spoke it very well—he was on the train as I departed, which I found actually not very agreeable, since some of my colleagues had already teased me very much about him.

But back to my report about the land here.

It is true that this plantation cannot be compared to those near São Francisco. It goes back to the grandparents of Mr. de Sousa, and the family has not occupied it for many years.[105] Even now, it is only really useful to the family as a working station, and nobody spends anything extravagant on it. My room, with all of its defects, is nevertheless the one made with the most stone, which is the reason why I cannot complain. I see that the family is much happier with itself here, and at least the parlor is bright and airy. The *sala de visita* [living room] is a big room with five windows and whitewashed walls. It is furnished with a wicker sofa, twelve Viennese chairs, a hammock, and a Singer sewing machine. There are no curtains in front of the windows here either, no carpet on the bare planks, no image adorns the wall—but I can confirm a rare and extremely advantageous exception in this country that a clock is always set to the right time! Dona Maria Luísa values punctuality, and this is something for which I am especially grateful: she values punctuality for the mealtimes, so

104. Ina is referring to Dona Francisca Miquelina de Souza Barros—"Dona Maria Luísa"—wife of "Mr. de Sousa," whose real name was Bento Aguiar de Barros. Ina refers to their children by their actual names: Maricota (Maria Isabel) and Albertina. She does not name the middle sister, Isabel; Eugênia, the youngest, had not yet been born. Their twelve-year-old brother, Luís de Souza Aguiar de Barros, born after Maricota, was at school in Germany.

105. Lying at least fifteen kilometers south of The Station, "Fazenda São Sebastião," in reality, was a portion of the enormous Fazenda São Luiz, owned by Dona Maria Luísa's father.

that after meals there is always a quarter or a half an hour of recovery time before the lesson begins again.

Every day at 9 a.m. and 3 p.m., we get together on the *veranda* for breakfast and lunch, respectively. The Brazilians call the dining room a *veranda*—diverging from our definition of a veranda—and the innumerable doors and windows that usually grace this room justify this name to a certain extent. One usually recognizes the rustic *veranda* by the fact that its outer door is at the same time the back door of the house and leads directly outside. Through these characteristics, the room exhibits qualities similar to those of a backstairs area in Berlin. It is like that here as well. The serving goes back and forth through this area: water, wood, supplies, laundry—everything goes in and out in big buckets and baskets on the heads of the blacks. Because the room is usually connected to the kitchen, and often with the chamber of the Negro women as well, it makes an admirable control post for the housewife, as in the kitchens of Dutch houses.

Dona Maria Luísa really exercises control in contrast to most of the Brazilian housewives. She is everywhere and oversees the Negro women right up to their very fingers. She herself bakes excellent white bread so that I can luckily escape the *biscoitos*, and she makes butter herself in the most cumbersome manner by beating cream in a bucket until it becomes butter. She also sews tirelessly with the Singer machine and helps make the clothes and linens for the children, yes, even shirts and winter jackets for the house—in short, she is more industrious than many a "German housewife" and under more difficult conditions on top of it all. She really impresses me and I like her very much. She also has a great sense of humor and was highly amused by my horror upon seeing the veranda here, which was supposedly made according to the "old style" about which I had been told in São Paulo. I will describe it to you.

This very large room, longer than it is wide, is neither made with planks on the ceiling nor with boards on the floor. The floor is laid out half with bricks, while the other half unabashedly reveals the mud on which stands the house, which, like all Brazilian houses, does not have a cellar. In this loamy soil there is a place for fire, around which the family gathers on cold evenings, just as in our country we gather around the ceramic heater. Of course with this furnishing, the lack of a ceiling is rather nice, since there is no other escape for the smoke other than the holes and cracks in the tile cover over the beams of the roof. On one side of this fantastic hall there is the dining table, where we eat breakfast and lunch. In the evening, by the glow of a stearin light, we drink tea.[106]

106. A stearin light was an odorless glycerin candle made from natural fats.

Right on the first evening, from my very own seat, I got an idea of the multifaceted usefulness of this veranda. While we drank, a Negro woman stood on the opposite side of the room ironing clothes, which already, as far as I was concerned, generated a certain horror in me from the outset. For in that corner, first of all, it must have been pitch black. Furthermore, she didn't move the iron at all for seconds, but rather, stared at us with her mouth agape. One can only hope that the iron wasn't that hot. Next to her, another woman was kneading dough for bread. This and the clock, as well as the relaxed nature of the whole family, had elicited the greatest satisfaction from me. Suddenly a new sight delighted me. You will not be able to imagine what it was, and that's why I want to say it right away: there was a boot-cleaning mulatto boy who had been placed in another secluded area of this amazing room. Thus I was confronted with exception number three: the total lack of a general Brazilian aversion to polishing! The satisfaction with my new lot grew. This small mulatto—he is also, by the way, the driver in the afternoon—was extremely funny to look at. The monotonous blackening of the shoes, executed at a slow tempo, had probably created an insuperable soporific effect, for every couple moments his activity stumbled, and he stood there with closed eyes and uplifted brush, leaning against the wall, until the falling of the polishing instrument or the rousing, "Well, Ivo?" of the housewife put him again into sleepy motion. After his work was finished, he had to bring the entire row of boots to the table, where the lady of the house examined them and then let the dirty little fellow go. After a couple moments, however, he came back in and reported: "Cesário is still bringing the pig, Senhora." "My God, how troublesome, it is so late!" The lady called: "Now that doesn't help anything, tell him to come, and fast!" "Cesário" came in through the famous back door carrying a small pig on his back. He put it on a table that had been shoved his way and began to carve it. Indeed, this veranda was a *non plus ultra* of versatility, and its extended usefulness as a baking room, a folding room, a polishing area, and a slaughterhouse—whatever one thinks of it all—saves the masters many extra steps and many words of abuse. Here there hasn't been any screaming as there was in São Francisco because from the start there is more control and there are therefore fewer mistakes. This is how the "old style" is—may it live long.

Your primeval-forest woman,
Ulla

São Sebastião

July 19, 1882

Dearest Grete!

I am completely happy—my long-sought-after wish has finally been fulfilled: I am horseback riding! A couple of days ago, I had my first and only lesson. It was not complicated. Dona Maria Luísa lent me her riding dress until one could be made for me, and she said, laughing, "Mais ne tombez pas, mademoiselle." [But don't fall off, Miss.] Then Mr. de Sousa helped me onto the horse and said with a smirk: "Não caia, mademoiselle." [Don't fall, Mademoiselle.] And when I sat on the horse, Maricota completed these ample instructions with a third variation on the same theme: she called down to me from her own horse, "But don't fall off, Miss" [original in English]. Then the three of us began to trot, with Mr. de Sousa in front and me in the middle, because it is safer. However, since my horse, according to the habits of all the local horses, always followed the horse in front of it, and I therefore didn't have to guide the horse in any way, all I had to do was sit still, which was not so difficult. Or perhaps, as Mr. de Sousa claimed, I was born with a talent for horseback riding. Since then, we have gone on two more little rides within the area of the plantation, and now I can go without any of my honored companions riding in front of me. Many of my fellow governesses, just as they are coming back fresh from Europe, will have to ride for hours on horseback at the train station until they reach their destination! The saddles for ladies come mostly from England and North America, although there are some local saddles. The ones for men are usually the result of local work—work that, by the way, also turns out to be excellent in this particular domain.

It is very funny to see how the blacks round up the horses when we want to go riding. There are no stalls here, neither for the cows nor for the pigs, nor even for the horses. They don't really take care of the horses other than to take them every once in a while to eat salt. Other than that, they run around free and eat whatever they find in the way of grass and herbs, which is often rather meager, since no one really does anything with the soil for this purpose. Furthermore, there is no real grazing land. If someone wants to use horses, then a young lad chases into the courtyard as many animals as random chance lets him capture. They then take those that they wish to have and let the others go free. The freedom given to the household animals is in itself quite nice, but as a result of this they don't get fat. And during the cold nights at this time of year, which are sometimes very cool in the highlands, many a poor animal will often freeze to death in the forest, especially the young ones. The de Sousas don't know how many cattle they own. Taking stock would only be possible with great difficulty, as the cows have calves in the forest and then, one fine day, they arrive with their offspring. Of course, there is absolutely no way to regularize the milking here. Usually, however, the cows come in to be milked, but when it is very cold, they stay in the forest. Then Cesário simply says: "There will be no milk today, Senhora; no cow has come inside." Everything is rather earthy under the aegis of Saint Sebastian.

The little black pigs, which eagerly multiply here, have it the best, although almost every day one of them dies, since the plantation consumes a great deal of them.

There are almost no slaves here since both Mr. de Sousa and Dona Maria Luísa don't like the slave economy. There are only a few blacks for immediate household service, and the work outdoors is done by the free workers. All of the remaining slaves that the family owns work on a second plantation, São Luiz, under a Portuguese administrator.[107] Mr. de Sousa only rides the nine hours once every two to three weeks to get there and back in order to inspect everything. São Luiz is a coffee plantation, whereas we only have sugar and cotton here and a sawmill, all of which demand less of a workforce than coffee production.

I believe that it is quite clever of the Brazilians to gradually break in the *camaradas*. It is, however, not easy, as far as I can see here. I would get annoyed to death dealing with such people! The *camaradas* are Brazilians, many of them half-Indians named *Cavoclos* [*caboclos*], as well as the impoverished descendants of Portuguese immigrants. They are a miserably poor and tattered folk, in their appearance far more wretched than the slaves, but they are free in a land of slavery.[108] The arrogance they have developed because of this

107. "São Luiz" (the actual name of the property where Ina was living) was Ina's fictitious name for Fazenda Vila Bela, the family's coffee plantation, which she said was located in Capivari, southwest of the Station (but actually in Dois Córregos). Correct property names probably were provided by a surviving, younger half-sister of Dona Maria Luísa and the translators' presumed octogenarian informant.

108. *Caboclo* applied either to an assimilated indigenous population or to those of a mixed ancestry of indigenous and Portuguese or African descent. Free laborers who were fixed tenants and sharecroppers usually were termed either *colonos* or *agregados* (dependents). They included refugees from the Northeast's Great Drought of 1877–80, several thousand of whom migrated to western São Paulo Province.

and the demands they make are unbelievable! In addition, they work about half as much as a slave at most, of course. The hair of our German estate owners would stand on end if they had to deal with such people! When those who are now here first arrived, Mr. de Sousa initially gave them material for their huts and ordered his own people to help build them. Then he gave every family an advance, a sum of money so that they could live until their own beans and cornfields began to deliver food. Of course, this advance was going to be taken bit by bit from their pay. Now, however, these people are "buying" everything that they need here, on credit from the house, after they have used the money. That is, they take bacon, flour, coffee, corn, and sugar in immodest amounts and then promise to work them off again. Since they often don't even go to work and usually have big families that consume many goods, however, their debts do not grow smaller, but rather, larger. Mr. de Sousa claims he can do little about this. If he were to deny them their food, then they would leave, and even if he made a contract with them, that would not make a bit of difference. Since they don't have anything, one can't take anything away from them, and one can't force them to work either. So he lets all of this go on and gets as much work as he can out of it. If it gets to be too much to bear, then he chases the people away. He sent away the last bunch with a loss of two thousand marks.

When one looks at these conditions, one can hardly be astonished at how the larger plantation owners struggle tooth and nail against the abolition of slavery. Where is the plantation owner supposed to get his workers? The Negroes who have been freed do not stay on the plantations, just as they have infrequently remained in other former slave states, and European workers are too expensive or inconvenient for them.[109] The Portuguese and the Italians only want to earn a lot of money in order to go back to their native countries with a small fortune, and the Germans come seeking the independent acquisition of land. The question of workers is an extremely difficult question here, exactly as it is in our country. It's just that, over there, there are too many workers and, here, there are actually no workers at all.

109. Although in the Paulista West (Ribeirão Preto, for example) some coffee planters (like Martinico Prado) were experimenting with European immigrants as a labor force, they could not be attracted in sufficient numbers until slavery was abolished. Then the floodgate of European immigration to Brazil opened. Immigrants' passage to Santos initially had been financed by the provincial government of São Paulo together with the planters. After 1888, immigrants had to pay the cost of their transatlantic transportation, as an advance on sharecropping earnings or on wages.

I discuss these conditions quite a bit with Mr. de Sousa and Dona Maria Luísa, who have, as it seems to me, very reasonable opinions about them. They themselves condemn slavery in principle and wish that it might stop, but they also have an eye open to the danger that might threaten the country directly following its abolition. Many of Brazil's wealthiest landowners would be impoverished and even completely ruined by abolition. Indeed, the issue becomes more difficult the further away the plantations are from the coastal areas, which are the first to receive immigrants.[110] On the one hand, then, one cannot be amazed that the Brazilians wish for foreign guests as a replacement for their slaves. On the other hand, it is certainly not the goal of our countrymen who come to Brazil to make themselves dependent yet again and to allow themselves to be hired out as the servants of a foreign nation. Whoever makes a life for himself and his descendants in a foreign country demands independence and his own stake in the country, and he does so justly. The Brazilians should draw on their own people for a working class, which they lack—just as they lack a class of craftsmen—and they could accomplish this with at least partial success if they tried to accustom the free children of the Negroes to regular work. However, precisely the opposite is what is happening.[111]

The emancipation law of September 28, 1871, commands every owner of slaves, among others as well, to educate these children in reading and writing. However, there are probably in the entire empire not even ten households that act according to this law. On plantations, following this law is actually impossible. Here in the country's interior there are no village schoolmasters

110. Coffee plantations in the Paulista West still relied heavily on slave labor. In the 1840s and 1850s, coffee planters had experimented with European immigrants as a labor force, but the immigrants found their status as indentured labor within a system of debt peonage discouraging. They chafed at the planters' unwillingness to live up to contractual obligations and "revolted." Planters became dissuaded from continuing the experiment following the wave of complaints made by European immigrants to their consular officials in the late 1850s, and the experiment waned, to be attempted again in the late 1870s, but only by a small number of planters.

111. Ina posed correctly the key question: Why did not free, native-born labor (including hundreds of thousands of ex-slaves) define an alternative work force after abolition? Historians today still debate this issue. In opting for post-1888 European immigrant labor under a *colono* system based on sharecropping and low or nonexistent wages, planters exercised greater control over that labor force because its basic unit was an immigrant *family*. The movie *Gaijin: A Brazilian Odyssey* (1980), by director Tizuka Yamasaki, herself the granddaughter of Japanese immigrants, illustrates such planter control through the story of a group of early Japanese immigrants to São Paulo's western coffee fields in 1907.

as there are in Germany. And even if there were—should the *fazendeiro* saddle up between twenty and fifty animals in order to send the little Negroes into the neighboring village, which is usually very far away? Or should he employ a special educator for the little group? One can answer these questions as one wishes—at any rate, nobody here is doing anything of the sort. Therefore, the freeborn children of slaves are being raised without lessons or any education at all.[112] They will live like savages, since they don't even have the advantage that their former masters are going to teach them some form of manual labor—as they did with the slaves. They are indeed free: Why should one take pains and spend money for the benefit of other people? One wouldn't get anything out of it.

Amazingly, even Mr. de Sousa and Dona Maria Luísa think this way—people who are otherwise quite humane and clever. One wonders if they are considering the fact that, by doing this, they are allowing a generation of "fellow citizens" to develop along with their own children who will be of the worst sort imaginable?!

But I see that I am preaching again and that I have graced you with a complete national economic treatise. But you wouldn't believe how all of these issues force themselves upon you here—even the most harmless of souls becomes a social politician.

And now I can't even add something light to the end of this letter so as not to leave you with this sociological lecture as a final impression, for the carpenter who works here has just arrived. He is going back to the city tonight and has agreed to take our letters to the post office as an act of courtesy. Mr. de Sousa only sends things on Thursdays to the post office—I have completely succumbed to the "old style" of writing.

Therefore, a farewell for today and there will be more next time from

Your Ulla

112. The 1872 average literacy rate among free Brazilians of both sexes was 17.7 percent, with men leading women by 10 points. That census awarded slaves a merely symbolic 1 percent rate.

São Sebastião

July 28, 1882

Dearest, best Grete!

Just imagine my joy—there is a plantation close by that belongs to American settlers—that is, to completely civilized people! No one told me about them until they came to visit us today—and nobody knew how valuable that would be to me![113] Oh Grete, even though these de Sousas are very nice, the Brazilians remain nevertheless foreign, even more foreign than all the other foreigners here, who are brought together by a certain feeling of belonging together as guests here in this country. In addition, the very essence and being of Germanic people are far more sympathetic than these Romans. Just at the sound of the English language, I breathed more freely, quite apart from the fact that Mr. Quimby and his sister-in-law really were very nice and sympathetic. Mrs. Quimby stayed at home with the little children while the oldest, a twelve-year-old girl, had already ridden along briskly.[114] It was last Saturday that they came and—"Do you want to come with us to church tomorrow?" they asked me suddenly.

"To church?" I replied, surprised—"Where?"

"Nobody has told you about our church yet? Well, it's not exactly a grand building, but at least we can hold our service every third Sunday. Come with us and stay the night; tomorrow, we can all go together if you want."

If I wanted! Of course I wanted to go. A horse was quickly saddled for me, and we galloped three miles, satisfied, until we reached Mr. Quimby's plantation. For I "galloped" now, at quite a brisk pace, and Mr. Quimby flattered my weaknesses when he said: "You look as if you'd been born and bred

113. The American neighbors were *Confederados*, families of defeated Confederate States of America war veterans, welcomed to Brazil by D. Pedro II, who wanted them to improve agricultural techniques (especially cotton cultivation) and to "whiten" the population. Refugees from the Old South moved to nine separate locations in Brazil, but only the colony in Santa Bárbara d'Oeste proved successful. About 154 families arrived there from Texas, Alabama, Georgia, and South Carolina, between 1866 and 1870. Then they were joined by others from colonies that had failed elsewhere in Brazil.

114. In the published multiple lists of *Confederados* living near the Santa Bárbara Station, the name "Quimby" does not appear, suggesting it is one of von Binzer's many pseudonyms. She may have been concealing the most prominent *Confederado* and his family, that of Col. William H. Norris, who bought land in December 1865, on Faz. Machadinho (also Bairro do Recanto). This same property was where The Station was built, the locale eventually becoming "Vila Americana." There were four distinct geographical groupings where American family clusters settled in the county.

on your horse" [original in English]. Mrs. Quimby received me warmly like an expected guest, and we spent the rest of the evening chatting and sitting in the hammocks.

The next morning, at nine o'clock, a small cavalcade rode off to church, as there were still some ladies and gentlemen from the area that went with us. As long as the road was on the plantation's property, it was not that bad, although you ought not to imagine anything more in the word "road" than a path only suitable for one horse. Afterward, however, it became so bad in some places that, in our country, people would probably have refused to try to ride on it. But Brazilian horses are not spoiled. Even unshod, they safely go on their way, and one can leave it to them to find the path confidently themselves during the difficult parts.

Our little society was exceptionally picturesque: the bright clothes and hats of the ladies, the white coats of the gentlemen, and the large, mostly white, parasols—everything gleaming, lit up by an already burning sun, here and there disappearing and reappearing between ferns as tall as men. As the horses trotted between the ferns, all of this reflected itself in a large puddle, almost like a sea, and the animals had water up to their stomachs.

I had never ridden out at this time of day, as we always chose early in the morning or late in the evening as a time for riding in São Sebastião. For that reason, I experienced the sun as particularly unpleasant. Unfortunately, the road did not reveal one single tree as far as the eye could see, aside from a few palm trees whose graceful, yet sparse, crowns provided no protection from the sun and threw no shadows on the ground. I then realized what sort of exhaustion can come upon you after only a three-hour ride under a tropical sun. The heat of the air would have been bearable, but the immediate effect of the sun is terrible! Everyone seemed to have the same sentiment as I did, for our conversations became ever more monosyllabic and finally fell into complete silence. Then, at a bend in the road, a long, straw-covered adobe building suddenly appeared.

"Who could have built a barn in the *mata* [a dense vegetation of brush and woods], so far from all the plantations?" I asked, full of surprise.

"That is the church," said Mr. Quimby with a half-smile and turned immediately into a small side road heading toward the building.[115]

115. Presumably, Ina visited a church opened in 1871 by thirty Baptists, one of two "fragile structures" (the other being the Hopewell Church, established in 1870 by thirteen Presbyterians on land that was part of Fazenda São Luiz) in the vicinity of the Santa Bárbara Station. This church definitely was not the better-known interdenominational chapel inaugurated at Campo in 1871, for the latter was entirely constructed of wood, surrounded by plantations, and accessible by a better road.

My surprise was almost horror—this was a church, this barn with adobe walls full of holes, a straw roof, window holes without frames, let alone windows?! But I could no longer doubt it: our society rode up, the gentlemen jumped off their horses, helped us from ours, and tied the animals to some trees next to the building. Then I noticed a number of other horses and mules that were standing around, as well as riders of both genders who were sitting here and there in the shadows or who were already in the "church," and whom Mr. Quimby and his family came up to greet. "How do you do?" was heard from all sides, and in between this came repeatedly the jovial, "How d'ye?" [originals in English] of the Southern states, and then they informed each other of all the happenings in this solitary place since the last "third Sunday of the month." A drink from the nearby well somewhat refreshed our worn-out spirits. Then we entered the building, where, after we swept the benches with a broom, we gratefully enjoyed the cool silence for a bit, while fifty to sixty people gathered there gradually, almost all of them without exception Americans coming from their plantations or from the colony Santa Bárbara.[116]

I watched the scene outside through a big hole in the adobe wall, noting how the congregation became more lively with the new arrivals, their horses and their mules grazing, and the colorful riding dresses of the ladies hanging in the trees. I had never sat in a church like this before. Behind me, a young mother tried in vain to calm her young, screaming child, who obviously did not enjoy the outing. Soon there sat down next to me an old, white-haired little mother who had previously amazed me when I saw through the wall how cheerfully she came riding up on her mule.

After a while the preacher came and the service began. He was still a young man without a gown or any other insignia of spiritual office. He stepped with great simplicity before the wooden altar (there was of course no pulpit) and, only a Bible in hand, he gave a very sophisticated, very beautiful sermon about Christ's answer to John the Baptist's question: "Are you he who should come, or should we wait for another?"[117] Grete, such a thing could make one pious. It was deeply moving to hear those words from the Bible being spoken there in that mud hut, in these tropical surroundings so divested of any other

116. The "colony" consisted of individual Americans, who, like Col. Norris, had purchased land very close to the Santa Bárbara Station.

117. The preacher had to have been the Rev. William B. Bagby, who, in March 1881, replaced the first Baptist parson at this Santa Bárbara church, Elijah H. Quillin. Bagby was a young missionary accompanied by his wife, Anne Luther Bagby. In 1883, the couple, who would spend over fifty years as missionaries and teachers in Brazil, departed for the Brazilian Northeast.

sacred objects, those we civilized people are accustomed to associate with the hour of the catechism or with the sacred halls of our churches—we who unconsciously evoked them in such an ambience. And they didn't sound any different than at home, neither less serious nor less solemn than in lavishly decorated cathedrals behind colorful banners with awesome columns rising upward. I had not been in a church for a long time, but I doubt that the most dazzling mass in St. Peter's Cathedral could have even approached the impression that our simple evangelical service in this lost outpost in the middle of Brazil made upon me. The thought of the omnipresence of Christ and the sermon—"God does not live in temples made by the hands of men"—asserted itself with a powerful immediacy and a certain poignant grandeur, even for those who were not seeking such an impression.

The oppressive heat had somewhat let up after a while, a light wind began to stir, and suddenly I saw through the holes in the adobe hut large drops of rain. . . . The saddles! The rain became stronger very rapidly, so that no other option remained than to bring the saddles and the riding clothes into the church if one didn't wish to have a highly unpleasant ride home. About sixty saddles and thirty riding outfits took a place in the corner of the church, and I thought with a smile about the fact that what appeared completely natural here would have probably seemed exceptional in a European church or chapel.

The rain stopped as suddenly as it had begun, and when the service was over and everyone had said their farewells for one month, the saddles could be put in place again.

We went home in a far better mood in the cooler, dust-free air. In the evening, Mr. Quimby and his sister-in-law brought me again to São Sebastião, promising to pick me up again soon.

But here is the old, portly Anna, calling at my door: "Cha, Senhora"—I am finished.

Write soon to your jaunty Amazon, Ulla

São Sebastião

August 5, 1882

Dear Gretel!

This letter will probably turn out a little scatterbrained, as I am writing to the barking of thirty-seven dogs. Since yesterday, there has been a hunting party gathering, and Mr. de Sousa has invited six gentlemen, each of whom has brought one or two horses and as many dogs as he owns. The bigger the pack, the greater and more impressive the hunt. Yesterday I saw the hunters flash by in the forest, following a roebuck—it looked quite good, and, at any rate, it was the sort that could be hunted as befits this country. But we never had any of the game. Two slain animals have been hanging on the wall of the tack room since yesterday, and when I asked Dona Maria Luísa when they would appear on the table as a roast, she smiled and said that roebucks are not fit food for people; they were for the dogs! I was about to get my dander up when I remembered at the right moment that Mr. Schaumann had, in fact, told me once that here deer meat is far too bitter for it to be enjoyed by human beings.[118] So then, we will continue happily along eating our *carne de porco* [pork meat], although I have to say that Dona Maria Luísa does everything in order to bring some variation to the food. We have eaten all sorts of animals, even armadillo one time, which tastes quite good, somewhat like tender veal or chicken. The armor of this tropical inhabitant is proudly displayed in my room as a decoration piece. Right after it has been skinned, the armor is quite soft and can be bent into any form you want. Afterwards, it will then harden and remain in that shape.

Indeed, I collect as many curiosities as I can, although this is much more difficult than one commonly thinks at home in Germany. We imagine the process of collecting curiosities as if one could simply snatch up arrows from the Indians and find other wondrous things on the side of the road. I now know that the objects here are very expensive and difficult to acquire. So I

118. Gustav Schaumann's pharmacy, founded in 1858, on the Rua de São Bento in downtown São Paulo, was named the Botica Ao Veado D'Ouro—the Pharmacy at the Golden Deer. A well-known center of homeopathic medications, it closed in 2008, still in the same location.

make do with a very modest cabinet of natural curiosities of my own collection. The Negroes bring me everything strange that they find outdoors, and they positively beam when I am happy about it. They call me *a professora que gosta dos bixos feios* [the teacher who likes ugly creatures], and almost every day I find some beetle or caterpillar or a strange plant arranged on my windowsill. I have already "preserved" a snake for myself—and indeed, a very pretty coral snake. In particular, I have a collection of charming nests, among which there are delightful hummingbird nests of different sorts and an even stranger, very large, nest made out of mud. This nest is made by a medium-sized bird that people here have named after its dwelling place: *joão-de-barro*, or mudjohn. The mud nest is somewhat bigger than a human head, and the entrance is so inventively designed—namely, toward the sides—that rain cannot get into the nest. On the inside, one can find the really soft, little nest.

My latest acquisition is an otter's coat and the most lovely skin of a black monkey that a *camarada* just recently killed on the plantation. And yesterday, Maricota, who is always dear and kind, brought me a very nice collection of twenty-one types of wood that she had collected by herself and cut into delicate, uniform samples. By the way, according to our standards, they waste wood here in São Sebastião to a terrible degree. For example, my chest of drawers, a heavy, clumsily made thing, was constructed completely from cedar, just like the crude furniture in the classroom is made out of the most expensive wood. Again, this is an example of one of the many incongruities in this country between waste, on the one hand, and deficiency on the other.

Evening: Gretel, I am beside myself with joy! Just now, Maricota interrupted me with the delightful message that we are going to the seashore at Santos, for five to six weeks of bathing! So soon I will see my beloved São Paulo again! First, we must go there, where we are staying one or two days in the house of Dona Maria Luísa's parents. From there, we will travel over the Serra [do Mar] to Santos, the large coffee port of the province of São Paulo. We are going to live in a house belonging collectively to the entire family, where those who want to bathe in the sea can stay. It is located on the *barra*,—that is, on the beach at the entry to the bay, outside the city.[119]

119. The "Barra," a popular vacation beach on the Bay of Santos, designated where the estuary emptying into the bay had deposited an enormous bar of silt and sand—precisely where

Adieu, adieu, I have to write quickly to Fräulein Meyer, who is for the moment also with the family in Santos. She will be happy to have company.

Your Ulla, happy

---

ships entered that channel in order to reach the port on the mainland side of the island. The beach house was owned by the Companhia Souza Queiroz, the export-import firm whose proprietors were the intermarried Aguiars, Barros, Souza Barros, Whitakers, and Souza Queiroz. Thus visiting nephew Luís Guilherme was the son of widowed Dona Ilídia Malfada de Souza Barros, sister of Dona Maria Luísa, and João Guilherme de Aguiar Whitaker (deceased), the son of Britain's vice-consul in Santos, who had married Angela da Costa Aguiar, Mr. Sousa's (Bento Aguiar de Barros) first cousin.

SANTOS

August 20, 1882

My dear and good Grete!

I'm telling you, this house is terribly poetic—pardon me, I have to chase away this wasp . . . so, what I wanted to say: a pure idyll! Outside, the waves are cresting and breaking—Good God! That is the fifth spider I have seen today that is as big as a hand!—and the sun is shining outside and makes the waves—not another fly in the inkwell?—glisten like silver. The garden is a little neglected, but for precisely this reason, so much the more romant . . . well, I just noticed that the cockroaches have also been nibbling at my new writing case!—romantic. It is indeed charming when we see the ships coming in from afar—oh these mosquitoes, forgive the blot—and I take out the binoculars immediately whenever a large ship comes into view in order to determine its nationality. Ah, poor me, the table in front of me is swarming with ants! Why on earth did I leave the sugar bowl there! So for the moment—a break in order to kill ants. . . .

Later: You see, my Gretel, that poetry here comes with difficulties attached. Everything here is an idyll with impediments. These *chakara* (that's what they call the buildings here that are half-mansion, half-country house) were doubtless built earlier for human habitation, but for a seemingly long time, cockroaches, spiders, lizards, and ants have been able to establish themselves here unchallenged and in such a homely fashion that one can hardly blame them now for not wanting to give up their uncontested position of absolute authority only with difficulty and very gradually.[120]

My first night here was nothing other than a constant "struggle with the insect," but since I spent all of my leisure time thinking about the best means of defense, it seems to me as if I am finally beginning to claim the rightful position of human being against these power-hungry fellow creatures. My bed is

120. In the 1880s, *chácaras* (which Ina misspells with a *k*, a letter not found in Portuguese) were coming into vogue as rustic vacation homes for the middle classes in São Paulo and Rio de Janeiro. Santos, at sea level, not only hosted armies of insects but also enjoyed a reputation as a pesthole for many diseases—yellow fever, malaria, cholera, and smallpox. Inland, the higher elevation of the plateau meant that those diseases were less prevalent.

in the middle of the room, and I have no furniture against the wall; I have conceded the wall to "the insect." By furniture I mean the washstand, a table, a chair, and my suitcase. The last serves as a chest of drawers and in general as a storage place for all my property except for my clothes. After having nailed down a wide, old curtain, I hung a bed sheet over my clothes and set them up in a picturesque manner on the wall, but I only use them according to the precautions such as one finds on the labels of medicine bottles: "Shake well before using." The way in which a collection of insects pile up on the floor after such a procedure teaches me how wise I am to follow these precautions. With my washstand I have at least the satisfaction, now that it is far from the wall, of enjoying the sole use of my soap and not finding it in the morning half-eaten by cockroaches. They seem to regard it as a quite particular delicacy. It cost me more thought to figure out how to bring my bed under the most favorable insect-conditions. The first night it stood against the wall to the great joy of the local spiders, cockroaches, lizards, and ants. The second night I pushed it away from the wall so that only the head of the bed stood against the wall, but even this, as I found out, did not essentially impede the movements of the aforementioned inhabitants of the house. So on the third day I pushed the bed into the middle of the room, and the comical position had the additional advantage of teaching me how to hold my balance in my sleep. For the first night that I spent "in the open air" like that began with me sliding from the side of my Spartan encampment, which had no walls on the side. Of course, this cost some cockroaches their lives. After this experience, I had then convinced myself that these pleasant little critters have a special preference for the striking strip on a matchbox, putting us at risk by obliging us to remain in total darkness, even with a full box of matches. I put the chair next to my bed, placed the candle one arm's length from my bed on the floor, and then put the matchbox along with the clock and my towel secretly under my pillow, on top of which I sleep—it being the size used by Brazilians—so very uncomfortably. Only the ant problem remained to be solved. This, too, I finally managed to do satisfactorily, by imitating what I had recently seen on a table in a train station restaurant: I placed all four feet of the bed in tin containers filled with water so that now—hurrah!—the insects remain limited as to the attacks they can perpetrate against me, those they can do only from the ceiling.

Other than that, these interesting cohabitants are valuable inasmuch as they care for our continual entertainment. Every morning when we drink coffee, the sugar jar has to go outside so that the ants can be smoked out, while Maricota and I fish them out of the milk. In the afternoon, we are now so used to the flies at the edges of the plates that I now imagine a meal without these ornaments as quite gloomy. In the evening, when the cockroaches become cheerful, this becomes the main attraction. Maricota and I usually sit in my room hunched over our Dickens, and next door in the dining room Dona Maria Luísa, her sister, and Mr. de Sousa are playing whist with a straw man. Suddenly we hear an unholy noise, people are screaming and everyone's morning slippers go flying. Then we, too, immediately grab our boots, ready at hand, and fling them against the door, since the endangered insect has flown in from the whist players' room through the crack in the door a hand's breadth wide toward us Pickwickians. It does this only to find its rather certain demise here, for I have practice in the destruction of flying cockroaches from my days at the colégio.

"Life in and with nature" is, generally speaking, the coat of arms on our banner. At around five o'clock in the morning, or at about the time when the moon, as a farewell, pulls his most sour face at the sun, every single inhabitant of the house jumps into the lap of the waves. Men and women, black and white, everyone marches in flannel bathing suits through the garden onto the beach into the water in order to refresh one's limbs in moonlight in the most beautiful harmony. There is a devil of a shrieking that deafens me for the entire coming day, and since bathing in the sea doesn't really appeal to me at any rate, after the first five days I withdrew myself from the throng. Now, as before, I bathe in one of the typically large and round tin tubs that the Negro women carry on their heads.

The evening tends to come to a close in an opposite manner, namely in the most harmless of ways. Our *chácara* is rather isolated; on one side there is a big garden and on the other side there is an uninhabited *chácara*. From the beach side, however, it is impossible to close off the house. Then in the evening, we make a barricade with a table and two chairs piled up in front of the glass door, and then we take leave for the night. . . . If I know you, this side of our beach idyll would appeal to you in particular!

The lessons are progressing as usual, it is only that—unfortunately, to the great disappointment of the family and my greatest joy—the piano lessons have ceased. Exactly for this reason, I regard this bathing season like a recreational trip!

But I haven't even told you how it was in São Paulo. We stayed there for two days and took up a lodging with Maricota's grandparents. On the first day, I spent the afternoon with the Schaumanns, and on the second day, I spent it with Fräulein Harras, who was staying with Fräulein Meyer. She, unfortunately, had already returned to Santos with her family. On the third morning we came back here, along the imposing road over the Serra with the funicular, and just imagine who was also going there—Mr. Hall![121] He sat next to me in the coupé and told me that he was going to Santos because he had been notified of a shipment of machines from England that he wanted to pick up from customs himself. Since then, I have not seen him again, but Grete, I believe—we were both happy about the fine machines having arrived at just that moment.

Oh Grete, I am so happy! And Brazil is truly very beautiful!

More later from your Ulla

121. "The funicular" referred to the celebrated final section of the Santos-Jundiaí line of the Sao Paulo Railway Company, Ltda. (*a Inglêsa*), which descended the escarpment of the Serra do Mar, from its highest point at Paranapiacaba to its foot at Piaçagüera, just outside Santos. Four sections of steel cable railroad relying on stationary steam engines lowered the cars along a 10.3 degree grade in successively longer stretches that increased from 1,781 meters (5,840') to 3,139 meters (10,300')—an impressive engineering feat completed in 1867.

Fig. 12. Petrópolis: Imperial Palace and residential neighborhood, 1875. *Photographer*: Marc Ferrez. Digital Image Courtesy of the Getty's Open Content Program. A neighborhood (foreground) adjacent to the Imperial Palace (in the distance) reflects the influence of German-speaking immigrants who settled in Petrópolis during the second half of the nineteenth century. Sharply pitched roofs constructed of wood shingles contrast markedly with the Portuguese curved tile roofs otherwise used in the city. Gingerbread trim on the houses proclaims the special identity of the immigrants and their Brazilian descendants.

Fig. 13. Petrópolis: Waiting for the arrival of the train, 1885. *Photographer*: Marc Ferrez. Digital Image Courtesy of the Getty's Open Content Program. In late 1881, Ina von Binzer could take the train to Petrópolis only half way up the mountain, but a year later the railroad reached the city, thanks to the construction of several spectacular bridges. Travelers disembarked at a station reflecting German architectural elements, greeted by a multiplicity of horse-drawn vehicles patiently awaiting their arrival.

Fig. 14. Petrópolis: Tourists taking a nature walk, ca. 1880. *Photographer*: Marc Ferrez. Digital Image Courtesy of the Getty's Open Content Program. Known as "the Imperial City" because Emperor D. Pedro I had purchased the land on which it was built, Petrópolis provided D. Pedro II with his summer residence for over forty years. Simultaneously, Petrópolis provided refuge for residents fleeing Rio de Janeiro during yellow fever season. In 1883, the arrival of the railroad sealed the special identity of the Imperial City as Brazil's first popular tourist destination, one offering beautiful natural vistas, clear and cooling mountain air, cascading waterfalls, and a range of classy European-style hotels.

Fig. 15. The Rua da Assembléia, downtown Rio de Janeiro, 1880s–1890s. Photographer unknown. Courtesy of the Museu de Som e Imagem. By the 1880s, "Centro," Rio de Janeiro's downtown, had become a more commercial neighborhood and, residentially, lower-middle- or working-class. The wealthier middle classes were abandoning it to the poor, who increasingly could be found living in tenements called *cortiços* (beehives), carved out of once-grand upper-class mansions and townhouses. Newly constructed homes on the hillsides of Laranjeiras, Cosme Velho, Santa Teresa, and Glória, as well as the appearance of beach neighborhoods in Flamengo, Catete, and Botafogo, testified to the city's spatial extension southward from the historic center. Coffee boomed, fueling both the exodus of middle-class sectors from Centro and the arrival of wealthy outsiders from the Paraíba Valley who residentially colonized the capital's southern flanks.

Fig. 16. The Arches of Lapa (Os Arcos da Lapa), Rio de Janeiro's aqueduct, ca. 1890. Photographer unknown. Courtesy of the Museu de Som e Imagem. An icon of the city of Rio de Janeiro, the Arcos were constructed between 1725 and 1744 of an extremely resistant type of concrete made from stone, lime, and whale oil. They carried water from a natural spring on the heights of Corcovado Mountain to the Largo do Carioca in the very center of the imperial capital. At the close of the nineteenth century, the Arcos were converted to an elevated tramway for streetcars connecting downtown to Santa Teresa, an adjacent, hilly neighborhood enjoying fabulous 360-degree views of the city and Guanabara Bay.

Fig. 17. Equestrian Statue of Emperor D. Pedro I, in the originally named Largo do Rocio, Rio de Janeiro, ca. 1875–80. *Photographer*: Marc Ferrez. Digital Image Courtesy of the Getty's Open Content Program. Ina von Binzer praised this earliest of monumental statues erected in the imperial capital, one still standing in today's renamed Praça Tiradentes. Brazil's first monarch, who went into permanent exile in 1831, is shown with the Constitution of 1824 in hand. He himself arbitrarily revised the country's first national charter after dismissing the legislators assembled to draft it. In the 1890s, with the establishment of the First Republic, the *praça* was renamed the Praça da Constituição (Constitution Plaza).

Fig. 18. Panoramic view of Laranjeiras and Sugar Loaf, Rio de Janeiro, ca. 1890. *Photographer*: Marc Ferrez. Digital Image Courtesy of the Getty's Open Content Program. Taken from the top of Corcovado Mountain, this vista looks down on the neighborhood of Laranjeiras and outward, toward Sugar Loaf in the distance. The intervening Botafogo Estuary, soon to be developed as the city's famed marina, is partly hidden from view. In the 1880s, coffee barons from the Paraíba Valley were building *palacetes* (mansions) in Botafogo, turning it into an elite residential neighborhood that in the 1890s would become home for a new class of republican legislators. Laranjeiras, a neighborhood of mansions belonging to the former imperial elite, continued to be an upper-class redoubt of beautiful gardens and secluded, spacious homes for the wealthy.

Fig. 19. Corridor of the Imperial Palms (Alameda das Palmeiras), Botanical Garden, Rio de Janeiro, 1885. *Photographer*: Marc Ferrez. Digital Image Courtesy of the Getty's Open Content Program. Although Ina von Binzer believed it overrated, the Alameda das Palmeiras is universally acclaimed for its stately grace. A year after founding the Botanical Garden in 1808, Regent Dom João VI planted a sole palm (*Roystonea oleracea*) that originated in the Caribbean. Regarded as the Palma Mater (mother palm), because all of the 128 trees in the Garden's Alameda came from its seeds, the tree first flowered in 1829, then grew to a height of 38.7 meters, and, finally, died in 1972, struck by lightning. Meanwhile, acclaimed as the "imperial palm," the tree proliferated so rapidly that its progeny became closely associated with the nobility of the Second Empire. Hence, the coffee barons of the Paraíba Valley lavishly propagated seeds from the "royal palm" throughout their plantations, cities, and towns (see fig. 5).

Fig. 20. Silva Prado Family Photos. Photographers unknown. Courtesy of the Acervo Danda Prado.

Top: Ina von Binzer, holding Vercingetorix (Martinho da Silva Prado Neto), São Paulo, 1882. This low-resolution print is the only known photograph of Ina von Binzer. The date and place, scribbled on the back, led to identification of the toddler, whom Ina called "Mucius" (after a youthful hero of Republican Rome), as the most recent child of Martinico da Silva Prado and Albertina de Morais Pinto, born January 3, 1881. The photo shows a smiling Ina, thriving in the household where the children she called "My Romans" kept her wondering about their father´s republican child-rearing practices, but happy to be living in an urban space that inscribed a German-speaking community and an English beau.

Bottom: Martinico da Silva Prado and Albertina de Morais Pinto with their twelve children, São Paulo, 1890. Lavínia, at twenty the eldest, is seated on her mother's right, while Caio Graco (father of historian Caio Prado Jr.), at eighteen and the second eldest, stands behind her, immediately to the right of Martinico, his father. Martinho Neto, seated on the floor below Lavínia, is now about nine. He will soon be off to Wiesbaden for his secondary education in Germany. Graduating in 1898, he will fulfill the family penchant for grounding the children's education in European culture.

Fig. 21. Delivering coffee at the Port of Santos, São Paulo, 1885. *Photographer*: Marc Ferrez. Digital Image Courtesy of the Getty's Open Content Program. Although the horse-drawn cart at left is delivering bags of coffee beans, by 1885 the railroad that reached the Port of Santos from the city of São Paulo as early as 1867 delivered almost all of the coffee produced in the interior. By 1888, Santos would surpass Rio de Janeiro as Brazil's busiest port. Abolition immediately opened the floodgates to European immigration, providing a rising labor supply that western São Paulo's entrepreneurial coffee planters exploited to the maximum. By then, the Port of Santos no longer was filled with sailing ships, but boasted docks visited by steamships that departed with bags of coffee for Hamburg and New York or disembarked tens of thousands of immigrants from Europe each year.

Fig. 22. Princess Isabel on the balcony of the Imperial Palace, displaying the law abolishing slavery, May 13, 1888. *Photographer*: A. Luis Ferreira. Digital Image Courtesy of the Getty's Open Content Program. The Imperial Palace, known as the Paço Imperial, was both royal residence and a seat of government. As regent, Princess Isabel signed the bill abolishing slavery into law in one of the rooms of the Paço after the bill's adoption by the Imperial Parliament. Moving to the balcony, she displayed the just-signed law to the waiting crowd of abolitionist supporters. Less an act of Parliament and more the consequence of the slaves themselves, who deserted the coffee plantations of São Paulo en masse in 1887–88, the abolition of slavery has been falsely interpreted as the "gift of the throne," thanks to Princess Isabel's signature on the bill.

Santos

September 22, 1882

To my dearest Grete!

Our beach idyll is coming to an end. Hardly eight more days will go by and the thirty-two pieces of luggage with which we came will be repacked and brought home to São Sebastião. I regret this from the bottom of my heart, for I have gotten so used to life in the *chácara*—in spite of the conditions here that are more suited to entomologists than to other mortals—that I have truly begun to love it. Whether or not the lack of music in our place of residence here could make a difference in this opinion—we'll just close a well-wishing eye and look the other way. By the way, as a replacement for the piano lessons I had to teach the only son of Dona Lídia, Dona Maria Luísa's sister, during bathing time. Dona Lídia is a widow and usually doesn't have her own governess, but always gives her Luís Guilherme (Ludwig Wilhelm) to one of her many sisters in São Paulo to have him as a pedagogical guest.[122] All of the *professoras* of the family already knew him and claimed to be tired of him. So I was then not very delighted to have been asked whether or not I would take him along with Maricota during her lessons, as I feared a repetition of my time in classical antiquity in São Paulo. But lo, he turned out to be a quite well behaved, even pleasant and very intelligent, thirteen-year-old boy. He was already playing at being a gentleman during walks, and I have noticed nothing wrong with him up until the present moment, other than the fact that he is somewhat stiff and claims to have gout in his feet. I am the fourteenth among the teachers that he has had in his rapidly alternating—as you can see—school career. He recently said to his mother that of the fourteen, I am the most rational. I am not a little proud of this, and you must admit that one ought not to deny him a certain capability of judgment in this respect.

Luís Guilherme is my most expert provider of creatures, like clams. Of course, I collect these sorts of things in a way that can even be directly dan-

122. Here Ina uses the actual names of "Dona Maria Luísa's" (Francisca Miquelina de Souza Barros) widowed full sister and her son: "Dona Lídia" was Ilídia de Souza Barros, who had married João Guilherme de Aguiar Whitaker, the son of the British vice-consul in Santos, and "Luís Guilherme" was that couple's only son—Luís Guilherme de Aguiar Whitaker. Thus a third generation of intermarried cousins was vacationing at Santos by 1882.

gerous for public safety. Both a small, empty room next to mine and my own windowsill are continually "fragrant" in the most penetrating way with seaweed and rotting clams. It is a true cross for me to bear, but I have had the following experience here: if the rage to collect has grabbed a hold of anyone, then nothing ends up being sacred anymore, not even one's own nose!

Today Mr. de Sousa is coming back from the *fazenda*, where he was making sure that his instructions were followed. During his absence, it was not exactly calm, especially since a couple of days before his departure, or rather a couple of nights, there was a break-in and robbery quite close to us. The morning of his departure he came up to me during breakfast with a big revolver and said that I am probably the most courageous of the eternally feminine company, and for that reason, he was laying the defense of the place in my hands. I have to confess that this was my first acquaintance with a revolver or with any other instrument of death, but I boldly accepted my role as the well-armed occupant of the *chácara*, and, only for the purpose of greater security—for myself—I had the thing explained to me by a German acquaintance in our neighborhood. Since then, it rests threateningly on my wall, and indeed, it makes an extremely terrifying impression contrasted with my calico clothes and dresses. It had its first effect on the Negro woman, who since that moment has been incapable of being persuaded to clean my room. Another precaution that we took was to collect all of the women during the day and parade them conspicuously without jewelry and in their worst clothing along the *praia*, that is, along the beach, in order to demonstrate to the thieves that there is nothing worth stealing in our house—a precaution that certainly did not fail to have the most striking effect on the thieves! Finally, we also refined the construction of the barricade in the evening. An available wicker sofa was added to the table, the number of chairs was increased to five, and the whole thing was made somewhat more "wobbly"; a couple of empty drawers crowned the work—that was my invention! And the whole thing, when it had been built up, always made a strong impression on all of us. Today we will probably go back to barricade number one, and I will again place the defense in Mr. de Sousa's hands.

Will he bring me a letter from my Grete upon coming back from São Sebastião? Adieu, my dear, the light is burning, Dickens is claiming his rights, and the hour of the cockroaches is approaching.

Your Ulla

São Sebastião

October 4, 1882

My good Grete!

Here we are again sitting in São Sebastião, and we are waiting for the heat and the sugar cane harvest. We anticipate the latter with great, the former with moderate, desire.

Our departure from the good old dirty *chácara* and our farewell to the bothersome insects was difficult for us, in spite of everything. Except for Mr. de Sousa and Dona Maria Luísa, we all had some form of consolation—the children had the rapidly approaching "sugared" season. I had the small, cheerful Lazão, my favorite horse that I always rode, with whom Mr. de Sousa, smiling, already had promised me a reunion at the station. It is true, riding is my most precious pleasure here—indeed, my only distraction—and when the solitude ever becomes too sad for me, I can be made happy again easily with a particularly beautiful ride.

The richness and charm of the tropical world is enchanting and gives us an almost intoxicating sensation when we ride slowly and silently along the edge of the forest in the evening. Sometimes, for a quarter of an hour, we are accompanied by the voluptuous fragrance of glorious orchids, which bloom in self-sufficient beauty here on their ancient and lonely stems deep in the forest. In the afternoons, in the bright sunlight, blue butterflies the size of one's hand flutter by, almost grazing the heads of our horses.

We also often take walks, and I use these opportunities to complete my collection of "natural curiosities." Just recently I found a whole quantity of huge, empty snail shells, and I could have a whole collection of snakes if I wished to preserve those that have been killed here. A couple of days ago, I killed a somewhat smaller exemplar of these monsters myself with my umbrella, and the young servant girl, when she goes on walks with the little ones, often brings back quite disgusting reptile corpses, for which we then construct a special "mass grave." However, I had to let my collection of beetles diminish right from the start; I could no longer bear the killing, Grete. Whenever I believed I had killed them with chloroform and then they laid themselves down on the window in order to dry themselves in the sun, they often regained their forces after an hour and crawled around sluggishly. That was too revolting for me; my cold-blooded nature seems to be restricted only to cockroaches and snakes. Of the former we have here, thank God, almost none at all, as in general, insects thankfully play a very subordinate role in this plantation situated at a very high altitude. Rather, we suffer most from the extreme atmospheric humidity now regnant, whose season begins again in summer, with the almost daily rains and thunderclaps. In a short while, I will have to make my room into a display stage, if all of my possessions are not to be overrun with mold. By the way, I have discovered an excellent way to prevent mold stains in gloves: You keep the gloves in a box with buckthorn wood—although you have to take the buttons off, lest they become tarnished.

Today my letter writing is being impeded, my dear Gretel, since black beans are being threshed in the open space right in front of my window. Six Negroes are standing in threes across from one another, and they are beating the beans with long bamboo sticks in order to dehusk them. This monotonous sound occurring at regular intervals has been going on since seven o'clock in the morning and has accompanied all of our school lessons today. The occasional singing of our threshers in Germany has been replaced here by a random, but rhythmical, and yet, often completely idiotic, phrase that the first thresher invents or utters, and that the others then repeat, and according to whose rhythm they then go to work. "Que bom cha, que bom" [What good tea, how good] is Cesário's ingenious invention, to whose rhythm the black bean bushes are then beaten. I can claim in all truthfulness that I have heard this imaginary tea being praised probably some thousand times today. By the way, I don't drink Chinese tea here anymore because it prevents me from going to sleep. Instead of this, I drink a lettuce tea in the evenings according to the advice of Dona Maria Luísa. At first, this tea had a dreadful taste for me, but I have now gotten quite accustomed to it, especially as it does indeed have a light calming effect.[123]

What I would give to have a small bottle of beer here in the evening! But that would be impossible to find on the plantations, as it already costs a milreal [i.e., one mil-réis], that is, two marks, for a bottle in the harbor areas! Brazil is, in general, a bad place for drinking. The Brazilians drink a small glass of port in the afternoon, just like we drink for breakfast, but it is usually of such bad quality that we at home would refuse to touch it. It is not even a

123. The leaves, sap (latex), and seeds of wild lettuce (*Lactuca virosa*) were used in nineteenth-century medications. They contain lactucarium, an opium substitute, used as a sedative or analgesic for calming babies or treating insomnia, whooping cough, asthma, and restlessness in children.

table wine that can be enjoyed in greater quantities. The water here in São Sebastião is quite terrible, and it is often totally yellow and muddy. I only drink the red wine from Lisbon that Mr. de Sousa ordered for me out of politeness. Brazilians are not connoisseurs of wine, and, in general, they drink little else than water and coffee. However, they do consume surprising quantities of these two drinks throughout the day.

Gretel, dedicate to me the first glass of punch that you drink after you hear my strong sighs, and do not ever condemn the student when he sings: "A lad like me drinks up entire barrels—entire barrels!" Perhaps he intends to travel to Brazil and is drinking his provisions, and, indeed, he is doing the right thing!

And with this snappy and daring phrase, I will end my letter for today.

Your Ulla

São Sebastião

October 27, 1882

My sweet Grete!

Today I am going to tell you a whole little story, and hopefully you won't find it too mean because it is about—a leper. The whole affair has occupied me so much, and it reminded me automatically of the poignant story by Xavier de Maistre, "Le lépreux d'Aoste," such that I cannot help but share it with my Grete.[124]

Some time ago, before our trip to Santos, I was with the children one evening, and we went walking toward the Negro on horseback who picks up the letters from the station for the plantation. "There he comes," I called joyfully, as something moved in front of us in the twilight.

"But that is not even a man on horseback," laughed the little Albertina. "That is Inacio."[125]

"Who is Inacio?"

"Well—Inacio, you know."

"Is he a Negro from the plantation?"

"Oh yes, but he doesn't work; he is sick."

"What is wrong with him?"

"I don't know, but he has a hole under his foot and on his hand as well, and nothing can cure it."

You know, my dear Gretel, that I have an almost pathological revulsion against all forms of skin disease, so I moved somewhat to the side as we approached the Negro.

A large and by no means insubstantial figure stood before us as we went by, with his hat in his hand. He grinned and murmured, "Sos kiss," and responded to the children's friendly, "Good evening, Inacio, how are you, Inacio?" by repeating, "Thank you, thank you, Senhora: good evening, my little lady, praised be Jesus Christ."

The horribly tattered and dirty clothes of the black man, his wild, woolly hair, and his big, shabby beard, unusually thick for a Negro, gave the man, who

124. De Maistre's "Le lépreux de la Cité d'Aoste" (1811) is a dialogue between a soldier and a leper confined in a tower in Aoste with a view of the Alps. Joaquim Maria Machado de Assis (1839–1908) was influenced by his stories.

125. Albertina was the youngest of the Sousas' three daughters.

was leaning against his cane and dragging himself along with difficulty, such a revolting appearance that the repugnance in me outweighed my sympathy by far. The children were not completely incorrect when they announced later on in the house, laughing, that the mademoiselle had been "afraid" of Inacio.

"What is wrong with him?" I asked instead of defending myself.

"*Quem sabe*! [Who knows!]" said Dona Maria Luísa. "He has holes all over his body and sores against which the most true and tested leaves and herbs do nothing. We almost believe now that he is leprous."

That was said so calmly just like that, as if she were saying that someone had the sniffles. Grete, a chill ran through my whole body. A feeling of unutterable misery for the unhappy one, whom fate seemed not to be able to humiliate deeply enough, overcame me. Negro—slave—leper! It was almost a relief to think that nothing worse could possibly have happened to him. What were his own thoughts on the matter? Would he call for help if he fell into water? Did he hate us, those who were healthy? I pondered this unlucky man the whole day, designated by fate to be a pariah, and his image frightened me in my dreams.

Several days later, someone told me that Inacio had been banished from the immediate surroundings of the courtyard. The Negroes had been forbidden any association with the man so that he would not be able to contaminate anyone with his miserable disease.

How pitifully egotistical is man! My first immediate and almost instinctive feeling was one of relief, relief that I would never again see the savage, limping form of the tattered leper. Only then, however, did I think about his misery and—eventually I attempted to forget this as well.

Soon thereafter I took my usual morning walk. As I was doing so, feeling my health and strength with a sense of joy, I belted out a jolly German song into the Brazilian landscape. . . .

Suddenly, however, the tune broke off in my throat—the leper was there, limping over to me!

Obeying the first lightning-fast impulse that overcame me, I turned around abruptly and was already going along the road at a hurried pace when I came to my senses.

"Noble be man, helpful and good"—I didn't even dare, Grete, to think seriously about this phrase, our favorite saying, as it came into my head. Shame on my insensitive haste! . . . [126] Then a voice appeared in my head seeking to

126. The expression comes from the poem by Goethe entitled "Das Göttliche" (The divine), written in 1783 and first published with Goethe's authorization in 1789.

exculpate me: his appearance had been so sudden that I had not even had a thought about the wretched Negro—But again, no, no, that didn't help. I was ashamed of myself, oh how very ashamed!

The next morning, I traveled along the same road at the same time. That was my penance. At the same place I met the leper, just as I had done so yesterday. His uncovered hair stood up in the morning wind, his clothing hung threadbare around his stout body, his thickly wrapped feet—everything reminded me of his illness. A shudder overcame me, and yet, I forced myself to go on. Then, as he stood about ten paces away from me, the black man turned sideways into the pathless shrubbery, and he walked by me in such a way as to maintain a rather large distance between me and him with the greeting: "Praised be Jesus Christ." My face burned with shame as I thought of my flight yesterday—how unspeakably petty that had been! I wonder if he thought the same thing? I wished that he had not avoided me so scrupulously.

On my way back, I did not see him, but from that moment the leper began to play a role in the life of my mind. I tortured myself with the thought of him, I found myself petty and contemptible in my timidity, then again, foolish and oversensitive in the struggle against a revulsion that everyone here bore openly toward the man; even the unfortunate object of this revulsion himself obviously recognized its validity. Why should I be the only one to bring myself to meet a man whom all other fortunate creatures fled!

Without any resolution in this internal struggle, I found myself the next morning again on the familiar path. As on both of the previous days, I met the leper. Again, he turned into the shrubbery when we were passing by one another. I noticed this time, however, that he wore cleaner clothes and a hat on his head, which he doffed in a lively fashion as he called out zealously "sos kiss" twice. It occurred to me that the poor outcast might receive with a certain satisfaction a morning greeting from one of those more fortunate people, from whose company his misery had banished him. The struggle inside me was over. I decided that he should no longer do without this small consolation.

The following morning I had gotten up and out of the house a little earlier, and, as a result, I met Inacio just as he was coming out of a small hut made of bamboo and adobe, nestled between ferns and brambles. When he saw me, he maintained distance.

"Is that your hut, Inacio?" I called over to him.

"Yes, Senhora, mine," he responded, beaming with joy.

"Where do you go every morning?"

"To get water for the coffee, Senhora."

How many days had gone by, maybe even weeks, and these were perhaps his first spoken words!

Every morning I brought the unhappy man a greeting from the world of human beings, and every time it was a satisfying sight to see his face light up gleefully in the distance behind the high brambles through which he gradually made for himself a road. And yet, my morning walk, which had formerly been the most pleasant part of my day, for a long time remained for me something I had to force myself to do. Above all, I did not sing and cheer anymore when I was on the road.

Then there was our trip to Santos, and thinking about the leper had been pushed into the background. Shortly after our return I was destined to be reminded of him again, as I saw one day that Dona Maria Luísa filled large paper sacks with coffee, rice, sugar, and black beans.

"For whom is that?" I asked.

"The lepers are there," came the answer.

"Inacio?"

"No, the lepers from Santa Bárbara, a whole bunch of these sick people who have formed a sort of colony and beg for their livelihood in order not to spread their horrible suffering by means of money* and going to merchants.** These helpless, sick people are better off in this way than in solitary banishment. For example, whoever has a leper as a slave usually sends him there. They do not suffer want, for everyone gives copiously to them.

"Why don't you let Inacio go over to join them?"

"He doesn't want to because he has a daughter here; we have often suggested it to him."

A sad and moving thought, a family of pariahs, which, cut off from the rest of the world through a common flight, becomes a brotherhood formed in mutual Samaritan exile—the freemasons of misery. . . .

I looked toward the company of sick people going forth, and their grateful "Praised be Jesus Christ" wounded my heart.

On the following day, I did not meet Inacio, so I assumed that he had gone off with his fellow comrades in suffering. On the next day, during the distribution of the rations, when we did not see him at his post behind the barrier, we sent an old Negro to go look for him. The job was a disagreeable one, and the report was uncharitable: Inacio claimed to be sick, or so he said,

* In Brazil there was almost exclusively paper money.

** Shopkeepers.

and yet he could not say what was wrong with him. The whole malady was therefore probably nothing other than physical torpor; he wanted to be served and to avoid the petty toil of cooking. I was surprised and hurt to see that this unkind statement was accepted without hesitation, and I thought about what was to be done if this should continue.

The next morning, however, I met the leper, who looked dirty and neglected, and whose unhappy facial expression and feeble greeting wrung from me the greatest sympathy.

On the very same day, a rain broke out whose intensity and length prevented me from going out for many days. I often thought about Inacio during this time and whether or not he had enough to eat and enough dry kindling in his hut. He was again absent from the distribution of the rations. I would look over in the direction of his hut many times a day and never saw a cloud of smoke going up into the air. Grete, I then struggled with a difficult resolution: Should I enter the leper's hut? A horror shook my whole body merely at the thought of doing so. But: "Noble be man, helpful and good," the warning resonated again in me. For what had I done up until then for the unfortunate man, how had I really been a Samaritan? I blushed at the thought of how much effort it had cost me to do the little that I had done. Actually it was even worse, as I had to admit that my avoidance of the sick man consisted less in the fear of illness—a fear that is always slight for me—but rather, was to be found almost solely in an unreservedly immense disgust. And so much the more did I believe that it was necessary for me to overcome my own impulses. I repeated to myself that I would have done nothing if I did not do this one thing. The struggle was difficult, and the bitter wrestling with myself almost put me into a feverish state. One moment I rejected the idea of entering the leper's hut as a crazy one, and I mocked myself for my imaginary Samaritan duties, especially when the priest and the Levite passed over such duties. May the Lord take care of his own vassals; what did that have to do with me! And then again, I was horrified by my own lack of charitability. I had the feeling that divine providence had purposefully led this unlucky man into my life, as if it were very much something that concerned me, me before all others, and that I, and not anyone else, would be committing an act of sacrilege if I were to leave him lying thus on the road.

I finally resolved to enter the leper's hut, but Grete—and this I will confess to you—the evening before, I had a wild, feverish hope of dying during the night. . . !

Early the next morning, there was a banging on the door. One of the lumberjacks who had come over here from the nearest colony reported that he had heard an audible groan coming from Inacio's hut as he walked by, but that he was afraid to go inside as the poor devil was certainly very ill. A Negro had been sent there in order to look after the poor man and to take care of him with medicine that would restore his strength. I began my lessons, but I could hardly hide my agitation. Just as we were taking a break, the messenger came back. He had found a dead man.

Gretel, a cry for redemption forced itself out of my human—as I was only human after all—breast, and I had to recognize with shame the validity of the phrase *homo sum.* But then, when vigorous crying had loosened my tense nerves, I was able to grant the unfortunate pariah eternal rest without thinking egotistical thoughts centered on myself, and I could not help but imagine that this phrase, which was almost the only phrase that I had ever heard out of his mouth, had almost certainly been his last: "Praised be Jesus Christ."

An old, almost unusable, oxcart was drawn up, and two Negroes carried away the dead man, who had been laid in a hammock, to his final resting place. The day was already descending rapidly into twilight when they came to the village and stopped in front of the residence of the chaplain in order to consult with him about the burial of the corpse in one of the graves that was always ready to receive the dead. But such a late burial, and, in addition, the burial of a black man—an impertinent request! There was a gruff communication to them that they would have to wait until the following morning. "But that's impossible, we have to go home, sir, where would we stay here overnight?" the Negroes remonstrated. "Allow us, then, to put the corpse ourselves in the churchyard and then go home." This request as well was curtly denied, so that the enraged people had finally threatened to place the corpse of the leper on the doorstep of the Christian clergyman. Then the priest ordered that the lepers in the colony be fetched and that these would look over the corpse during the night in front of the gate of the churchyard. The silent brotherhood of the sick then came, and these outcasts of humanity held the nighttime vigil for their former comrade in misery, whom human beings had themselves pushed out of their community even beyond death.

I remember that during that night, the brightly gleaming constellation of the cross [the Southern Cross] stood in the sky. But now I often reflect whenever I see this holy sign: Why does it shine on the earth! I don't wish to add anything more for today, my Gretel, but I will send this away as soon as possible with the next letters.

Sua Ulla

São Sebastião

November 17, 1882

Today the children and I had the same feeling as the horseman that rode over Lake Constance; we had a nice scare in retrospect. During our walk, the glorious weather enticed us to extend our journey rather far away, and we came across a large sugarcane plantation. We saw in one spot that the barely ripe sugarcane had been cut out in a large, square-shaped pattern. We were all surprised about this odd harvest, cut out in pieces, and we talked about it when we came home. "Oh, those are *maraus*, Senhora," Cesário, who was there at the time, said. "I recently thought I saw smoke rising up late in the evening over there in the forest, but it was too dark and foggy to distinguish anything exactly."

You can imagine my fright when I received the following answer to my question, "What are *maraus*?"

"Oh, you have to watch out for them very carefully and, from now on, you aren't to wander off so far alone. *Maraus* are slaves who have run away and become savages; they have fled into the forest and live there just like wild beasts, plundering the neighborhood wherever they can.[127] Together, they steal the necessities of life, usually from the plantations, and, less frequently, they plant some beans and corn for themselves in the forest. They are even more dreaded than the Indians. In recent years, Negroes that have been let free and are too lazy to work join up with them. These bands are terrible wounds for Brazil, and they would be even more terrible if not for the fact that they often die because of their savage lifestyles. In general, their ability to reproduce is limited; women seldom join these bands, and so we hope that within a generation, they will be gone."

From now on, I will hardly have the courage to do more than slink around the house in a cowardly manner, for these *maraus* have most definitively ruined my delight in our more far-reaching walks.

The oppressive weight caused by the presence of this black race—and the fact that slavery is ultimately a far greater curse for the slaveholders than for the Negroes themselves—is being revealed most forcefully at the very moment that slavery must be given up. What, for God's sake, are these millions of free black people going to do here! At home in Germany, where people

127. Applied here as a local variant on *quilombola*, *marau* referred to an escaped and therefore a free-roaming slave who kept moving to avoid capture.

have almost no idea about the conditions of the Brazilian interior, many will think (and I probably would have claimed the same thing had I stayed in Germany) that the slaves would certainly stay on the plantations of their former masters and work there for wages as free people. The very poverty of their situation would teach them to become industrious workers and valuable citizens! Here, however, I can see that nothing like this will happen. Even a comparison with the conditions in the North American Union is inappropriate. First of all, they do not have any examples of industriousness here as they do over there. The North American respects work and those who do work; he himself will labor and unabashedly use his hands. He despises only the inferior racial status of the black person. The Brazilian, less scrupulous, and, on the other hand, more arrogant, although less educated, precisely despises work and those who do work. He himself will not work if he can avoid it somehow. He regards doing nothing as an attribute of the free man. How can one therefore expect that the slave, raised in beastlike ignorance, is able to, or will be able to, extract himself from such tendencies and form his own independent philosophical opinion?! He will calmly reiterate the opinion of the white race and work as little as possible, and how little this "possible" is can only be measured here on the spot, influenced by the gentleness of tropical nature and the simply unbelievable lack of ambition of these people. Since I have come here, I have accrued an interest for these things that, of course, infinitely surpasses what I had in former times. I read much about these matters, and then I came to the realization that many a connoisseur of the tropics has come to the same conclusions as those that I have reached here.

Smarda says exactly the same thing in his dictum: "In the tropics, no one works for pleasure—why should the Negro, who is free of wants, do so?"

Lewes writes: "Hunger is the true fire of life, that from which all impetus to work and activity stems, and we can look wherever we want to, we find in hunger the motivating force that sets the immeasurable chain of making and doing into motion. If food is present in abundance and easy to procure, civilization will become impossible."[128] That is true here: the necessities for life

128. Ina refers to Ludwig Carl Schmarda (1819–1908), an Austrian zoologist whose scientific travels in the Southern Hemisphere took him to Brazil, Argentina, Chile, and Peru and produced his three-volume study, *Reise um die Erde in den Jahren 1853–1857* (Braunschweig: G. Westermann, 1861). Her reference to Lewes is to George Henry Lewes (1817–78), English philosopher and self-taught scientist who engaged in discussions of Darwinism, positivism, and religious skepticism—better recalled as the life partner and soul mate of novelist George Eliot (Mary Ann Evans). Lewes studied in Germany for several years as a young man, and the couple began their unconventional "marriage" in Weimar and Berlin in 1854, where Lewes researched and completed his multivolume *The Life and Works of Goethe*, published in 1855.

are present or at least easy to procure, and ambition [*Ehrgeiz*] or lust for gain [*Erwerbssin*], which would suffice to push the slave to labor for himself, is foreign to the temperament of both the slave and those who have been freed, with few exceptions. Why should these attributes suddenly be found in their children, who are growing up amid complete idleness? And the ingenious Fernando Schmid (Dranmor), the forty-year-old observer of Brazilian life, claims in his main article:

> Fieldwork is detested by no one more intensely than the free Negro. It is not like the Southern states of the American Union, where one has the following philosophy: "When the sun is burning on your head, earn from the sweat of your brow that with which you will be able to cover the nakedness of your body when icy frost covers the earth." In Brazil, that blessed place—or rather in those districts where, unfortunately, only compulsory labor produces all of the important tropical commodities—the African race is superior to ours inasmuch as it knows how to wallow year after year in a life of plenty, a life that fits perfectly with its aspirations. As soon as this race ceases to be subject to discipline, it doesn't need to worry about its daily bread, which is easy to procure. A regeneration in terms of mentality is out of the question.[129]

The same thing is happening here in Brazil that happened in Jamaica according to an article from an older issue of the *Economiste Français* that recently fell into my hands. The paper says: "Next to the abolition of differential duties, not taking into account the leavening of the differential tax, it was the emancipation of the slaves that wiped out the prosperity of the formerly flourishing English possession of Jamaica. The Negroes gave in to idleness, and even today they do not earn that which they need to survive from the plantations: the island needs to hire one hundred thousand 'coolies.'"

I have the impression, according to my own observations, that, initially, Brazil is going to suffer horribly because of the abolition of slavery. This will happen especially because they have not yet decided to create better conditions for European and, specifically, for the most useful Germanic immigrants. Brazil will suffer from two events: on the one hand, because of the decline in the labor force in the countryside, and, on the other hand, because of

129. Presumably, Ina is quoting from Dranmor, "Lied aus der Verbannung." See n. 79, above.

the sudden deluge of its cities with noxious and, in the best-case scenario, useless, elements of the population.

One now understands rather well what Brazil can expect and hope for from the first two generations of its free, black fellow citizens. Only a small, declining portion of the men are staying behind as free agricultural workers in the countryside. Only a small percentage of all of them have become, if not particularly helpful, at least not disruptive or harmful members of the free society. An increase in work and productivity from the black population beyond the most modest needs of its own people, however, an increase that would be beneficial for the entire country, be it in the realms of agriculture or industry, will probably remain inconceivable until many decades go by—if it is even possible at all.

I have already written to you about the old, abused slaves that have been freed, and how they are often exposed to the most intense misery. I once read that an old Negro woman froze to death because she could not find a place to stay the very night of her emancipation in a small, high mountain town. Indeed, the number of both male and female beggars with whom the emancipation of slaves has graced Brazil's cities is practically overwhelming. I do not know whether it is some form of irony that moved the police in São Paulo to provide them all—with numbers! The younger women, especially the mulattas, are to a large extent morally depraved, and they certainly would not even come near any work if they could somehow exist without it. The older women take advantage of others as much as they can. They eat today with their former masters, the next day with their parents, one time in the kitchen with slave friends, another time they will throw together a cheap lunch consisting of bananas and some bread. Anyone who knows the sleeping place of a Negro woman knows that it can be set up anywhere. A mat and a towel over one's head are easy to find. They earn the little money that they do still need usually by washing or sewing, or else they sell fruit and candy in the streets. But one ought not to conceive of their labor as anything even approaching a regular or serious occupation. Even when they do accept employment, the most important thing for them remains to change their line of work very quickly.[130]

130. For the most part, this litany of pessimistic conclusions on the future behavior of former slaves in postabolition Brazil emanates from information von Binzer has received from her employers rather than from her own eyewitness observations. In fact, many emancipated slaves fled São Paulo's coffee fields for the provincial capital in order to seek better terms of employment than were possible in the interior's still-slave-dominated workforce. Otherwise, most planters preferred not to hire them to work alongside their slaves.

In addition to all that, there are now (1882) about one million slaves in Brazil.[131] What will the conditions be when all of them are emancipated? And this point in time is not in the all-too-distant future, for emancipation is making daily progress. True, the state [emancipation] funds are not sufficient for the distant future, but the grassroots [abolitionist] organizations are helping, and innumerable slaves are being freed through private initiatives.[132]

A relative of Mr. de Sousa who is very rich just emancipated all of his slaves, which came to about three hundred; he replaced them, incurring enormous costs, with "colonists" from Switzerland and Tyrol. And this example is not the only one of its kind. One also sees many German names among the number of such noble gentlemen. It has now become customary that during particularly joyous family occasions or other events, one expresses one's joy by freeing one or more slaves. The birth of a child, the happy return of a son who had been sent to Europe to be educated, a particularly rich harvest or a successful business venture—in each case, many a slave receives his *carta.* It has recently been divulged to me that when Maricota's brother, Bento, returns from Cassel, the factotum here, Cesário, will be given his *carta.*[133]

A great number of slaves are emancipated through the power of a slave owner's last will and testament. But their owners keep testaments strictly secret, since otherwise they would exist in perpetual fear of being poisoned.[134]

Solitary [without children or parents or grandparents] persons will even sometimes make their slaves—of course, free—their beneficiaries, to whom they bequeath the plantation.[135] However, this form of humanity seems to me

131. Two years later, in 1884, Brazil's slave population numbered 1,241,000, excluding those yet unmanumitted by the Rio Branco Law of 1871. The latter pushed the figure to at least 1.5 million individuals in captivity. Robert Conrad, *The Destruction of Brazilian Slavery, 1850–1888* (Berkeley: University of California Press, 1973), 291 (table 10).

132. Ina was confirming the recent trend witnessing the growth of abolitionist societies that raised funds to manumit slaves, a political manifestation of the growing impatience with the 1871 Law of the Free Womb for freeing relatively few slaves.

133. The *carta* was the *carta de alforria*—the emancipation certificate, colloquially known as the "letter of liberty" (*carta da liberdade*). "Bento" was Ina's pseudonym for Luís de Souza Aguiar de Barros, the "Sousas'" only son, who was studying in Kassel, Germany.

134. The much older tradition was "posthumous manumission," by means of a clause in a will, but it usually was conditional. The freed slave had to observe stipulated conditions, including proper deference to the decedent's family members and a defined period of service to the former owner's heir. Disobedience could result in a reimposition of the condition of slavery.

135. According to inheritance law, only individuals lacking living descendants and ascendants (parents and grandparents) possessed full testamentary freedom to name their own "universal" heirs. Until the 1871 Law of the Free Womb, in order to inherit, a slave first had to be freed.

not wholly appropriate, since in these cases, within a short amount of time, the blacks are the proprietors of an uncultivated wilderness. Indeed, these very people leave their plantations in order to lead the idle life of a vagabond in the cities, a life that corresponds far more to their inclinations than to a well-organized, hardworking existence. For this reason, a lady from Minas Gerais who recently died probably knew what she was doing when she decided that one of her plantations would be assigned to her thirty-two emancipated Negroes for beneficial use only [i.e., in usufruct] for a certain number of years, and then it would be given to two charitable foundations.

Dona Maria Luísa, however, just recently told me about the most sensational case illustrating how dangerous imprudent humanism can become. An old black woman, who earlier had belonged to her, had come to her some time ago in order to complain about her distress. She had become one of the inheritors of her new mistress's plantation at her death, and, she explained, now the place was in terrible condition. Some of the former slaves and the current owners did the planting and harvesting. The lazy ones then demanded that they live off the others' toil, and the others, of course, denied them this request. Because of this, there had been bloody brawls in which almost half of the Negroes lost their lives. "No," she concluded with complete conviction, "our master did not leave us a blessing by bequeathing to us the *fazenda*—for that he is going to Hell!" This seems to me, however, to be far too harsh a prediction for the blessed slave baron and his certainly well-meaning last testament. Nevertheless, it was enormously bad judgment for him to have made the slaves into masters without a period of transition, to suddenly give independence to beings that had been educated only as dependents. All of this obliges us to stop and think, doesn't it? The situation sounds like it is "attractive" and well founded, but I can guarantee you that it is not. I can only tell you, Grete, that now I would not like to be in the middle of a large plantation run by slaves.

But now you will probably have had enough of Negroes and slavery, and now Albertina is coming in order to fetch me to look at the tallest sugar cane that I have ever seen in my life!

Adieu, my dear Gretel, just write to me in time for Christmas. Your letters would have to be sent next week already. Have you considered that?

Your old Ulla

São Sebastião

December 5, 1882

My dear Grete!

"The tallest sugar cane that I have ever seen" is standing at a corner of the veranda. Here, the solemn procession of the longest sugar cane is similar to the harvest wreath procession in Germany. The sugar harvest is in full swing and—everything is sticky. It is horrible. The children are chewing from morning until evening on *cana* [sugar cane], which they sometimes nicely peel and then have cut into little pieces for them. More often than not, however, they simply suck on it, as much as the skin of the cane will allow, and then spit it out around themselves. You would not be able to see the smallest Negroes over the last couple days without sticks of sugar in their mouths; and as for their attempt to chew these sticks, only the comparatively small grinding skill of their jaws might provide one with some comfort.

Now the raw *cana* period is over, and we have come under the sign of syrup, a quite dubious progress indeed.

Yesterday they set up the machine that is supposed to grind the sugar cane and squeeze out the juice, and this morning the children triumphantly brought me a large bowl of sugar juice before breakfast that had just gushed forth from the freshly squeezed stalks. It is a greenish liquid, relatively clear and as thin as water, but it does not taste as disgustingly sweet as one might imagine. Both big and small devour it by the liter.

This juice drains through pipes into large vats where it is boiled and thickened into molasses, which, aside from a somewhat more refined taste, corresponds exactly to our notion of syrup. This afternoon, the *melado* [molasses] period began, and we had some at the dining table together with *canjica*, and, since then, the children have had to change clothes two times. Everything is wallowing in the sugar harvest, even—or, rather, above all—the pigs. They get the bagasse that has already been pressed, and, as a result, they have been gaining quite a bit of weight.[136]

136. *Canjica* is a corn pudding, made by cooking fresh (green) corn kernels with milk, sugar, and spices, especially cinnamon. The bagasse are the crushed stalks of cane left after the sugar juice is crushed from them—a food for livestock. The molasses (*melado*) is not a syrup that is a final product, but on its way to being set up in molds to become sugar crystals.

Nature in its entirety around the *fazenda* smells, but not unpleasantly, like the cooked juice. When the molasses is thick enough, it crystallizes in large wooden containers. In order that this happen more rapidly and more effectively, the molasses is covered with—cow dung! At least most of the smaller plantation owners do it like this, according to Dona Maria Luísa. Here, however, thankfully, they use an especially thick form of mud that can be found on the plantation.

For the most part, it is only the state government that owns installations adequate for large-scale production of sugar in Brazil. The state refineries utilize machinery that is much more modern. The *fazendeiros* usually only plant what they need for their own consumption, and whoever cultivates sugar in larger proportions usually sells the raw *cana* to the state.[137]

December 11: We have entered into a new sugar phase: the molasses has completed its proper transformation into yellow caster sugar, and this sugar is now lying around in great heaps after having been shaken out onto mats in the courtyard in order to dry.[138] Grete, do you know what pleases me most about the whole affair? That I am not always around, for otherwise I would probably be incapable of enjoying anything sweet. I don't even want to bring up the countless mosquitoes, flies, wasps, bees, and ants that take their twopence from the pile of sugar. But since there is no fence protecting these sweet mountains, cats and dogs also come by as guests and wish to take part in the common sugar delight of São Sebastião. However, the initial, still rather dark, sugar is only for the Negroes to use for their coffee, although I have my suspicion that it is also being smuggled into the kitchen to use for our food. The sugar for the masters goes through a process of refinement, but only here on the plantation and in the most primitive manner. It never becomes quite light in color. And absolutely white sugar is something that many Brazilians will never see, no matter how long they live. There are no cubes of sugar here,

137. Ina referred to the technological revolution of the 1870s that witnessed small, steam-powered sugar mills (*engenhos*) being replaced by the enormous "factory in the field" industrial plant that represented the modern sugar refinery (the *usina*). Former small producers then became suppliers of raw cane (*fornecedores de cana*) to the *usinas*, which were not necessarily owned by the state.

138. Caster sugar was refined sugar whose crystals are small enough to fall through the holes of a caster (shaker) when it is shaken, in contrast to the thick, light brown granules (semi-refined) that Ina has already noted were to be found at nineteenth-century Brazilian tables.

even in the best houses, and the children were recently highly amused to see in their French reading book that someone was speaking about a "lump" of sugar; they thought this was a wonderful slip on the part of the author. You know, Gretel, on the whole, I believe, we can be happy with our country, in which only beet sugar is a native resource—it seems to me to be somewhat more appetizing at any rate. Put them into the famous punch bowl: Germany and—its beets!

Your Ulla

São Sebastião

December 18, 1882

Gretel, my dear Gretel, just imagine, I am traveling to São Paulo for Christmas! The Schaumanns have invited me, and I am going there on December 22. I can barely contain my joy! How different it will be than last year! And I am going to see all of them again. The dear people, the Schaumanns above all, and Miss Meyer and the little Harras and—and—everyone!

Oh Gretel, I am, as you know,

Your so happy

Ulla!

São Paulo

December 28, 1882

My one and only Grete!

If this isn't a pretty Christmas with German people, German songs, German festive cakes! But the tropical sun is glowing brightly and burning us all, as if it wanted to avenge itself for our immersion in the customs of the cold, northern homeland. The banana trees outside seem to rustle unhappily, and the palms are shaking their heads as if they wanted to say: "How could you think of gloomy pine trees when you are looking at us!" And yet—and yet, Grete! Dranmor's "sole, snow-covered pine" has followed me all day long, for the Christmas tree was lacking even if everything else was like Christmas, with everyone amicably acknowledging their guests with plentiful gifts. Indeed, that so much poetry can be attached to such a tree! My brother always said that he did not feel the Christmas spirit until various wax blotches covered the floor and it smelled of burnt pine needles in every room. I knew earlier that because of this statement, which was always said half-teasingly, he felt the poetry of Christmas more than he ever would have wanted to admit. But how correct he was! This is something that I am just now noticing when I seek in vain the "aroma of Christmas."

And even outside—oh Grete, how much more beautiful is a white, snowy square in Berlin with pines standing in long rows than this sun-drenched southern garden with its roses and palms. . . .

I am ungrateful, really, I must be so, for the people are so infinitely dear to me and the country has such a fairy-tale beauty. And yet I can't help it that the refrain of the song that we just recently sang keeps buzzing through my head: "It is indeed nice in a foreign country, but it will never be a homeland!"

Yesterday, I went to visit a governess who has a piano in her schoolroom and owns an album of German folksongs. We were six German girls in all and we sang the entire album right up until the final, famous song. We sang so much that I am still hoarse today. Oh, greet it for me, greet for me my beautiful Germany and its joyous song!

December 29, evening: I have just come back from the English family that I had met at the time of my antique Roman cultural experience. They invited me for Christmas pudding. Mr. Hall brought me home, for he was there as well, as he is indeed very good friends with the Emersons. But I have no idea, Grete, what has happened to him since that time when he drove with me to Santos. He did not say a word the entire time, so that we just walked next to one another in complete silence, for I, too, did not say anything. And here, in front of the door, he was odd as well. First he held my hand tightly for a certain amount of time and looked at me (he has really captivating blue eyes!) as if he wanted to say something; then he let me go all of a sudden, uttered a curt "good-night" [original in English], and was so rude that he ran away before I had even opened the door. What do you have to say about that, and what should I think about it? Was he perhaps hurt that I had not spoken at all on the way over here? But it was his duty to begin speaking about something, and I really didn't know what to say, Grete. It was quite funny. Sometimes I can chatter the blue down from the sky, but just now absolutely nothing occurred to me that I could have said, or those things that did occur to me were idiotic. Now, the whole thing is a matter of indifference, and I don't even need to think about it anymore.

Tomorrow I was actually supposed to go with the Emersons to the place where they keep the machines. He was going to show us some interesting things, but now I will no longer go. Rather, I will seek out my past acquaintances from the time of classical antiquity, from whom I will, however, only find the smaller heroines. The bigger ones will probably have remained in the colégios. The Brazilians don't really care about Christmas.[139]

Adieu for today, my Gretel.

Your Ulla

P.S.: December 30. Morning. The mailman just brought me an invitation from Santos to a New Year's Eve ball in the local "Germania" [Club] for "Fräulein" Schaumann, her brother, and the "visitor." That would be me, and that means the blue silk dress did not make the journey from São Sebastião in vain! How funny it is to be able to go to a ball over here, and moreover to a German ball. But it will be very hot!

139. Again, Ina resorts to her "classical antique experience," implying the Roman-named children of Martinico and Albertina da Silva Prado—or at least their younger daughters. She was correct in observing that Christmas was not considered an important holiday—New Year's (Reveillon*)* being much more important for parties and balls.

Santos

January 2, 1883

Dear Grete!

The ball is over and the blue silk dress as well. We danced a lot, but it was terribly dusty and hot in the small hall. What else should I tell you about it—you know what a ball is like. It is actually a childish pleasure, is it not so, Grete? Basically, I was bored.

There was, besides us, only one other German merchant there from São Paulo. I had believed that many people would be invited from there. Oh, Grete, many pleasures of youth are really quite foolish! I will now be very sensible and will gradually fit myself back into the mold of the old virgin. That is really the only proper thing to do!

How are you? Hopefully better than

Your Ulla

That is, there is actually nothing wrong—

São Sebastião

January 9, 1883

Grete my dear—he was here! Mr. Hall! Mr. de Sousa just bought new machines, and Mr. Hall was so conscientious that he oversaw the assembly himself. I was so surprised and terrified! But I have to tell you the whole story, it was too funny! Just do not be surprised if a melon plays the main role in my story—it deserves it!

When I came back from São Paulo and arrived in Santa Bárbara at the Station, Cesário was already there with his wagon. I would rather have ridden, but since I had luggage with me, we had to drive. Santa Bárbara is famous for its glorious watermelons, which are cultivated there by the North American settlers.[140] Because the wagon was there for once, I decided to buy the biggest one that I could find. "That one weighs a good twelve to fifteen pounds," the boy from whom I bought the melon grinned, and he carried it to the wagon for me.

"Now Cesário," I said, satisfied with my brilliant purchase, "where are we going to put this splendid object? It is for the children."

Cesário stroked his black, woolly hair.

"Hmm, Senhora, there isn't any room anywhere."

"What?" I exclaimed, "a whole wagon and no place for a melon? There is a box here under the seat."

"In that box there is Senhora's handbag, meat from the village, and some white bread, nothing more is going to fit in there."

"So take it on the horse."

"Yes Senhora, gladly, but it is going to fall to the ground because I have four mules and the whip."

"Well, then, it will ride proudly next to me on the seat. Give it to me," I decided, since, in fact, the wagon did not seem to have any other place for the beautiful fruit.

The small open vehicle had gotten stuck on an uneven grass square behind The Station building, and pulling it back up over the ups and downs of the square was no small feat. But Caesário knew how to handle his animals.

140. The Confederate émigrés are still recalled today for having introduced Georgia rattlesnake watermelons from the American South to the province of São Paulo, in addition to techniques for cultivating Upland cotton, the wheelbarrow, and the steel moldboard plow. Known as the *arado de Sta. Bárbara*—the "Santa Bárbara plow"—it was first manufactured in 1869 by a Dutch emigrant from Texas who accompanied the *Confederados*.

He had in his vocal repertory an incredible amount of encouraging calls and adorned them in the most skillful manner with small, appropriate lashes of the whip. The mules finally made a decision and sallied forth.

"Ho-ho," I screamed at the same time, for the melon had fallen out of the wagon. The only thing that I was able to do during the sudden outbreak of energy from the mules was to keep my hat on my head, catch my umbrella (as it was on its way out of the wagon), and then to remain in the wagon myself, which I was only able to do with the help of the most complex equilibrium-maintaining stunts—"Stop, Cesário, my watermelon!"

Luckily, it lay unharmed in one of the shallow places in the uneven field. Cesário climbed down from his horse and brought it back to the wagon. "It's not a good situation, Senhora," he said, grinning at the large fruit helplessly. But I was confident: "I'll just hold on to it better," I said, and Cesário got back onto his horse.

He repeated the whole series of flatteries, threats, and exhortations for the mules. When those animals finally resolved to move again, they managed to bring the wagon along with its entire contents, umbrella and watermelon included, happily outside of the fatal grassy area.

A mighty puddle underneath the barrier that marks the boundary of the train station brought the glossy fruit once again into not insignificant danger. It only escaped this danger when I dedicated both of my hands to securing its safety, thereby sacrificing the right side of my calico dress to the water spraying from the wheels of the wagon. But now the road ahead of us looked much more peaceful. I attempted to steady the large, green ball with only one hand, and the success was satisfactory, although the pleasure of having to hold the big thing for four hours was already beginning to appear to me in a dubious light. At the very least, I wanted to open the umbrella. After all, I didn't need to burn myself into a Moor because of the stupid melon! Grete, I can still see myself, how I slowly, slowly loosened little by little the tight grip with which I held the melon, then carefully raised my hand and followed attentively the movements of the fruit with my eyes. Indeed, the fruit was still wobbling under my outspread fingers in a way that inspired a lack of confidence. But it really worked! I could let it go for a moment!

The umbrella was open and the melon was left to its own devices—how relieved I was! But I just had to observe it a little bit . . . a glance from the side: everything in order.

But couldn't it slip out of my fingers from the front? Another glance—no, it's in the same spot over there.

But perhaps it could slip away under the handrail. . . . A third glance! No, it couldn't get through that way. . . .

The area through which we were driving became very pretty. Solitary palm trees on the billowing hills stood out picturesquely in a silhouette against the southern sky and—only a quick turn to the left: yes, there it is—and there the small settlement, grazing cattle—oh, no! The melon! What? It fell from the same spot. . . .

You have an idea about how the cumbersome thing tortured me, the eternal turning this way and that of the head was simply unbearable, I would have rather just held it in place!

Finally we came to a bend from which point I knew that the road would ascend for a certain time—hurray, I was once again the master of both of my hands! "Here it can't fall," I cheered, and I believe that I actually smiled at my smooth yet mischievous tormentor. But, but, Grete, here I was calculating the bill before the waiter, or rather, before the willfully acquired fruit. The thing truly had the most perfidious caprices that one had ever seen in a watermelon. From the front it was impossible for it to fall out, but now, in accordance with the light trot of the mules, it began to collide against the side of my body at thirty-second intervals with a vehemence that was absolutely impossible to ignore and against which passive resistance was impossible.

I was outraged at the melon, at myself, at the boy who sold it to me, and who, while still grinning, emphasized the fact that it weighed twelve to fifteen pounds. It was as if he had known how the immense creature would behave. An attempt to balance the melon on my lap in front of me without steadying it with my hand failed because of a row of savagely powerful blows from the melon directed against the area around my stomach. It was impossible to cope with the devilish thing by means of tricks. It was resourceful.

A particularly lively exclamation of rage on my part led Cesário to suggest that the nuisance be placed on the floor of the little wagon and held with my feet. This seemed to me a brilliant idea! But nothing ultimately came of it. The heavy fruit rolled away from my feet, which were attempting to contain it, toward the front of the wagon, and when I then tried to hold it even tighter with my angry energy, the smooth thing just slipped to one side, and I had to perform all sorts of gymnastic exercises in order to keep it from falling beneath the wheels. For one moment, the thought flashed through my mind of what a relief it would be to dispatch it altogether, but then again I reflected: "No, not after so much trouble!" I then placed the melon again between my feet, this time balancing it on its tip. That went well for a while, and I thought that I had truly and finally gained the upper hand over it, when suddenly Cesário thought it would be a good idea to send the right wheel of the wagon into a deep rut while the left one stayed on level ground—yes, no amount of resistance could have done anything! Indeed, I clung to the armrest of the little wagon, my lips willfully pressed together, and I also tried with all my strength to force the melon to submit to the same force of inertia, but, Grete, we are not equal to the vehemence of a fifteen-pound watermelon determined to have its way: both foot and fruit slipped away, and the malicious melon flew out of the wagon and lay in outrageous tranquility in the dust of the road before I could even recover from the fear of almost being catapulted from the wagon along with it. Cesário had already come to a stop and given me the fruit, yet again undamaged, with the same embarrassed grin that he had the first time. I, on the other hand, gave vent to my anger in German against the melon. But, since I had already tortured myself such a long time fretting about the thing, it would have been foolish to lose my patience in this final hour. I gave the melon its former place on the seat of the wagon and condemned my left hand yet again to continue thwarting its attempts at flight.

The wagon spluttered along.

The sun had already hidden behind the clouds some time ago, and single droplets fell from the sky as if they were hesitating. I have to confess to you, Gretel: I had in the meantime become so annoyed and vexed that a small, indignant blow of the fist hit the melon as if it were unmistakably responsible for this tribulation as well. A despairing exclamation accompanied this blow: "And I don't even have a raincoat!" All of this occurred, however, without hindering the hard-hearted melon from its annoying wobbling and jerking around. Only Cesário let out, *au hasard*, the occasional, "Sim, Senhora," which was modulated along with German exclamations.

The rain quickly became stronger, and my open umbrella had soon become just a rain pipe that emptied itself onto my shoulders, my hat, and into my collar, respectively, depending upon the movements taken by the wagon. And in addition to all this, the melon! The thing lay in a state of relaxation dripping with rainwater. Eventually dust gathered lovingly onto it. The dirt had soon given an indefinable color to the white glove that was sliding around it trying to hold it into place. I could have cried with rage! With an officious hatred I looked at the large, recalcitrant melon, considering whether, during the remaining hour of the journey, I was going to be vexed by whatever new chicanery it decided to undertake, or moreover, by the fact that I would be unable to resist hurling it right out of the wagon. A sudden, violent collision with a stone forced the melon to initiate a corresponding attack against the side of my body. This decided the question. I resolutely snapped shut the useless umbrella and with both hands I took hold of the abhorrent fruit and was about to cast it out of the wagon.

"What do you intend to do with the beautiful watermelon?" asked a voice in English behind me at that very moment, and I saw, turning around, a horseman immediately behind the wagon. . . . Grete, I could have sunk into the earth with shame! It was Mr. Hall. And I was in such a state! My dress was full of mud, soaked with rain, I had dirty gloves, and my face was enraged by the large green fruit—I was petrified with fright and I wished that he were—yes, just imagine, honestly, I wished that he were thousands of miles away rather than standing there in front of me at that moment! He rode slowly next to the wagon, while I stared red-faced and embarrassed at the melon that I still held tightly in my hands. "Well?" he said, and smiled [original in English]. Then I looked at him and we both laughed.

"The big thing has become too insufferable," I said. However, I began involuntarily to hold the "insufferable" thing, I have no idea why, with a renewed gentleness.

"Give it to me," said Mr. Hall, "I'll carry it for you the rest of the way."

"Oh!—but how?"

"Here in this bag; I can hang it like this on my saddle . . . you see, like this!"

"Oh, thank you!"

Grete, if only I had not looked so disheveled! I was positively delighted that it was no longer far to São Sebastião. But where did Mr. Hall intend to go, and where did he come from?

I shied away from asking him, but I would have so gladly known. Besides, we spoke little in general, but I had the presentiment that he had to be going to São Sebastião.

Another road appeared up ahead, and I wanted to verify my suspicion.

"You shouldn't make any detours on my account," I said. Gretel, this remark had certainly been intended as subtle, and I thought that he would not notice anything, but he made such a funny face at it, and I became so red, that I instantaneously cursed these words ten thousand times more intensely than the perfidies of the melon.

"I am on my road," smiled Mr. Hall.

"Yes, are you also intending to go to—"

"To São Sebastião, yes, just like you, I am coming from the Santa Catarina *fazenda*."

"But what—?"

He seemed to take delight in exciting my curiosity about what he wanted in São Sebastião, until he finally told me about the business matter with his machines. So we arrived together at São Sebastião. You can imagine that the de Sousas were not a little surprised to find that we knew each other very well—or rather well—at any rate, that we were already acquainted with one another.

He stayed only one day, but this time it was as if *I* had been predestined to behave foolishly. What could he possibly think of me now!

When he wanted to leave around evening time, he came to say farewell to me. I was alone in my schoolroom singing. I stood up from the piano and gave him my hand. Then he held it again tightly in his hand just as he had done that evening in São Paulo, and he looked at me just as he had done before as well. This time, however, he said something—it was not much—only "Ulla"—but, Grete, it was as if I had never before heard my name spoken out loud. My head began to spin for a moment and my mind was numb, and then—I, a stupid, ill-mannered goose, ran away, and I did not reappear until he had already left. Will I then remain forever childish?

Your naughty Ulla

He also told me that the Emersons wanted to invite me to an upcoming ball. I am looking forward to it immensely—a ball is a delightful thing, don't you think so, too, my dear Grete?

Heavens, what could he possibly be thinking of me!

São Paulo

January 1883

Ulla von Eck
George Hall
Fiancés

Sweet Grete, it was at the ball!
I have always adored balls, you know!!
Now I will no longer write you.
We will both be coming soon—I as

Your overjoyed Ulla Hall

How funny that sounds!

Suggestions for Further Reading

HISTORIES

Acerbi, Patricia. *Street Occupations: Urban Vending in Rio de Janeiro, 1850–1925.* Austin: University of Texas Press, 2017.

Araújo, Ana Lucia, ed. *The Politics of Memory: Making Slavery Visible in the Public Space.* New York: Routledge, 2012.

Beattie, Peter. *Punishment in Paradise: Race, Slavery, Human Rights, and a Nineteenth-Century Brazilian Penal Colony.* Durham, NC: Duke University Press, 2015.

———. *The Tribute of Blood: Army, Honor, Race, and Nation in Brazil, 1864–1945.* Durham, NC: Duke University Press, 2003.

Bethell, Leslie. *The Abolition of the Brazilian Slave Trade: Britain, Brazil and the Slave Trade Question, 1807–1869.* Cambridge: Cambridge University Press, 1970.

Borges, Dane. *The Family in Bahia, 1870–1945.* Stanford, CA: Stanford University Press, 1992.

Castilho, Celso Thomas. *Slave Emancipation and Transformations in Brazilian Political Citizenship.* Pittsburgh: University of Pittsburgh Press, 2016.

Conrad, Robert Edgar, ed. *Children of God's Fire: A Documentary History of Black Slavery in Brazil.* University Park: Pennsylvania State University Press, 2000.

———. *The Destruction of Brazilian Slavery, 1850–1888.* Berkeley: University of California Press, 1973.

Cowling, Camillia. *Conceiving Freedom: Women of Color, Gender and the Abolition of Slavery in Havana and Rio de Janeiro.* Chapel Hill: University of North Carolina Press, 2013.

Cowling, Camillia, Maria Helena Toledo Machado, Diana Paton, and Emily Ward, eds. *Motherhood, Childlessness and the Care of Children in Atlantic Slave Societies.* New York: Routledge, 2020.

Dávila, Jerry. *Diploma of Whiteness: Race and Social Policy in Brazil, 1917–1945.* Durham, NC: Duke University Press, 2003.

Dean, Warren. *The Industrialization of São Paulo, 1800–1945.* Austin: University of Texas Press, 1970.

———. *Rio Claro: A Brazilian Plantation System, 1820–1920.* Stanford, CA: Stanford University Press, 1976.

Eakin, Marshall C. *British Enterprise in Brazil: The St. John del Rey Mining Company and the Morro Velho Gold Mine, 1830–1960.* Durham, NC: Duke University Press, 1989.

Eisenberg, Peter L. *The Sugar Industry in Pernambuco, 1840–1910: Modernization without Change.* Berkeley: University of California Press, 1974.

Eltis, David, et al. "The Trans-Atlantic Slave Trade Database." SlaveVoyages. www.slavevoyages.org. This is a massive, free-access online database recording all slave ship voyages to the Americas, sixteenth through nineteenth centuries.

Ferrez, Gilberto. *Photography in Brazil, 1840–1890.* Translated by Stella de Sá Rego. 1976. Reprint, Albuquerque: University of New Mexico Press, 1984.

Fraga, Walter. *Crossroads of Freedom: Slaves and Freed People in Bahia, Brazil, 1870–1910.* Translated and with introduction by Mary Ann Mahoney. Foreword to the Brazilian edition by Robert W. Slenes. Durham, NC: Duke University Press, 2016.

Frank, Zephyr. *Dutra's World: Wealth and Family in Nineteenth-Century Rio de Janeiro.* Albuquerque: University of New Mexico Press, 2004.

———. *Reading Rio de Janeiro: Literature and Society in the Nineteenth Century.* Stanford, CA: Stanford University Press, 2016.

Garrigus, John D., and Christopher Morris, eds. *Assumed Identities: The Meaning of Race in the Atlantic World.* Introduction by Franklin W. Knight. Arlington: Texas A&M University Press for the University of Texas, 2010.

Graden, Dale Torston. *From Slavery to Freedom in Brazil, 1835–1900.* Albuquerque: University of New Mexico Press, 2006.

Hahner, June E. *Emancipating the Female Sex: The Struggle for Women's Rights in Brazil, 1850–1940.* Durham, NC: Duke University Press, 1990.

———. *Poverty and Politics: The Urban Poor in Brazil, 1870–1920.* Albuquerque: University of New Mexico Press, 1986.

Holloway, Thomas H. *Immigrants on the Land: Coffee and Society in São Paulo, 1886–1934.* Chapel Hill: University of North Carolina Press, 1980. Reprint, 2012, 2017.

Johnson, Walter, ed. *The Chattel Principle: Internal Slave Trades in the Americas.* New Haven: Yale University Press, 2004.

Karasch, Mary. *Slave Life in Rio de Janeiro, 1808–1850.* Princeton: Princeton University Press, 1987.

Kiddy, Elizabeth W. *Blacks of the Rosary: Memory and History in Minas Gerais, Brazil.* University Park: Pennsylvania State University Press, 2005.

Lauderdale-Graham, Sandra. *Caetana Says No: Women's Stories from a Brazilian Slave Perspective.* Cambridge: Cambridge University Press, 2002.

———. *House and Street: The Domestic World of Servants and Masters in Nineteenth-Century Rio de Janeiro.* Cambridge: Cambridge University Press, 1988.

Levi, Darrell E. *The Prados of São Paulo, Brazil: An Elite Family and Social Change, 1840–1930.* Athens: University of Georgia Press, 1987.

Lewin, Linda. *Surprise Heirs*. Vol. 2, *Illegitimacy, Inheritance Rights, and Public Power in the Formation of Imperial Brazil, 1822–1888.* Stanford, CA: Stanford University Press, 2003.

Love, Joseph L. *The Revolt of the Whip.* Stanford, CA: Stanford University Press, 2012.

Marcus, Alan P. *Confederate Exodus: Social and Environmental Forces in the Migration of U.S. Southerners to Brazil.* Lincoln: University of Nebraska Press, 2021.

Marques, Leonardo. *The United States and the Transatlantic Slave Trade to the Americas, 1776–1867.* New Haven: Yale University Press, 2016.

Mattoso, Katia M. de Queirós. *To Be a Slave in Brazil.* Translated by Arthur Goldhower. New Brunswick, NJ: Rutgers University Press, 1986.

Miki, Yuko. *Frontiers of Citizenship: A Black and Indigenous History of Postcolonial Brazil.* Cambridge: Cambridge University Press, 2018.

Nazzari, Muriel. *Disappearance of the Dowry: Women, Families, and Social Change in São Paulo, Brazil, 1600–1900.* Stanford, CA: Stanford University Press, 1991.

Needell, Jeffrey D. *The Sacred Cause: The Abolitionist Movement, Afro-Brazilian Mobilization, and Imperial Politics in Rio de Janeiro.* Stanford, CA: Stanford University Press, 2020.

Prado Júnior, Caio. *The Colonial Background of Modern Brazil.* Translated by Suzette Macedo. Berkeley: University of California Press, 1971.

Read, Ian. *The Hierarchies of Slavery in Santos, Brazil, 1822–1888*. Stanford, CA: Stanford University Press, 2012.

Schwarcz, Lilia Moritz. *The Emperor's Beard: Dom Pedro II and the Tropical Monarchy of Brazil.* Translated by John Gledson. New York: Hill and Wang, 2004.

Schwarcz, Lilia M., and Heloisa M. Starling. *Brazil: A Biography*. Translated from the Portuguese. New York: Farrar, Straus and Giroux, 2018 (orig. pub., 2015).

Silva Dias, Maria Odila. *Power and Everyday Life: The Lives of Working Women in Nineteenth-Century Brazil.* Translated by Ann Frost. New Brunswick, NJ: Rutgers University Press, 1995.

Skidmore, Thomas E. *Black into White: Race and Nationality in Brazilian Thought.* New York: Oxford University Press, 1974. Reprint, Durham, NC: Duke University Press, 1993. Rev. ed., 2014.

Stein, Stanley J. *Vassouras: A Brazilian Coffee County, 1850–1900.* Cambridge, MA: Harvard University Press, 1957. 2nd ed., Princeton: Princeton University Press, 1985.

Stepan, Nancy Leys. *'The Hour of Eugenics': Race, Gender, and Nation in Latin America.* Ithaca, NY: Cornell University Press, 1996.

Tomich, Dale, ed. *Slavery and Historical Capitalism during the Nineteenth Century.* Lanham, MD: Lexington Books, 2017.

Tomich, Dale W., et. al. *Reconstructing the Landscapes of Slavery: A Visual History of the Plantation in the Nineteenth-Century Atlantic World.* Chapel Hill: University of North Carolina Press, 2021.

Toplin, Robert Brent. *The Abolition of Slavery in Brazil.* Studies in American Negro Life. New York: Atheneum Books, 1974.

Viotti da Costa, Emilia. *The Brazilian Empire: Myths and Histories.* Rev. ed., with a new chapter on women. Chapel Hill: University of North Carolina Press, 2000.

Xavier, Giovanna, Juliana Barreto Farias, and Flavio Gomes, eds. *Black Women of Brazil in Slavery and Post-Emancipation.* New York: Diasporic Africa Press, 2017.

TRAVEL ACCOUNTS AND STUDIES, AUTOBIOGRAPHY, AND BIOGRAPHY

Agassiz, Professor Louis, and Mrs. Agassiz [Elizabeth Cabot Cary]. *A Journey in Brazil.* Boston: Ticknor and Fields, 1868. Note: Many reprint editions are now available.

Araújo, Ana Lucia. *Brazil through French Eyes: A Nineteenth-Century Artist in the Tropics.* Albuquerque: University of New Mexico Press, 2006.

Brant, Alice Dayrell Caldeira. *The Diary of "Helena Morley."* Translated and with introduction by Elizabeth Bishop. New York: Farrar, Straus and Giroux, 1957, 1995. Reprint, New York: Ecco Press, 1978 (orig. pub., 1942).

Burton, Capt. Richard Francis. *Explorations of the Highlands of Brazil: With a Full Account of the Gold and Diamond Mines* [. . .]. 2 vols. London: Tinsley Brothers, 1869. Reprint, Westport, CT: Greenwood Press, 1969; Chestnut Hill, MA: Adamant Media Corp., 2005; Sidney/Marrickville, Australia: Wentworth Press, 2016.

Denis, Pierre. *Brazil with a Historical Chapter by Bernard Miall and a Supplemental Chapter by Dawson A. Vinsin.* Translated by Bernard Miall. London: T. Fisher Unwin, 1911. Reprint, Stockholm: Utan Press, 2012 (orig. pub., 1909).

Diggs, Cerue K. *Brazil after Humboldt: Triangular Perceptions and the Colonial Gaze in Nineteenth-Century German Travel Narratives.* Burton-upon-Trent (Staffordshire), UK: Waterstones, 2012.

Fontes de Oliveira, Natália. *Three Traveling Women Writers: Cross-Cultural Perspectives on Brazil, Patagonia, and the United States for the Nineteenth Century.* London: Routledge, 2017.

Gardner, George. *Travels in Brazil: Principally through the Northern Provinces and the Gold Districts, during the Years 1836–41.* London: Reeve Brothers, 1846. Available from the Gutenberg Project as *Travels in the Interior of Brazil, Principally through the Northern Provinces, and the Gold and Diamond Districts, during the Years 1836–1841.* www.Gutenberg.org.

Gerassi-Navarro, Nina, ed. *Women, Travel, and Science in Nineteenth-Century Americas: The Politics of Observation.* Palgrave Studies in Literature, Science, and Medicine. Cham, Switzerland: Palgrave Macmillan, 2017.

Graham, Maria Dundas [Lady Callcott]. *Journal of a Voyage to Brazil and Residence There, during Part of the Years 1821, 1822, 1823.* London: Longman, Hurst, Rees, Orme, Brown, and Green, and J. Murray, 1824. Reprint, Charleston, SC: BiblioBazaar [Bibliolife], 2007.

———. *Maria Graham's Journal of a Voyage to Brazil.* Edited by Jennifer Haywood and Maria Soledad Caballero. Rev. ed. Reprint, Anderson, SC: Parlor Press, 2011.

Grinberg, Keila. *A Black Jurist in a Slave Society: Antonio Pereira Rebouças and the Trials of Brazilian Citizenship.* Translated by Kristin M. McGuire. Chapel Hill: University of North Carolina Press, 2019.

Hahner, June E., ed. *Women through Women's Eyes: Latin American Women in Nineteenth-Century Travel Accounts.* Wilmington, DE: Scholarly Resources, 1998.

Kidder, Rev. Daniel P. *Brazil and the Brazilians Portrayed in Historical and Descriptive Sketches.* Philadelphia: Childs and Peterson, 1845.

Kidder, Rev. Daniel P., and Rev. James C. Fletcher. *Brazil and the Brazilians Portrayed in Historical and Descriptive Sketches.* Boston: Little & Brown, 1857–79, nine editions. Available in numerous reprint eds.

Koster, Henry. *Travels in Brazil.* London: Longman, Hurst, Rees, Orme, and Brown, 1816.

Laerne, C.F. Van Delden. *Brazil and Java: Report on Coffee-Culture in America, Asia, and Africa, to H.E. The Minister of the Colonies.* London: W.H. Allen & Co., 1885. Reprint, Whitefish, MT: Kessinger Legacy Reprints, 2015; Delhi: S.N. Books World, 2020.

Lery, Jean de. *History of a Voyage to the Land of Brazil.* Translated and with introduction by Janet Whatley. Los Angeles: University of California Press, 1990. Originally published as *Histoire d'un voyage* [. . .] *1578* (Paris: Antoine Chuppin, 1578).

Mulhall, M.G. [Mrs. Marion McMurrough]. *Between the Amazon and Andes, Or Ten Years of a Lady's Travels in the Pampas, Gran Chaco, Paraguay, and Matto Grosso.* London: Edward Stanford, 1881.

———. *From Europe to Paraguay and Matto-Grosso.* London: Edward Stanford, 1877. Reprint, Oxford: Oxford University Press, 2006.

Nabuco, Carolina. *The Life of Joaquim Nabuco.* Translated and edited by Ronald Hilton. Stanford, CA: Stanford University Press, 1950 (orig. pub., 1928).

Nabuco, Joaquim. *Abolitionism: The Brazilian Anti-Slavery Struggle.* Translated and edited by Robert E. Conrad. Urbana: University of Illinois Press, 1977 (orig. pub., 1883).

Pfeiffer, Ida. *A Woman's Journey round the World from Vienna to Brazil, Chili, Tahiti, China, Hindostan, Persia, and Asia Minor.* London: Office of the National Illustrated Library/Open Library, 2012 (orig. pub., 1852).

Pratt, Mary Louise. *Imperial Eyes: Travel Writing and Transculturation.* 2nd ed. London: Routledge, 2007.

Staden, Hans. *Hans Staden's True History: An Account of Cannibal Captivity in Brazil.* Translated and edited by Neil L. Whitehead and Michael Harbsmeier. Durham, NC: Duke University Press, 2008. Originally published as *Warhaftige Historia* [. . .] *1557* (Marburg, 1557).

Toussaint-Samson, Adèle. *A Parisian in Brazil.* Translated by Emma Toussaint. Boston: James H. Earle, 1891 (orig. pub., 1883).

———. *A Parisian in Brazil: The Travel Account of a Frenchwoman in Nineteenth-Century Rio de Janeiro.* Edited by June E. Hahner. Wilmington, DE: Scholarly Resources, 2001.

Tristan, Flora. *Peregrinations of a Pariah, 1833–1834.* Translated, edited, and introduction by Jean Hawkes. London: Virago Press, 1977, 1986 (orig. pub., 1838).

Walsh, Rev. John. *Notices of Brazil in 1828 and 1829.* London: Richardson, Lord & Holbrook, 1831.

BRAZILIAN NINETEENTH-CENTURY NOVELS IN ENGLISH TRANSLATION

Alencar, José de. *Iracema: A Novel.* Translated by Clifford E. Landers. Foreword by Naomi Lindstrom. Afterword by Alcides Villaça. New York: Oxford University Press, 2000 (orig. pub., 1865).

———. *Senhora: Profile of a Woman.* Translated by Catarina Feldman Edinger. Austin: University of Texas Press, 1994 (orig. pub., 1875).

Azevedo, Aluízio. *A Brazilian Tenement.* Translated by Harry W. Brown. New York: R.M. MacBride & Co., 1926. Reprint, New York: H. Fertig, 1976. First published in Portuguese as *O cortiço* (Rio de Janeiro: B.L. Garnier, 1890).

———. *Mulatto.* Translated by Murray Graeme MacNicoll. Edited and with an introduction by Daphne Patai. Madison, NJ: Fairleigh Dickinson University Press, 1990 (orig. pub., 1909).

———. *The Slum.* Translated and foreword by David H. Rosenthal, afterward by Affonso Romano de Sant'Anna. New York: Oxford University Press, 2000. First published in Portuguese as *O cortiço* (Rio de Janeiro: B.L. Garnier, 1890).

Machado de Assis, Joaquim Maria de. *The Alienist, and Other Stories of Nineteenth-Century Brazil.* Translated, edited, and with an introduction by John Charles Chasteen. Hackett Classics. Indianapolis: Hackett, 2013.

———. *Esau and Jacob: A Novel.* Translated and edited by Elizabeth Lowe. Foreword by Dane Borges. Afterword by Carlos Felipe Moisés. New York: Oxford University Press, 2000 (orig. pub., 1904).

———. *The Good Days! The Bons Dias! Chronicles of Machado de Assis (1888–1889).* Translated by Ana Lessa Schmidt. Foreword by Greicy Pinto Bellini. Hanover, CT: New London Librarium, 2018.

———. *Helena*. Translated and introduction by Helen Caldwell. Berkeley: University of California Press, 1984. First published 1876 by B. L. Garnier (Rio de Janeiro).

———. *Quincas Borba: A Novel*. Translated by Gregory Rabassa. Introduction by David T. Haberly. Afterword by Celso Favoretti. New York: Oxford University Press, 1999. First published 1891 by B. L. Garnier (Rio de Janeiro).

Index

Note: The entry "Binzer, Ina Sophie Amalie von" is restricted to the discussion of that author in the Introduction to this book and several biographical footnotes. Otherwise, she is indexed under her authorial pseudonym, "Eck, Ulla von."

Where an entry is a fictive name from von Binzer's letters, the person's actual name appears next to it in brackets. The reader is referred to the latter by "*See also actual name.*" Where an entry is an actual name that von Binzer rendered as fictive in the letters, then the fictive identity is noted at the end of the entry and the reader is referred to it by "*See also.*"

Ina von Binzer's five unnumbered footnotes are indicated by one or two asterisks following the page number (e.g., 92n*).

Ina von Binzer (1855–1929)

was a German writer who worked as a governess in Brazil from 1881 to 1883. She was the author of several novels, a children's book, and a number of articles and essays. Her letters have been translated into Brazilian Portuguese as *Os meus romanos*.

Linda Lewin

is professor emerita of history at UC Berkeley and author of the two-volume *Surprise Heirs*.

Gabriel Trop

is associate professor of German in the Department of Germanic and Slavic Languages and Literatures, University of North Carolina, Chapel Hill.